THE
TECATE
JOURNALS

LIVINGSTON PUBLISHING COMPANY
18 Hampton Hall Drive
Livingston, N.J. 07039

THE
TECATE
JOURNALS

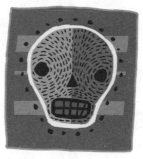

SEVENTY DAYS

ON THE RIO GRANDE

Keith Bowden

THE MOUNTAINEERS BOOKS

THE MOUNTAINEERS BOOKS
is the nonprofit publishing arm of The Mountaineers Club, an organization founded in 1906 and dedicated to the exploration, preservation, and enjoyment of outdoor and wilderness areas.

1001 SW Klickitat Way, Suite 201, Seattle, WA 98134

First edition, 2007

Manufactured in the United States of America

Copy Editor: Alice Copp Smith
Design: Peggy Egerdahl
Cartographer: Linda M. Feltner
Cover Artwork: *Green and blue skull* © Images.com/Corbis

Library of Congress Cataloging-in-Publication Data
Bowden, Keith, 1957-
The Tecate journals : seventy days on the Rio Grande / Keith Bowden.
—1st ed.
    p. cm.
    ISBN 978-1-59485-077-6 (pb)
    1. Rio Grande—Description and travel. 2. Rio Grande
Valley—Description and travel. 3. Mexican-American Border
Region—Description and travel. 4. Bowden, Keith, 1957—Travel—Rio
Grande. 5. Canoes and canoeing—Rio Grande. 6. Rio Grande
Valley—History, Local. 7. Mexican-American Border Region—History,
Local. I. Title.
    F392.R5B69 2007
    917.64'40464—dc22

                    200702382

FOR SALLY DENNISON, MY LOVELY AUNT

Contents

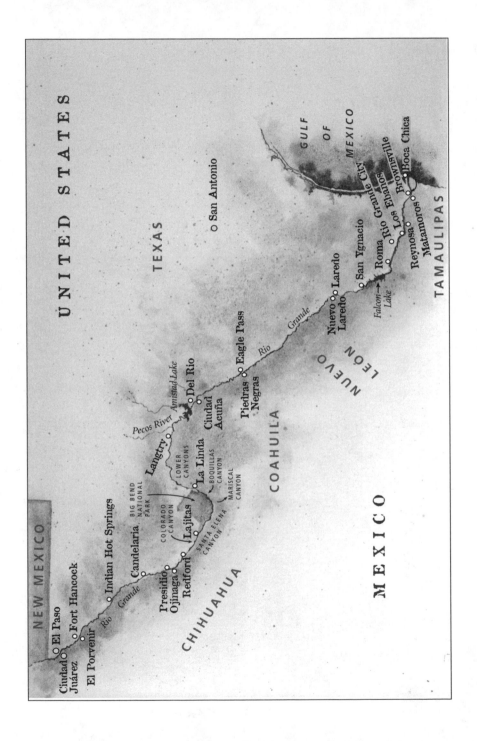

Prologue: Between Two Worlds

WHEN I FIRST GLIMPSED THE RIO GRANDE, I mistook it for a sewer drain. It was December 1973. I was sixteen and hitchhiking from home in eastern Pennsylvania to my best friend Tony's house in northern California. I'd caught a ride through El Paso, Texas, which sits on the north bank of the river. Those who have traveled that interstate know there isn't much river to look at. By the time the Rio Grande reaches the northern outskirts of El Paso and begins to form the international border for its final 1,260 miles to the Gulf of Mexico, the flow has been reduced to an ankle-deep trickle of contaminated water. In fact, the first time I looked at it, I didn't see it at all.

What I did see—and it made a profound impression on me—was the abject *colonia*, or shantytown, which to this day sits on a dusty rise on the Mexican side immediately adjacent to the freeway. It appears so close and the river so tiny that upon first glance, the *colonia* seems to be an El Paso slum on the periphery of downtown. When I saw its poverty, I asked the long-haired man giving me a ride if El Paso had any neighborhoods worse than the one beside us, which was the worst I had ever seen in my sixteen years of middle-class American life. He chuckled and said I was seeing Mexico, not El Paso, and what I had been mistaking for a sewer drain was the main channel of the fabled Rio Grande. I thought he was joking.

I found the squalor of the *colonia* both disquieting and fascinating. Cardboard shacks with roofs of plastic sheeting lined random, unpaved paths in no clear order. I could see chickens wandering among the hovels, and emaciated dogs slumping as they sniffed hopefully at trash in the dirt. Cars that appeared to have been resurrected from junkyards bounced slowly through the maze of seemingly temporary encampments. Incredulous, I asked my driver, "Do people really live there?"

"Oh, sure," he said, "but that's one of the better ones. They can be a lot worse than that."

It was nearly impossible for my sheltered mind to assimilate what my eyes saw, let alone to conceive of an environment "a lot worse than that." Now, when I glanced back at the modest skyscrapers of downtown El Paso and saw them juxtaposed against the miserable makeshift structures in their shadows, those high-rises suddenly looked luxurious.

My father was transferred to Houston, Texas, only six months later. His patience had been stretched beyond its wide limits by my dropping out of high school the previous year and hitchhiking all around the U.S., so he made me a deal: If I would attend school, get a part-time job, and stay out of trouble, he would allow me unlimited freedom to hitchhike wherever I wanted when school wasn't in session, as long as I could get the release time from work. During spring break of my senior year, in March 1975, I decided to hitchhike to Monterrey, Mexico, some 450 miles southwest of Houston, despite the fact that I spoke no Spanish and had never been to Mexico. On that trip, I saw the Rio Grande for the second time, as I crossed the international bridge at Laredo.

The river here is as wide as at any point along its entire course between El Paso and the Gulf of Mexico, and I was struck by the contrast in its size relative to the trickle I had seen fifteen months before. In Laredo, although the sweep of the river pales in comparison to the Missouri, the Mississippi, the Yukon, and the St. Lawrence (the only four North American rivers longer than the Rio Grande), at least it looked like a real river, with vegetation lining its banks and water coursing through its channels. I stood looking down at the dark water on a warm March night, my feet straddling the international border, one foot in Mexico, one in the U.S., and watched the city lights twinkling on its inky surface. Then, I entered Mexico for the first time—alone, naïve, and underprepared for the experiences that awaited me half a river's width away.

Immediately I had the overwhelming sense that I was entering a foreign world, a feeling I still experience thirty-one years later, despite my familiarity with the place. In that short walk across the bridge, one moves from the First World to the Third, from North America to Latin America, from English to Spanish. Cross that river and you're in a world that more closely resembles the one at the bottom of South America, five thousand miles distant, than the one on the other side of the bridge. I found the contrast so discomfiting on my first visit that I had to summon all my determination not to retreat to Texas.

The beginning of my thirty-year love affair with Latin America was inauspicious. Nearly paralyzed by my inability to speak, read, or understand even the most basic Spanish, I struggled just to eat. Although I did reach Monterrey via a second-class bus that same night and booked a room in a hotel ("hotel" is the same in either language), I returned to Laredo, and the comfort of an English-speaking world, within twenty hours. Re-crossing the Rio Grande and relieved to be back in my comfort zone, I resolved to learn Spanish so that I would never again feel so alienated in my neighboring country.

Mastering Spanish was a continuing struggle despite two great teachers—my second-year Spanish professor at Acadia University, a Chilean exile whom I later married, and our daughter, who for most of her life willingly used English only when she wanted her gringo father to buy her ice cream. When my wife was granted amnesty to return to Chile in early 1984, I followed her ten months later. Despite the fact that I'd minored in Spanish for my undergraduate degree and had traveled extensively in Mexico and Central America, my daughter, at age four, expressed her frustration at my limited Spanish by telling a friend, "Don't even talk to him. He's lost in a world of English."

I didn't give up, though, and thanks to my time in Chile and my daughter's neglect of her English, I slowly achieved a degree of mastery of the language. Put it this way: when she was five, my Spanish, though American-accented, was at least as competent as a five-year-old Chilean girl's. As she turned six and began attending school, my Spanish improved to the level of a first grade student. It was a slow yet delightful process.

My marriage wasn't nearly as delightful, and in January 1987 I returned to the U.S. and Texas to pursue graduate studies at Sul Ross State University in Alpine, a hundred miles north of the Rio Grande. I had left Texas to study in Canada in 1977, and, except for brief periods, I'd spent the intervening ten years outside of the U.S. One result was that my résumé had developed no clear focus or direction. More importantly, I'd become detached from American sensibilities, and I found on those occasions when I returned to the U.S. that I no longer fit in. I was an American on the outside only. In some respects, my five years in Canada defined me more than did my youth in the U.S.; in other respects, my daughter and my many experiences in Latin America tied me to that end of the hemisphere. Mexicans call Mexicans who divorce themselves from Mexican culture *pocho* or *coco*. *Coco*, or coconut, suggests pejoratively that a person is brown on the outside but white on the inside. You might say I had become an inverse "coco."

My first two months in Alpine passed dismally. Since most of my classmates were considerably younger than I and much less interested in the world outside Brewster County, I had difficulty assimilating. But halfway through the semester I played basketball with a group of guys at the university gymnasium, and because I wore a T-shirt with the logo of a professional baseball team on which one of my brothers pitched, they asked if I played baseball. When I said yes, they invited me to join a quickly assembled team that was traveling to a tiny border town named La Linda, in the state of Coahuila, to compete against the local team, a group of miners, the following weekend.

La Linda doesn't appear on most maps, nor does the road leading to it. This tiny mining village, now abandoned, was created by Dow Chemical Company because its geologists found fluorspar in the rugged mountains about twenty miles south of the river. Dow built a one-lane bridge linking the company town to a point in Texas about ten miles downriver from the eastern boundary of Big Bend National Park.

To call this corner of Texas/Mexico scenic wouldn't begin to do it justice. The river courses through spectacular canyons whose walls rise as much as two thousand feet directly out of the river, and the river gives the only access to the most breathtaking sections. If you look on a map northeast of Big Bend, you'll see a large triangle of land completely devoid of markings other than the ribbon of the Rio Grande.

My first trip to La Linda, however, was memorable not for the river but for the change it produced in my life in West Texas. I mixed easily with the Mexicans, and by the time we parted that night for the long drive back to Alpine, I had become the starting pitcher for the La Linda mine baseball team—a switch of allegiance that riled some of my classmates at Sul Ross but gave my dismal graduate school existence a boost it sorely needed. Clearly, I was a lot more at home on the river with Mexican miners than I was in an American university.

After fourteen months of playing weekend baseball in myriad dusty border towns and studying literature during the week, I received a phone call from my wife announcing that our daughter had developed a tumor above her right knee and that they were coming to the U.S. for treatment. I quit school, joined them in Memphis, Tennessee, at St. Jude's Children's Hospital, and spent much of the next eighteen months watching cancer emaciate the most beautiful and spirited eight-year-old girl in the world. She died in February of 1990, some months short of her tenth birthday.

The most difficult transition from being a parent to being childless is that one must revert to the self-centered life of the time before one became a parent. In my case, adjusting to that proved even more difficult than dealing with the devastating grief and the nightmarish memories of her illness. I've never been a guy who found himself impressive, likable, or even tolerable. In fact, my one source of pride was having been resilient enough to tolerate myself without the aid of antidepressants. As a father I was at my happiest because I could focus all my attention on my daughter; apart from her while she lived, I was often miserable. The reality of our absolute and final separation required that I reconstruct my life to avoid slipping into inexorable self-pity.

As if by an act of divine compensation for the death of my daughter, I was hired by what was then called Laredo Junior College a few months later. As many natives are fond of saying, Laredo is the most Mexican of all border towns. Put another way, it's the least American of all American cities in terms of culture, architecture, and government. Approximately ninety-seven percent of the population is Hispanic. Over ninety percent are "first language Spanish." A majority of the residents speak both languages with native fluency, but among themselves they often speak "Spanglish," typically formed with Spanish verbs, Spanish articles, Spanish modifiers, Spanish prepositions, and an occasional English word, especially nouns that are taught in the early grades of public school: days of the week, numbers, names of school supplies. I fell in love with Laredo and its people.

During spring break of that first year, 1991, Rob Boushel, a close friend from my undergraduate years, and I traveled out to the Big Bend, rented a canoe, and paddled the Rio Grande's Colorado Canyon, a sheer canyon formed by lava, near the western boundary of the national park. That brief taste of the river made us curious enough to return the following spring break, this time to attempt the remote Lower Canyons, beginning at La Linda.

Given that we were novice canoeists running a very remote section of river with white water rated Class IV (on a scale that goes only as high as Class VI); given that we had no map or guidebook to warn us of approaching dangers; and given that we ended up capsizing twice, losing nearly all of our food in the process, and having to walk a twenty-mile dirt road to pavement and our car in Langtry because we had insufficient supplies to continue by river, one would expect this experience to have discouraged me from ever embarking on a wilderness boating trip again. The reverse occurred.

Due to the challenges, isolation, and beauty of the Lower Canyons, this unpopulated river corridor became the primary focus of my life. I wanted to know every turn of the river, every rock in every channel of every rapid, every canyon wall, every animal path of the entire 137-mile length of that section of the river.

For the next thirteen years, I rafted the Lower Canyons every chance I got—twenty-eight trips in all, some longer than three weeks, some as short as one week, and most of them alone. I wrote newspaper articles about my adventures, took copious notes and thousands of photographs, and corresponded with a growing network of people I met on the river.

A wonderful thing happened in this long process. I found a home in the Lower Canyons, acquired a profound sense of belonging on the river where it defines the remotest section of the Texas-Mexico border. When I decided to take a leave of absence from my teaching job in December 2004 to begin my exploration of the entire 1,260-mile stretch of the Rio Grande from El Paso to the Gulf of Mexico (the other 600 miles of the river are in Colorado and New Mexico), I hoped to expand that sense of belonging to the entire river as it forms the border. Years ago one of the banks in Laredo ran an ad campaign with the slogan "Some people see a border; we see a bridge." I looked at the international bridge and saw it as neither bridge nor border: I saw the river, my home.

With few exceptions, everyone tried to discourage me from taking the trip. I was accused of everything from having a death wish to being ignorant of border realities. One typical reaction: "You'll never make it." Another: "People die every day in that river." People cited a plethora of dangers: drug cartels, *coyotes* (those who smuggle undocumented workers), the Border Patrol, predatory wildlife, and the river itself—its infamous pollution, numerous rapids, perilous currents, and geographic isolation.

Since I could find no published account by anyone who had made the journey, no guidebook for any section below the Lower Canyons, and no one who knew the specific dangers in those sections of river I didn't already know, I had to rely on strangers, each of whom knew only a short stretch of it. I learned that people who studied or patrolled the river looked at it through a very narrow lens. Environmentalists could specify levels of contaminants in the water to parts per million. Birders could point out the exact tree on which they had spotted an Altamira oriole or a plain chachalaca. Border Patrol agents knew the precise crossing points of an intricate web of smuggling paths. Fishermen could recite a long list of good fishing holes and the exact times of day to fish them. Powerboaters knew the sites of docks and little else. But nobody knew the whole river. Border Patrol agents couldn't tell a thing about birds, pollution, or fish. Fishermen knew nothing about smugglers, rapids, or nonaquatic wildlife. I tried to piece together as much information as I could, but most of my interviews yielded little useful information.

Before leaving on the trip, I had emailed the International Boundary and Water Commission (IBWC) main office in El Paso to inquire about the presence of dams in the river. This agency oversees the river, monitors its water flows and lake levels, and polices the stipulations of the 1944 treaty signed by the U.S. and Mexico to share and regulate the flows of the Rio Grande. I inquired about the dams because in August of 2004 two Border Patrol agents had drowned at a dam near the Los Indios International Bridge in the Rio Grande Valley. I had been unaware of any dams below Falcon Dam, the massive structure eighty miles southeast of Laredo. The official who answered my inquiry specified three dams but made no mention of the one that had claimed the lives of the two B. P. agents. I worried that I could be swept into a life-threatening situation. If

B. P. agents in a powerful motorboat had died at a dam, I didn't like my chances in a canoe.

Although nobody could tell me much about the river, an undeniable attraction of the trip was not having any idea what lay ahead. Each turn in the river offered a vista I had never before seen, each drop a rapid I had never before run. It was all new to me, and I was happy I had no guidebook to lead me through each day. Each move I made, then, would be a calculated gamble. If I passed one good campsite, would I find another before dark? If I didn't scout a rapid, would I smash the canoe? I worried about the Border Patrol, but I knew I might have to rely on its agents for information. I worried about running white water, but was eager to see rapids that had blocked steamboats a century and a half earlier. I looked forward to meeting Mexicans on the riverbanks, but I worried about those same encounters. With no advance knowledge of anything save the existence of international bridges in Presidio, Del Rio, Eagle Pass, Laredo, Roma, Rio Grande City, Reynosa, Progreso, Los Indios, and Brownsville, I was exploring an uncharted world. Never mind that this same world was under more surveillance than any other ribbon of land on the entire continent. I would see so few people and so few signs of people that it was difficult to imagine I could be anywhere but on a very remote river.

The bottom line was that, in the months ahead, most of the time I wandered around lost on the river. If the current and shores hadn't defined the course, I'd never have reached the end.

—◆◆◆—

I decided to begin the trip by mountain-biking on a rough road along the river on the Mexican side. At Presidio, Texas, a friend would bring my canoe and take the bike to storage. I would then boat the final 960 miles to the Gulf.

The choice of a mountain bike came about because I'd heard rumors that a thick growth of salt cedar trees blocked the river below the El Paso Valley. People told me the river was "channelized," meaning that it splintered into hundreds of tiny streams that flow between closely spaced salt cedars, which sometimes form an impenetrable barrier, choking the river with overhanging limbs and fallen trees.

To check it out, I drove a desolate stretch of road on the Texas side of the Rio Grande, looking for a good place to cross on a mountain bike if the channel didn't provide enough water or space for canoeing, but I never could find a way to the river because ranch fences blocked the desert that borders it. Not long after the pavement ended, I encountered two Mexican men who desperately flagged my car to a stop. Their faces bore the bruises of beatings, and cracked coagulated blood accented the swollen welts on their sunburned skin. They had been assaulted and robbed the night before while hiking a mountain pass in an attempt to circumvent the Border Patrol checkpoint on Interstate 10. One asked if I would drive them to Mexico. "We don't want to stay here," he said. "Your country is a dangerous place."

— ◆ ◆ ◆ —

Border violence is not a new phenomenon, but in the last thirty years the gruesome nature of the ever-increasing number of murders shocked even the most hardened observers. When the *San Antonio Express-News* border correspondent Jesse Bogan visited the night before my departure, he confided that one rival drug cartel in Nuevo Laredo (our sister city) was purportedly feeding its enemies to a lion—yes, literally, a lion. To his disappointment, I said I didn't find that ghastly act especially macabre, given the hideousness of past murders, few of which were even reported in the media.

Whatever apprehensions I had when I first decided to take the trip multiplied after my long research process led me to print media. The border goes unnoticed except for its stories about drug-smuggling violence, hundreds of missing young women in Juárez, deaths of undocumented workers attempting to circumvent Border Patrol checkpoints, and the disappearance of more people than ever vanished during the military dictatorships of Chile and Argentina combined. News reports of shoot-outs in the streets of Nuevo Laredo, Reynosa, and Matamoros have become so numerous that tourist-related businesses in those cities are nearly deserted. Kidnappings have soared to an alarming level. In Nuevo Laredo alone, twenty-seven Americans disappeared in the four months before I began my trip. Seemingly every person on the border can not only relate a battery of horror stories but also name a relative, friend, or classmate who was the target of such horror.

When I first arrived in Laredo in 1990, I befriended a young baseball player at the college where I teach, a Laredo native who had garnered all-state honors the year before for his outstanding play in high school. I spent many hours throwing batting practice to him in the hitting cage, and I listened patiently to his allegations that our college coach treated him unfairly "because I don't kiss his gringo ass." He confessed that his young girlfriend, the niece of a local drug lord, was pregnant. I liked this kid, and I sensed that I performed an important role in his life, primarily because he had grown up without a father. We began playing on the same team in the Nuevo Laredo semi-pro leagues on Sundays, and it was there that I watched his transition from scholarship athlete to narco-thug.

Ricardo, as I will call him, made a swift descent into the Nuevo Laredo drug-trade underworld, and his transformation from innocent adolescent to cold-blooded killer was total. He did not return to the college team for his sophomore season, electing instead to marry his pregnant girlfriend and enter the family business her uncle had gained international infamy for leading. The uncle, then the subject of an international manhunt and a standing member of the FBI's "Ten Most Wanted" list, had stepped out of his vehicle during rush hour at one of Laredo's busiest intersections, and at close range had promptly emptied the magazine of his assault weapon into the skulls of three enemies. Then he successfully eluded police for many months.

The first suggestion that Ricardo had entered his in-laws' business occurred early that same fall, when drug-sniffing dogs at the Border Patrol checkpoint leaving Laredo hit on a suspicious scent in the back of a pickup truck carrying the college baseball gear to an away game in San Antonio. Although Ricardo was no longer a member of the team, he trailed the pickup as it traveled north. B. P. agents found thirty-seven pounds of marijuana stashed in a bat bag, and though three of Ricardo's former teammates were apprehended and interrogated, no arrests were made. Ricardo later bragged to me that he had used the team as a cover to smuggle "a hell of a lot of loads." When I expressed my disappointment, he implicated several players on the college team in the small-time operation.

A few months later, Ricardo committed a series of violent acts that shocked the Laredo community. First, in broad daylight, he and an accomplice charged into a seafood restaurant during a crowded lunch hour and assassinated two rivals point-blank. When his rivals reciprocated by targeting one of his cousins, Ricardo retaliated by emptying more than thirty cartridges into a car sitting in a local drive-through convenience store. Remarkably, not a single bullet hit the driver, its intended target. Several months later, Mexican newspapers reported that Ricardo had been arrested in Monterrey, Mexico, for a series of armed bank robberies. Amazingly, a high-ranking police official there posted his bail, and Ricardo continued the slaughter of his enemies.

The last time I saw him—a chance encounter at the same Nuevo Laredo baseball fields where we once were teammates–he boasted that he was killing fifteen people a month "as part of business." I assailed his barbarism as "chicken shit" and demanded he explain the logic behind his feeble statement that his sadism was justified by his need to provide for his baby. After Ricardo struggled through several "You don't understand"s, I fired back, "I understand this: when I first knew you, Ricardo, you were a good person, a great baseball player with a good future ahead of you. Now you're bragging about killing people. Killing people! Don't you get it? People with babies and mothers and little sisters. That's what you do. You kill people and you brag about it. I can't accept that."

Ricardo buried his head in his hands and wept like a child. In a quivering, penitent voice, he said, "I'm going to try to change."

Whether or not Ricardo's words were sincere, I cannot say. I never saw him again. Within weeks, he joined the long list of players in the narcotics trade whose bodies are never located. A rumor surfaced that he had been hacked into five hundred pieces, the first hundred or so while he was still alive, which were then distributed in the back reaches of a ranch.

His cousins avenged his murder, and then they too were murdered in the continuing cycle of vengeance that wipes out each generation of new players, only to give way to a new generation of Ricardos who continue the same cycle. Unlike Ricardo, many of the victims are merely in the wrong place at the wrong time.

One of those people was another former student of mine, who for six years dated one of the baseball team's most likable players, until they had a lover's quarrel just after they finished two years of college. Alicia (not her real name) then began dating a young man who was at the center of the ongoing drug wars. Their courtship was destined to be brief. After only a few weeks, Alicia disappeared.

Some weeks later Laredo police received a phone call from yet another ex-student of mine, who offered to lead them to her body in exchange for witness protection. Apparently, his fears for his safety were justified; his specific instructions leading to the discovery of her corpse were among the last words he ever uttered, and hours after the fateful phone call, he joined the long list of the disappeared.

Police found Alicia buried in the basement of a house under construction in a good neighborhood of Nuevo Laredo, Mexico. The details of her death, presumably related by the informant, are chilling. She and her date were apprehended by members of a rival drug gang and forced into the basement of the house, where Alicia was raped repeatedly. After each violation, they sliced off one of her fingers, until all ten were removed. Finally, they killed her and turned their attention to their original target, the new boyfriend, who had been made to watch the ordeal for the previous seventy-two hours.

His fate seemed, by comparison, benign. His enemies tied him to her corpse in the conjugal position and buried him alive.

❖❖❖

In the long list of my fears on the river, being victimized by another human was only one of many. I knew firsthand that the human element I should fear the most was myself. Any micro-mistake I made could quickly turn into a large problem. Because of the isolated nature of much of the river, emergency assistance or medical help is days—in some parts, weeks—away, even assuming one can even reach that help. With the noteworthy exceptions of the area in and on either side of Big Bend National Park and the two large lakes, Amistad and Falcon, nobody floats the river except for Border Patrol surveillance boats near a few of the cities. In the past, I had gone as long as twenty-two days without seeing another person on the river. My biggest worry was what I'd do if I sustained a disabling injury a hundred river miles from the nearest access to help.

I did have a long history of finding myself in dire situations along the river. In one terrifying encounter, I found myself in the path of a charging mountain lion, which did not see me until it reached my campfire. We faced off for about thirty interminable seconds while I tried to overcome the paralyzing fear that rendered me a trembling and defenseless wimp, at once mesmerized by the beauty of the animal and immobilized by my fear of it.

As I watched the animal peering at me from forty feet, I considered two options: I could dive into the river on that icy December morning, or I could try to shout at it in hopes of scaring it away. Reasoning that my retreat to the river might signal to the mountain lion that I feared it, I opted for intimidation, and decided to bellow the most menacing shout I could muster. But my terror had nearly robbed me of the ability to breathe, and when I tried to summon a territorial roar, the sound I made was pathetic–a whimper that wouldn't have frightened a small child. But it worked! The cougar raced off in the direction from which it had come, disappearing into a cave about halfway up the canyon face above my camp.

In fact, the Rio Grande offers habitat to a number of species that could quickly ruin a canoe trip. In my previous trips, I had encountered lobos (Mexican wolves, smaller and less aggressive than their northern cousins, but a wolf is a wolf), black bears, wild boars, countless coyotes, rattlesnakes, copperheads, scorpions, and—for me the most terrifying—bulls, one of which had charged me in camp before dawn one morning, leading a dozen cattle behind it. I barely eluded this stampede by leaping across my campfire, and I was so afraid that I then did something I do only in extreme emergencies: I boarded my raft in pitch darkness and floated downriver to a beach around the next bend.

So there was plenty to fear on this proposed trip, and there were plenty of critics to stoke those fears in the months leading up to my departure. When two of my closest friends came forward to offer their company on separate sections of the adventure, I agreed. Tony Meyers, my boyhood friend who is like a brother, committed to the mountain-biking section of the trip, and Scott Hayes, or "Hayesy," a frequent companion of mine on rafting trips in the Lower Canyons, committed to the La Linda–to–Amistad Dam section. I would be on my own for the remainder of the trip, but with Tony along for the beginning, and Hayesy along for the most isolated part, I felt somewhat reassured.

By not going the entire route alone, however, I did feel I was compromising the spirit of the trip. Moreover, I battled daily the fear that by accompanying me, either Tony or Hayesy might fall victim to some accident, wild animal, or illness. That such a thing might happen on my watch nagged at me for weeks as the trip neared, particularly in the case of Tony, who is the father of three children.

We would have to bike much of the distance between El Paso and Presidio on a rough road on the Mexican side, passing through remote villages where few gringos had traveled. Although Tony had retained a remarkable amount of the vocabulary he had learned in high-school Spanish classes thirty years earlier, he wasn't close to being fluent, and I worried that this could be dangerous if we found ourselves in a tight spot.

Few people look more gringo than Tony. At six feet three inches, this fair-skinned, blond Mormon couldn't be mistaken for a Latin American even if he had had a native's fluency in Spanish. Maybe it was foolhardy of me, but I thought that my comparatively dark complexion might escape notice, at least while I was moving quickly on a bicycle; teamed with Tony, I knew I'd have no chance of blending in. As a pair, we would appear to the locals as exactly what we were: two large gringos on a curious adventure. We would make an easy target if anyone decided to relieve us of our belongings. And it would be a very long walk out of there if anything were to happen.

I never did confide my fears about the trip to Tony, preferring instead to accept the logic that he could just as easily die in a car wreck in his daily commute in Sacramento as he could riding the backcountry of the Chihuahua border. I kept secret from him the stories of Ricardo and Alicia, laughed off my previous encounters with wildlife as "That's what makes trips fun," and agreed to meet him on the west side of El Paso, six days before Christmas, to begin what would become one of the most fascinating weeks in our lives.

El Paso Valley

Dec. 19–20

On a brightly sunny Sunday morning, I found Tony awaiting me in the shadow of a copper smelter, his mountain bike saddlebags already packed and loaded. For once in his life, he'd arrived ahead of schedule. I'd been emphasizing to him during daily phone calls over the previous weeks how important it was for him to be timely. I had hired a man to accompany me to El Paso for the sole purpose of driving Tony's truck to Presidio, where we'd end the biking part of my trip, and I was paying the man by the hour.

My father was also along to move my car to Langtry, Texas, where it would sit for the first half of my trip. Although I'd seen Tony dozens of times over the years, Dad hadn't seen Tony since the early '70s. Their reunion might have consumed our precious biking time, but my father seemed eager to be on his way. I wondered if I would ever see him again. Given his increasing age and growing list of maladies, and the dangers of my trip, the possibility that I wouldn't merited at least a passing consideration. In that pensive moment, I felt relieved about Tony's companionship on the initial stage of the long trip.

Tony's and my approach to outfitting ourselves for the biking trip offered a study in contrasts. Tony was straight off the cover of *Outside* magazine. In his saddlebags he carried a BlackBerry, twin walkie-talkies, a digital videocamera, a new tent, three fragrant Cuban cigars smuggled in from his recent fishing trip to Cabo San Lucas, Italian biking pants and shirt, special biking shoes that clipped into his pedals, and water bladders with valved hoses. Add to the total his light-as-a-feather, full-suspension mountain bike and its custom tires; an impressive assortment of energy bars, electrolyte fluids, and hydrating gels; a wad of cash; credit cards; and a box of award-winning California wine.

A disciple of voluntary simplicity, I was stripped down to a change of clothes; a week's worth of sardines, instant oatmeal, crackers, beans, and chewing tobacco; a sleeping bag; a bottle of cheap whiskey; and enough pens and paper to record every word and tire rotation along the entire three hundred miles of river we would parallel. Instead of tailored saddlebags, I used my plastic laundry basket from Target and a backpack so old that the zippers no longer closed.

The contrast in our gear was consistent with the difference in our two characters. Outgoing and gregarious, Tony thrives as the center of attention, while I prefer solitude and quiet. He's nearly always well-groomed, and I'm the kind of guy who looks into the mirror and groans "Oh, not you again!" Tony comes from a family of cerebral doctors, and he, a civil engineer, has always been the athlete in the group. On the other hand, I'm the most educated in a family of athletes, and am regarded by my relatives as "the cerebral one." Tony's fine neighborhood houses several of the NBA's Sacramento Kings, while I live in a poor barrio three blocks from the border, and most of my family members say the only good thing about my marginal living arrangements is that I'm still alive.

Tony is a big guy who spends enough time in the gym to maintain a lean and powerful physique. He is so fit that twice he has completed what he calls "rim to rim to rims," meaning that by running and hiking, he went from the North Rim of the Grand Canyon to the South Rim and back in one day, a distance of more than forty miles. I accompanied him for part of one of those hikes and didn't walk right for a week afterward. Tony attacks life, charging down the highway at high speeds, tailgating drivers on a California freeway while talking on his cell, eating his lunch, and changing a CD. He is the kind of guy who packs more living into a single day than most people do in a week.

Despite our having little in common except sharing many of our happiest childhood memories, Tony remains my best friend because his enthusiasm for life, his undying optimism, and his perseverance make him the most determined person I know. He tries to be many things to many people, but when I hang out with him, I marvel at how fully he invests himself in whatever we're doing.

We seemed a mismatched pair as we boarded the bikes and set off along the narrow sidewalk between the highway and the river fence, pedaling toward the El Paso skyline with an enthusiasm yet to be diminished by the physical demands of carrying that much weight. By the time you factored in the drinking water, I carried close to fifty pounds, and Tony's freight had to be more than double that.

Our route began below the 828-foot-high smokestack at the ASARCO smelter, a plant that produces copper from iron ore mined in Mexico. Despite the plant's location on prime real estate close to downtown and the neighboring University of Texas at El Paso, there isn't a home for over a mile around it. In 1975 ASARCO, facing studies suggesting it was responsible for lead poisoning in children who lived in the nearby neighborhood, bought the entire community and relocated its residents. Thirty years later the area remains vacant, a gaping hole on El Paso's affluent west side.

We followed the river past the very shantytown I had seen on my first trip to El Paso thirty years before, until we reached the fringe of downtown and climbed a steep bridge to cross Interstate 10. We arrived in a delightful residential neighborhood in the foothills below the university, with a fine view of downtown El Paso and its less-scenic twin city, Ciudad Juárez.

The twin cities form "the most populous metro area on an international boundary in the world," according to the El Paso County official website. Despite the fact that Juárez is one of Mexico's wealthiest cities and El Paso one of the U.S.'s poorest, the per capita income of El Pasoans is roughly five times that of their Mexican neighbors. As Tony and I looked at the panorama below, we had the impression that the economic disparity between the two was even greater. The immaculate skyscrapers of El Paso shimmered in the brilliant sunshine, while immediately behind them lay a nondescript urban sprawl that stretched to the southern horizon.

"Is it as poor as it looks?" Tony asked.

"No, but all the money is over the horizon on the south edge of Juárez. The rich in Juárez are as rich as the elite of El Paso and probably richer."

Palatial estates hide behind fortresslike walls on the city's south side, each home maintained by a small army of hired help. The stark difference between the two cities is in how their poor live. Juárez's middle class survives on less income than El Paso's poor, and its poor on less—far less—than El Paso's homeless.

The land on which El Paso sits was part of Mexico until the Mexican–American War, but El Paso didn't prosper as a city until the railroad reached it in 1881. Juárez, on the other hand, was an established agricultural community long before Mexico gained independence from Spain, and was primarily a stopover point for travelers heading between settlements in present-day New Mexico and Chihuahua.

We coasted down a steep decline into the west side of El Paso's center, until we reached Paisano Street, which parallels the river as it cuts through the south side of downtown. Throngs of pedestrians jammed the sidewalks, and we navigated through heavy traffic by weaving in and out between the cars. We cut through a neighborhood in the shadow of the downtown international bridge, at a much faster pace than the congested Sunday traffic, to César Chávez Highway, a four-lane divided thoroughfare that hugs the riverbanks all the way to the edge of El Paso.

Even though I had already ridden freight trains or driven in a car on this precise route through downtown more times than I could count, I couldn't say I had done the entire border if I skipped this section. And, to my surprise, I didn't find it boring. Our pace, about twelve miles an hour, allowed us to see so much more than I'd ever seen from an automobile, and the mountain of gear piled on our bicycles drew the favorable attention of hundreds of motorists, who honked their horns and waved at us.

A few miles of pedaling brought us to Chamizal Park, near the international bridge of the same name. "Chamizal" comes from the Spanish word *chamisa*, or saltbush, and the park commemorates the signing of the Chamizal treaty in 1963 to resolve a heated border dispute between the two countries over a redirection of the Rio Grande, caused by flooding. For nearly a hundred years, the two nations had feuded over the land, known as El Chamizal. Under President Kennedy, the dispute was finally resolved, and the agreement called for the construction of the concrete channel that now carries the river.

Like nearly all rivers, the Rio Grande has a long history of flooding, but because it forms an international border for two thirds of its distance, flooding here has caused unique problems. In fact, much of the riverbank we biked along this first day on the east side of the river was formerly on the west side. Elephant Butte Dam, built in 1916, more than a hundred miles upriver, has been effective in limiting flooding in the El Paso Valley. Nowadays, flooding in the river's main channel is very rare; a complex system of dams and diversions nearly always keeps the flow well within the concrete channel.

The obvious conclusion one draws while gazing at the Rio Grande in El Paso is that man has tamed, or, more accurately, drained it. The river enters the El Paso Valley with little water, and it leaves, most months of the year, with next to none. Although the city taps its drinking water from wells rather than the river, when wells are drained, much of the rainwater recharges them before finding its way into the river. For sixty miles below El Paso, large farms grow thirsty crops like cotton and melons year-round, which take large draws from the Rio Grande. El Paso's average annual rainfall is less than nine inches a year, and it counts three hundred days of sunshine. When you factor the water demands of at least two million people on both sides of the river into the requirements of an agricultural belt of some one hundred fifty square miles, it's surprising that any water ever leaves the El Paso Valley. Add to the mix a long drought, and it's a wonder crops aren't shriveling in the fields. In fact, as we biked through El Paso, the reservoir at Elephant Butte held only five percent of normal capacity, a level threatening to dry up towns and farms all the way from Truth or Consequences, New Mexico, to Presidio, Texas.

Late that first afternoon, we turned off the river road and made the six-mile climb to the interstate to get a motel room in a clapboard building behind a small truck stop. Although it was only 4 o'clock, the clerk said the motel had filled and directed us to the motel in Fabens, about eight miles away on the interstate. We ignored the on-ramp signs prohibiting nonmotorized vehicles and pedaled on the edge of the wide shoulder, aided by wind gusts at our backs thrown by one semi truck after another. This experience hardly fit my idyllic conception of the long trip, but I found solace in knowing that by the same hour tomorrow, we'd be entering a world few people are fortunate enough to experience.

◆◆◆

When Tony awoke the following morning, he immediately wanted to do something he does more of in one day than I do in most weeks—eat. I have never known anyone who eats so incessantly. During our frequent stops the day before, Tony would retrieve snack food from one of the myriad pockets on his bike's saddlebags and spend the entire break furiously chewing. I sensed his biggest fear about our trip was that he would run out, and the very manner in which he attacked his rations at every opportunity suggested he worried most that our tight schedule wouldn't allow him enough time to eat the extraordinary quantities he consumed. As we walked to the restaurant, I asked if he thought he carried enough food to last the next week. "Shoot, I have enough to last two guys ten days," he said. "I think I brought too much."

"Even if you didn't," I said, "we'll find little stores along the way in the Mexican villages. But the selection will be really thin, so if there's anything you can think of that you need, we need to buy it here in Fabens."

We ordered eggs and beans for breakfast, and before our meal came, Tony grilled me about just what we would be able to buy in the Mexican villages and how often we would encounter stores.

To each question, I shrugged and replied, "I don't know."

Back at the motel, Tony did a close inventory of his rations. He had so much food that the inventory process took him half an hour. "I have more than enough," he said, "so if you get tired of sardines, I'll be happy to share."

The road linking Fabens to the interstate proceeds toward an international bridge several miles away, but only Highway 20, a two-lane road dividing cotton fields, would allow us to travel parallel to the river, which of course was my goal. Tony's enthusiastic early-morning charge put him so far ahead that I could barely see his bike in the distance. I watched helplessly as he missed the Highway 20 turn and proceeded toward the international bridge.

I tried to enlist help from passing motorists. The first couple wouldn't even roll their windows down to hear my plea, but the third guy at least gave me the opportunity. I hurried through my story and then said, "So can you tell my friend that I'm waiting back here?"

The man stared at me and replied in Spanish, "I don't speak English."

I rushed through the story again in Spanish, but the light changed to green, and the guy said, "Sorry, but I'm turning here."

Then a sheriff's deputy approached and I flagged him over. He seemed disappointed that my little emergency didn't involve a crime, but he agreed to go look for Tony.

Five minutes later, the Spanish-speaking man who had denied my request reappeared and pulled over to tell me that he had gone out of his way to relay my message to Tony. "I don't think he under-stood me at first, but now he's coming back and he should be here in a few minutes," he said. A moment later the sheriff's deputy arrived, confirming what the other man had just told me.

When Tony arrived, winded from his three-mile detour, he searched through his saddlebags for the two walkie-talkies. He handed me one and instructed me how to use it, eating the whole time he was explaining. These, he claimed, would prevent any more unnecessary detours. Mr. Voluntary Simplicity, I was not enthusiastic about carrying a device. Five miles outside of town, we pulled over for a rest break, and while he was making quick work of yet another snack, I said I was turning the walkie-talkie off to save the batteries.

But he called my bluff. "Don't worry; I brought plenty of extra batteries."

I worried. The thought of listening to Tony's walkie-talkie voice saying "¿Qué pasa, mi amigo?" every five minutes for the next week made me anxious. Tony mixed in some CB lingo with his gringo Spanish, saying things like "That's un grande ten-cuatro." At first, I tried having fun with the walkie-talkie, using CB radio slang I had memorized from my many hitchhiking trips in the '70s, but that grew old even faster now than it had in my youth. For a couple of hours, I had the sinking feeling that I might have to toss the walkie-talkie into a cotton field and then pretend I'd misplaced it.

Tony's eating capacity was clear, but I hadn't considered how much he could drink. The pace of our biking meant that we were going to need plenty of water, and by the time we approached Fort Hancock early that afternoon, what I had guessed would be a two-day supply of water was almost gone. At a laundromat we found a couple more gallons, but Tony worried that it might not be enough, and almost as if to prove his point drank another quart.

Mexicans strike out on challenging adventures with far less water than we had, so Tony's consumption caught me off guard. I had grown used to their stoicism, but realized that Tony took a more logical approach. After all, our purpose was to have fun, not push limits we didn't have to push.

After Fort Hancock, the countryside became so barren that even cactus didn't grow. I could see dwarfed creosote shrubs and spindly tumbleweed, but little else. Below us, the river threaded through a valley now bordered by large, craggy mountains, but we could see no water, only the ribbon of salt cedar trees that obscured the river.

Salt cedar, or tamarisk, is a non-native species that was introduced to the American West from Europe in the 1800s to control erosion from flooding. To say it succeeded in that mission is an understatement of distressing proportions: These trees consume at least twice as much water as any of the native species, and they multiply at an alarming pace, rapidly overtaking all other plants. Mature salt cedars drink as much as three hundred gallons of water daily, and then secrete salt through their scalelike leaves. This salt inhibits the growth of native plants, choking out riparian trees like cottonwood and willow.

A century ago the Rio Grande's banks were lined with cottonwoods; now salt cedar has grown in so thickly that in most places you can't see the river unless you're within twenty feet of it. And thanks in part to the salt cedar's tremendous thirst, there isn't much river to see even at that distance. Studies suggest it may even abet flooding by choking creek beds that would otherwise help to divert floodwater. It also provides poor habitat for animals, birds, and insects.

 Salt cedars do, however, give the otherwise drab winter desert a fiery breath of color as the green leaves change in late autumn to a burnt yellow.

Late in the day, Tony and I began the last stretch of paved road—eleven miles that closely parallel the salt cedar as the river dips into a wide canyon. By now, the traffic had thinned so much that we rode carefree down the middle of the pavement, and as the sun dropped low, we began looking for camp. I wanted a site near a large source of firewood, preferably mesquite, which is so dense with natural oils that it burns far longer than any other hardwood. Just as I was telling Tony how to spot a mesquite tree, I saw a large one near an arroyo off the sparsely traveled desert two-lane road. We walked the bikes through the sand to the base of the tree, and I began snapping off dead branches for our camp.

In the desert in winter, the air cools quickly once the sun has set, and although we had been sweating on the bikes a couple of hours earlier, we were huddled close to the fire by the time dusk descended. An hour later, we rummaged through our gear for our warmest clothing.

We were now at the outer reaches of the El Paso Valley, and very few people lived in the remote desert that awaited us the next day. We were very likely to be the first two foreigners ever to bicycle through there. If something should go terribly wrong from this point on, we would be far from help. The next tiny town on the U.S. side was two hundred miles distant, and we knew almost nothing about what we would find in Mexico. The area had a reputation as a drug-smuggling corridor, and we had no idea how we would be received.

On the Narco-Trail to Indian
Hot Springs

Dec. 21–22

The two-hundred-mile stretch of the Rio Grande between Fort Quit-man and Presidio, Texas, is called the Forgotten River. No paved roads access the river here, and the total population along its banks likely numbers fewer than three hundred people, though a census count would take so long that the population would change before it could be completed. Nearly all the residents live on the Mexican side.

There are only two ways into the area: one by river, when there is a river, and the other by a very rough dirt road that parallels the river on the Mexican side. This road is little more than a one-lane four-wheel-drive trail. It offers no services whatsoever beyond a handful of small signs pointing the way at forks that lead inland south of the river. I had learned of the road by purchasing a Joint Operations graphic map (essentially a pilot's map, used by the military and the Border Patrol) produced by the Defense Mapping Agency in Washington, D.C.

I had talked to dozens of people who live on the periphery of this area and found only one who had ever bothered to explore any part of it. When I told another guy my plan to bicycle the Mexican side, he warned me, "That is unlikely to be an adventure you're going to think was a very good idea once you get so far into it that you can't get out. You won't make it, but hopefully you'll still be able to turn around when you realize just how foolish it was to even try."

I didn't pass this bit of advice on to Tony while we were breaking camp that brisk December morning. I also neglected to tell him about the small mountain of border books I had devoured in preparation for the long trip. One, Charles Bowden's (no relation) *Down by the River*, dealt in part with a continuing series of horrific murders in and out-side Juárez. Another, William Langewiesche's *Cutting for Sign*, devoted a chapter to the Brite massacre in 1918, in which the Texas Rangers retaliated for a group of Mexicans' murderous raid on the Brite Ranch south of Marfa, Texas. The rangers went to El Porvenir, in the very corridor we were about to explore, and shot fifteen Mexicans point-blank. Yet another book detailed the unbridled violence committed in the 1980s by Pablo Acosta's drug cartel in and around Ojinaga, located at the end of our planned bike ride. If you want uplifting, reassuring news about the border, stay away from print media. I concluded that the only reason I hadn't read any horrific stories specific to the Mexi-can road we were about to travel was that it's inaccessible to journalists; when a body disappeared there, no one came around to notice.

As we were breaking camp, I discovered that my bike had a flat tire, and we didn't have the right wrench to remove the wheel. Tony carried an impressive supply of tools, spare inner tubes and patching material, but we learned that his wheels were different from mine. For a moment I cursed my potentially disastrous oversight, but then felt relief that we were only five miles past a truck stop. I had no choice but to borrow Tony's bike and backtrack to the interstate, hoping to find a wrench at the windswept truck stop where the highway sepa-rates from the river.

The truck stop seemed frozen in another era, its few patrons and workers eerily silent. On the dusty and disorganized shelves, I found the channel lock pliers I needed, and then tried to locate a valve corer, but neither the girl at the register nor the elderly man she consulted knew what I was talking about. Outside, I found three young guys painting posts, and I asked them about getting a valve corer from the tire shop whose sign I'd seen in an outbuilding. The one English-speaking guy said I'd have to wait until midafternoon for the man with the key to the tire shop to return. He asked where I was going on the bike; my answer made them all pause in their work and move closer. We switched to Spanish.

"How's the road down to Indian Hot Springs?" I said.

"I hope you have good tires on that bike because it's rough," one guy said.

"And you're not going to find anything on the way. No stores, no people, no nothing," said another.

"Is the bridge still there?"

"Yeah, but it's not much of a bridge, barely wide enough for that bike."

"Is there anywhere before the hot springs that I can cross the river?"

"If you want to sink into the mud up to your waist."

As I mounted the bike, the English-speaker said, "Be careful. It's dangerous out there."

Tony changed my inner tube and we pedaled hard down the last nine miles of pavement. At the beginning of the dirt road, we found an old man sitting next to a shack. He gave us drinking water from a cooler and a rough idea about what to expect on the dirt road between his home and Indian Hot Springs. When I told him I intended to go all the way to the Gulf of Mexico, he asked in Spanish, "Is it far?"

Although I found this question amusing, it portended the startling ignorance of geography I would encounter among the locals in the months ahead. Few people had clear ideas of the distances between familiar points, and many mistook the locations of towns and cities. One man thought Laredo was located just below Amistad Dam, the actual site of Del Rio. Countless others, on both sides of the river, estimated distances of ten or twenty miles as "a mile or two." Many had no clear idea what the Gulf of Mexico was, and, especially when talking to Mexicans, I learned to say my destination was *el mar* (the sea) rather than *el golfo*. Mexicans were usually proficient in giving directions, but nearly always gave distances in how long it would take in a truck rather than in miles or kilometers. Most of the Americans I met knew nothing of the Mexican side of the river.

Once we left the pavement, we made slow progress. The road undulated in a series of rises so steep that we had to brake on our way down and walk the bikes at least part of the way up. With each mile, we saw fewer and fewer signs of human existence. For the first hour, we saw no other vehicles. At one scenic rise, from which we could see the dirt road roll for miles in each direction, we stopped to take pictures and rest. Here Tony shot video and, trying to liven up the otherwise eventless footage, called me on his walkie-talkie: "Hey, Keith-o, what's your 20?"

"My 20 is about twenty feet away from you!"

Suddenly, the roar of a nearby truck engine startled us, and we moved the bikes to allow the as-yet-invisible vehicle to pass. A moment later the truck careened out from behind a sandy hill and sped away from us. The driver apparently never saw us. After a couple more miles of roller-coaster biking, we met the same truck as it returned. This time the driver stopped at the unlikely sight of our overloaded bikes. He was perhaps thirty-five years old, a Mexican-American rancher, dressed in cowboy hat, Wrangler jeans, and a western shirt. We began a cheerful conversation in the middle of the road.

"When I tell *mi señora* that I saw two gringos biking out here, she's going to tell me I've been out in the sun too long," he laughed.

"How's the road between here and Indian Hot Springs?" I asked.

"That's where you're going?

"We're going all the way to Ojinaga, but we want to cross the river there and bike on the Mexican side."

He let out a low whistle and turned his eyes away from me, looking at a distant range of mountains above the Mexican side of the river.

"*Supongo que hablas español porque no vas a encontrar a nadie que hable inglés*" (I suppose you speak Spanish because you're not going to find anyone over there who speaks English).

"*Claro que sí hombre*" (Of course, man), I said.

"*Mira,*" he said, turning to Tony. "It's going to be a slow trip, so I hope you're not in a hurry."

"Do we have to cross any mountains?" Tony said.

"You'll have two big hills to get over–no, three. The first isn't too bad. You'll do fine, but the second is going to take you way up. The third one takes you pretty high too, but it's not so steep, just long," he said. After a long pause, he added, "But that second one is going to be tough. You'll be walking most of the way."

When I asked him to compare the road on the Mexican side to what we had already traveled, he chuckled as if to dismiss any basis for comparison. "Well, that Mexican-side road is going to be a lot rougher. It takes you *way* up over that pass." He gestured toward the sky as he talked. "And watch out for the weather. The weathermen are saying a norther is due tonight and it may snow."

He said most of the villages we would pass had a small store and that there were a few families in each pueblo or *rancho*. "Listen, when you get to Indian Hot Springs–and if you hurry you might make it there before dark–say hello to Chuy for me. He looks after the place."

Our spirits buoyed by this encounter, we raced the bikes down the dusty road. Several miles on we rounded a bend in the road to find a sign: PRIVATE RANCH. TRESPASSERS WILL BE PROSECUTED. Tony said, "How seriously do you take this sign?"

"Very."

I gazed down at the river snaking through the valley below us, scouting for a possible low-water crossing into Mexico. Access to the river looked steep, and the riverside fields were fenced.

"But I didn't come all the way out here to turn around. Let's go!" I said.

Few things cause me more paranoia than trespassing in the state of Texas, but this time this ranch was simply too remote for me to worry. I never considered turning around. Still, I kept our pace brisk as I led us across the ranch before we were spotted. Despite the flat terrain, sandy patches made the going slow, and I thought of those bad dreams where an enemy is in hot pursuit but your legs move only in slow motion. Just when I decided to relax and let whatever happened happen, the sound of an approaching vehicle forced us to move off the narrow road. My heart sank when I saw a Department of Public Safety cruiser, the Texas equivalent of the highway patrol. I figured we were busted.

"Oh shit," Tony muttered as the patrol car screeched to a stop, raising a cloud of dust.

The two officers turned out to be congenial and more curious about our trip than concerned about our trespassing. They were en route to Indian Hot Springs themselves.

"We're going down there to tough-talk the caretaker," one said. "We hear he might be involved in marijuana smuggling."

They had driven all the way from Abilene, a city at least four hundred miles away, and I grew suspicious and uneasy. If they'd come one hundred miles from El Paso, I could understand, but Abilene was just too far. Despite their pleasant demeanor, I was relieved when our brief visit ended, although my relief was tempered by the thought that we'd surely run into them again. The road dead-ended at the hot springs.

We had been pedaling hard for hours when the DPS officers sped by on their way back toward the pavement. As the sun dipped behind the mountains behind us, we reached an abandoned ranch on a rise above the river, and knowing Indian Hot Springs lay close, we decided to set up camp in a pasture between the road and the river. Littered with piles of cowshit, the pasture offered a less than ideal site. I sensed Tony's displeasure with the site as I bounded off in search of firewood. With a norther on its way, we would need an impressive stack for the night in camp and the next morning.

Just then, a pickup truck approached slowly from the direction of Indian Hot Springs, and its driver scrutinized us as he drove past. I waved him over.

"How much further to Indian Hot Springs?"

"Not too far. Maybe one mile." I sensed he wasn't comfortable speaking English, and he left.

Ten minutes later, he returned and stopped. This time we spoke only in Spanish.

"Why are you going to Indian Hot Springs?" he asked.

"Actually, we're going to Ojinaga," I said, "but we want to cross the bridge at the hot springs. Do you know the place?"

"Of course, I'm the caretaker there."

I introduced myself to Chuy and told him about our meeting the rancher who had sent him greetings. "Well, you can camp here if you want, but it's going to be very cold tonight, or you can stay at the guest house at the resort. There's no heat in there, but you'll be out of the wind."

I wouldn't have cared if the night's weather were the best all year; I wasn't refusing a stay at Indian Hot Springs for a night in a dusty cow pasture. I had seen pictures of it on the Internet. Tony and I tossed our bikes and gear into the back of Chuy's truck, and he drove us to the stucco-walled guest quarters just inside the wrought-iron gate of the ranch's entrance.

Now in his mid-fifties, Chuy had worked at the resort since he was sixteen, crossing the river from his native village, Ojos Calientes, on the pedestrian footbridge we would cross the following day. He seemed eager for our company, although he was, by nature a shy and taciturn man accustomed to keeping quiet around gringos. While we settled into our simple rooms, he drove down to his casita next to the resort's spacious main building to fetch beers for us. Tony retrieved one of his precious Cuban cigars and gave it to Chuy when he returned.

Chuy knew the Mexican side of the river well, and I asked question after question. He said that Ojos Calientes, the tiny village visible immediately across the river, was home to four families. The biggest village in the area, Bosque Bonito, had another twenty families and a store that sold beer. He could not give us a precise distance to "Bosque" (as he called it), but said the trip took an hour by pickup truck if the road was in good condition.

"And if it's not?"

"Then you're better off on horseback."

While Chuy smoked cigarettes (he'd pocketed the cigar), I sensed it was a new experience for him to be treated with respect by a gringo; he appeared uneasy but not unhappy with his new status. Like so many Mexican ranch hands in the U.S., he was humble, proud, and stoic. Men such as Chuy often seem aware of their relative good fortune in holding jobs as ranch hands on the American side, paid in American dollars, but at the same time they live every day conscious of the in-justice of having to do so. Almost without exception, Mexican-born ranch hands earn less money, garner less trust, and face more difficult living conditions than their American-born counterparts.

When I asked Chuy about a late-model Cadillac parked outside the ranch gate, he said it belonged to a gringo who had gone to a ranch in the hills across the river. The man had vehicles on both sides of the river and he came and went often. I found this to be an unlikely story, especially given the rough road conditions. Aside from the DPS patrol car, the other three vehicles we'd seen on the road were pickup trucks, as were the half-dozen vehicles parked inside the gate of the resort. This wasn't the sort of environment for any vehicle with low ground clearance. My wariness made Chuy uneasy, and a minute later he excused himself and went home.

Tony's and my gratitude for Chuy's hospitality intensified during the night, as the northern cold front arrived and brought with it an icy rain that blew in sheets for hours. Neither of us slept well, what with the rain and howling winds, and about halfway through the night, we found ourselves witnessing a suspicious transfer of contraband right outside the side window of our guest quarters. A pickup truck arrived. We heard men's voices speaking hurriedly in English as they transferred a bale from the bed of the pickup to the trunk of the Cadillac. Then they raced off in a short caravan in the direction of the pavement, and Tony called to me from the other room, "Wow, did you hear all of that?"

"Yeah," I said. "First, the state troopers from Abilene, then Chuy, now this. Man, I can't wait to see what tomorrow brings."

Tony laughed. "This is so cool!"

At daybreak, we awoke to a wintry morning, the temperature hovering right at freezing, the north winds stout, a sleety rain gusting. I had little enthusiasm for biking in such conditions, and Tony needed some time to repair the three inner tubes I had already punctured. Each time the rain eased for a few minutes, I went out to explore the riverbank and the hills above the resort. From above, the resort looked like a hacienda, with a low rock wall defining its perimeter and a spread of stucco buildings surrounded by manicured pastures. The hot springs themselves were encased in a building near the main house. I was surprised to learn that they weren't true hot springs because they required a motorized pump to transport the water to the bathhouse.

I could see the small, spread-out village of Ojos Calientes on the *vega*, or fertile lowland, across the river. A brightly painted white chapel sat in its center, looking like part of the set for a spaghetti Western film. In between the resort and the tiny village, the burnt-yellow ribbon of salt cedar above the hidden river defined the border. Dark, foreboding mountains rose beyond the little village, and downriver the ribbon of tamarisk disappeared into a sheer canyon some four hundred feet deep. The transcendent beauty of this vista caused me to pause there long after the freezing rain started again in earnest. You can spend a lifetime on the border and never see anything quite so perfect.

I walked to the river's edge to look at the frail suspension bridge, which swung violently in the wind. Its twin steel pipes and rotting plywood walking surface affixed by baling wire looked jerrybuilt. Twin braided steel cables acted as handrails. I doubted this bridge would hold my weight, let alone the weight of Tony and me with our loaded bikes. Then a man appeared in a clearing on the Mexican side and scaled the stairs leading to the bridge. The plywood floorboards creaked and sagged with each step he took, but he appeared unconcerned about the bridge's trustworthiness. He marched across and disappeared in the direction of Chuy's casita.

At midday, as the rains and winds began to ease and Tony finished repairing the inner tubes, we loaded the bikes. Tony tried to lighten his load by leaving behind his box of merlot, but I found room for it in the corner of my plastic laundry basket. Just as the steely gray skies began to brighten, we went to bid good-bye to Chuy. We found him aloof, but when Tony passed him a tip of fifty dollars, his face brightened momentarily. Still, his apparent uneasiness with our presence made me hurry through our farewell.

With a raw north breeze stinging our faces, we marched toward the footbridge to Mexico.

Chihuahua Welcomes
the Gringos

Dec. 22–24

Ojos Calientes, Chihuahua, the village I'd glimpsed from my lofty perch, sits at the confluence of the Rio Grande and a wide arroyo that drains the Sierra del Pino. We counted six houses as we biked sandy paths toward the arroyo, four of which appeared to be occupied. Other than a battered old pickup truck rusting beside one run-down house, we saw no evidence that this village had been exposed to either the twentieth or the twenty-first century. The crude adobe dwellings seemed to sag into the ground, and the only noise we heard came from roosters roaming beneath the mesquite trees, pecking at the sand. I sensed that the few residents of this tiny settlement were peering at us from inside their houses, but then I noticed that none of the structures had windows. A wisp of smoke emanated from the adobe brick chimney of the last house, and I felt relief when we reached the arroyo, which Chuy had told us to follow until we found the main road. When I had asked him how far, he had replied in Spanish, "In a pickup truck, it only takes a few minutes."

Tony and I spent close to half an hour pushing the bikes because the surface of the arroyo was soft, unpacked sand and then loose pea stone. But at least we stayed warm doing it. Just as we reached the main road—a narrow, rutted, four-wheel-drive track—an old Ford pickup approached slowly from the direction we would go. Water splashed out of both sides of the truck bed, and a pony towed by a frayed rope followed behind. As the truck drew near, I saw the source of the splashes: a large uncovered vat used for transporting water from a mountain spring stood in the back of the truck. The truck made slow progress as it approached us on the rugged road. I was certain we were the first mountain bikers this rancher had ever seen, so I was both curious and apprehensive to see his reaction.

The Ford came to a stop next to me, and a handsome man in his thirties rolled down the window. I could see past him in the cab to four precious little girls, ranging in age from about three to seven, staring wide-eyed at me. Flanking them on the far side of the cab sat their mother, an olive-skinned woman who bore a close resemblance to all four children. The girls' eyes grew so large at the close sight of me that I found it difficult not to return their stare. The man's gaze suggested that I needed to explain just what the hell Tony and I were doing wandering around so far from the gringos' natural habitat. Out the corner of my eye, I saw that the happiest member of the group was the pony, who was using his brief rest stop to feed on the scrub growth.

"We're going to Ojinaga," I said, and the man glanced at the bike as the woman broke into a wide smile.

"It's very far," he said. "And where did you start?"

"In El Paso, Texas."

"That's also very far. Don't you have a truck?

I smiled and said, "Yes, but it's more fun to ride the bike."

I offered him a sack of hard candy to give to the girls, as all four pairs of big brown eyes stared at my blue ones. Although he was neither warm nor welcoming, I found the man's reception reassuring. We were no big deal, perhaps a little *loco,* but harmless enough that he would feed his girls the hard candy I had offered. I counted this first meeting a success.

The road heads southeast from Ojos Calientes. Stark mountains rise above the foothills to the right, and the wall of Mayfield Canyon across the river on the Texas side defines the left. Twenty minutes of rough riding brought us to a desolate fork, where a small blue highway sign pointed to Bosque Bonito, thirty-five kilometers away. My biggest fear, I had confided to Tony when he first suggested that he accompany me, was getting lost in this far-off backcountry. My detailed aviation map hadn't been updated in over twenty years, and despite the unchanged-for-centuries look of the first village we'd visited, I worried that much could have changed in the layout of these remote roads. A rainy-season flood could reroute a road miles from its previous course; a change in state government might bring favors to one large ranch at the expense of another and thereby change the direction of connecting roads; roads could have become impassable due to lack of use, as a whole generation of backcountry Chihuahuans emigrated to the U.S. to seek work that paid enough to feed and clothe themselves. Seeing the road sign pointing the way to Bosque Bonito alleviated, at least temporarily, my fear of losing our way.

Because of our late start, we knew we would have to make camp well before reaching Bosque Bonito, a good four- or five-hour bike ride away. The road led over a mountain pass, undulating even more than our roller-coaster ride of the previous afternoon. We'd walk the bikes up a steep rise of several hundred yards, only to have to inch them down the treacherous back side of that rise. Then we'd repeat the rise and fall time after time, until finally, late in the afternoon, we crested the last pass and found our reward: a spectacular 360-degree vista, made even more impressive by a sky that held black rain clouds, with scintillating blue patches below wispy streaks of high clouds, all in motion. Far over our shoulders we could see mountains we had passed two days before; ahead, those we would pass in the coming days. In declining light, we raced down a sinuous stretch of road that ended in another wide arroyo. A two-ton truck carrying a half-dozen head of cattle passed just as we pulled off to scout for a camp.

In three hours of hard going, we had traveled a mere ten miles. We decided to camp at the base of a thirty-foot dirt cliff that rose above the arroyo. I had learned from years of camping alone in the Chihuahua desert to scout a site thoroughly before deciding to stay. I checked the ground for animal prints and scat in a wide area around camp. I noticed a few mountain lion and coyote prints along the base of the cliff, but no signs of a hunting trail. Camping on or near the hunting trail of mountain lions terrified me. While Tony and I scavenged for firewood, I paid close attention to the direction and number of mountain lion prints. Once I felt certain that cat tracks posed no imminent danger, I attacked every dead mesquite limb within four hundred yards until we had a beautiful pile of my firewood of choice. Tony tucked the fire up against the base of the cliff and fashioned two makeshift seats by digging into the dirt wall on each side of the roaring blaze.

We opened a bottle of whiskey to celebrate our first night in Mexico.

Tony and I first became friends as ten-year-olds, and we still enjoy behaving like silly children when we hang out together. Alcohol just adds fuel to the fire. Due to my unspoken concerns about dangers on this remote section of the border, I'd been uncharacteristically reserved; now that we had arrived, I reverted to character. Around the campfire, we revisited our youth with story after story, giggling like the kids we were when we'd first met.

— ◆ ◆ ◆ —

Bosque Bonito translates as "beautiful forest," but it would take a lot more whiskey than we'd drunk the previous night to find this place beautiful. The nearest thing to a forest stood far below, where a ribbon of salt cedar formed the banks of the Rio Bravo del Norte, as the Rio Grande is known in Mexico. The village sits on a windswept plateau high above the river, and there wasn't a single tree over ten feet tall near the settlement. I couldn't figure out why the original settlers had chosen this as the town site, and even less why they'd given it this name.

We found a loose collection of about twenty houses forming a community along about a half mile of the main road. The two forks in the road led to the same spot, a cluster of five or six ramshackle structures that formed a circle at the village's center. Where Ojos Calientes had appeared archaic, Bosque Bonito looked modern, complete with the detritus of contemporary life: trash strewn everywhere, rusted vehicles, dismantled appliances, and broken windows. Only my eagerness to find a store kept us from hightailing it toward the distant mountains.

I located two shivering men working under the hood of an old Chevy truck, neither of whom seemed surprised by my appearance. They directed me to the store, which turned out to be merely a front room in someone's home. Despite my repeated knocks, no one answered the door. I had the uncanny feeling that I was being watched.

Just below town, Tony and I found a road sign pointing toward the next village, Lomas de Arena ("Sand Hills"), and we bounced down the rutted road in the direction of a high range of mountains that blocked the horizon ahead. This range held the pass that would take us "way up," but in order to reach the mountains, we had many miles of gradual ascent before us.

About three miles out of Bosque Bonito, we reached an unmarked intersection in the road. One fork led toward the river, the other from it, neither well traveled. We consulted my map but found the markings on the map inconsistent with the physical reality of the intersection. We paused for ten minutes, debating the possibilities.

Finally, one of us had to make a call. Waiting for someone to come along so we could ask directions wasn't an option. It was now early afternoon and we had seen exactly one vehicle all day, which, added to the two we had seen the day before, totaled three in our twenty-four hours in Mexico. In the distance, toward the river, we could see a ranch house. We pedaled toward it, but before we reached it, we came to yet another fork, and here the road deteriorated in both directions. This convinced me to pursue my original inclination to go inland.

At least for the first few miles, the road seemed to support my decision. It became wide and relatively smooth, suggesting that it carried more traffic than the river road. But a couple of miles later we reached yet another fork, and again we stopped to consult the map. It's a disconcerting feeling to stand at one of those forks and look far out into the distance, seeing each road snake for miles through the desolate country: you know that at best you could go an hour or two and reach a dead end, and that at worst you could ride fifty or more miles of uninhabited backcountry before finding someone who could alert you to your mistake.

Eventually, Tony matched the lay of the terrain to our location on the map, but the map didn't show this new fork. We agreed to take the left fork that led directly to the mountains, but we had our doubts as we plodded toward the base of the range ahead.

And plod we did. The beginning of the ascent was a long series of switchbacks. We had to walk all of them. The reward for the strenuous work of pushing the bike up one steep grade after another, hour after hour, was the vistas that opened to us after each new climb.

For the previous fifteen years, every weekday morning I'd gone to the nearest baseball field or track and, after running a mile or two of warm-up, run fifteen 110-yard sprints; but the grueling task of pushing my loaded bike up the steep grades of this mountain range made me feel as if I'd been a couch potato for that decade and a half. Tony, whose bike carried far more weight than my own, must have truly suffered. Still, he pushed ahead, never complaining.

The road narrowed through a very tight canyon and rose so steeply that each step made my thighs burn. The Mexicans had poured concrete on the narrow thoroughfare to help combat erosion from heavy rains, and it gave us better traction as we pushed. Despite the bitter cold, I found myself drenched in sweat, and the salt stung my eyes.

From the summit, we could see the Chinati Mountains, sixty miles away, in glorious detail. Tony pointed out where he believed each of our three previous camps had been. If not for the frigid wind and the absence of firewood, this site would have made a spectacular camp. We had to press on to lower ground.

And what an express ride it turned out to be! The road descended on a compact and rock-free surface, which allowed us to reach exhilarating speeds as we raced to beat darkness to the river valley far below. Twenty minutes later we sped into the hamlet of Lomas de Arena, a pueblo sitting on the talus slope some two hundred feet above the river, slightly more than halfway between El Paso and Presidio, Texas.

The village extends along the road for almost a mile, and we reached the end of it without finding a store. Diverting onto a sandy path leading toward the village church, we reached a modest home with fresh laundry hanging on the line and the sound of a television set emanating from its interior. I called out a loud greeting, and within seconds saw the faces of two small children staring from the nearest window. A moment later, their father, a slight man of about thirty years, emerged. I asked in Spanish if he could direct us to the store. He looked hard at both of us for a moment, then turned back in the direction we had come, saying in very good English, "It's back over there on the other side of town."

Tony was having problems with his bike chain, so I struck out alone in order to save time, and with the help of two more people I met along the way, located the store at the next-to-last house. A large man with massive hands emerged from his living room into the tiny, dimly lit room, not much larger than a closet, that served as the store. His matter-of-fact greeting lacked warmth. Knowing Tony's need to consume gallons of liquid each day, I bought bottles of Gatorade and fruit juice before asking my favorite question: "*¿Se vende cerveza?*"

Yes, he had beer, and I bought a six-pack of Carta Blanca. He followed me outside, and upon seeing my bicycle, became curious about my trip. He changed from a suspicious and protective head of the household to a warm ambassador for his small community, calling his wife and children out into the dusty yard to meet me and see the bike. Unfortunately, I could not linger; the sun had already set, and we still had to find camp and collect firewood. I felt rawness in the air that portended precipitation, and sure enough, as I mounted the bicycle, the man warned, "They say it's going to snow."

We found a wide, sandy arroyo just at the edge of town and pursued it around several bends until we felt confident that the light of our campfire would be invisible from the road. In near darkness, we raced to find firewood, tossing it into the arroyo and then retrieving it with the aid of flashlights after dark. We drank the Carta Blanca while settled next to the fire, and had a supper of canned beans that I'd bought at the store.

Just as I drifted toward a deep sleep, I felt snowflakes falling on my face.

—◆◆◆—

I awoke at first light to a glorious sight; the entire arroyo was carpeted by an inch-deep fresh snowfall. Everything looked so pristine that I hesitated to spoil it by stamping my footprints through camp. But as Tony stirred in the tent, dressing and rummaging for food, I decided to restart the fire. I saw bobcat tracks fresh in the snow at the periphery of our site.

As we huddled around the campfire, Tony voiced his concerns about our limited water supply. He began collecting snow to melt for drinking water, but sand had mixed with it.

"I'll get us some water," I said, but he kept collecting snow, and in thirty minutes he had about a pint of silted water. "I'm serious. I'll get us some drinking water first thing this morning."

Tony looked grave, as if he'd already resigned himself to a slow death by dehydration. Usually I drank a half gallon of water before getting on the bike, hydrating myself for a good part of the day while we were stopped and the water was easy to access, but I was concerned for Tony, and today I drank only one cup. I could see that my ability to deliver drinking water soon would determine the course of the day.

As our bike tires cut a slippery path through the fresh snow on the road, I calculated that the half gallon of water we carried would hold us over until we reached Pilares, the biggest town so far, only half a day ahead. An hour out of camp, I reached a group of adobe houses and shouted to get the attention of any residents, but no one answered.

A mile on I saw an old man next to a modest house high above the road, and I shouted up to him, asking for drinking water. He invited me up the steep path. I parked my bike in plain view in the road, careful to allow enough room for a truck to pass.

Juan Saucedo, a 68-year-old father of five grown children and former president of the Ejido (agricultural cooperative) Emiliano Carranza, greeted me with a warm handshake as I reached the dirt yard in front of his house. While I answered his questions about my trip, he had his sons fill my jug from the family's supply of drinking water, housed in 55-gallon barrels sitting under a plastic tarp at the side of the house. I declined his offer of a cigarette but accepted his offer to go inside for coffee. But, I said, we had to wait for my friend to arrive. Juan's eyes grow wide with amazement as I pulled out the walkie-talkie and radioed Tony. When a few moments later Tony responded, even the two adult sons paused while filling the water jug to stare at the source of Tony's crackling voice. Their wonder at the walkie-talkie was surpassed only by their curiosity about what we were saying in English.

"My friend doesn't speak Spanish," I said, "but he loves your country."

Juan smiled proudly. When Tony arrived, Juan's youngest son, Ramón, was very curious about him. Ramón had learned some phrases of English and seemed disappointed that my Spanish gave him no excuse to practice. Tony, on the other hand, gave Ramón a great opportunity. I noted that both Ramon and his father looked far more often at Tony than at me, no doubt in part because Tony's appearance is decidedly more gringo than mine.

Juan and I entered the dimly lit kitchen of his home and seated ourselves at the kitchen table while his wife boiled water for our coffee. A couple of minutes later, Juan asked, "Where is your friend?"

I walked out the door to find Tony cleaning the mud from the bottom of his biking shoes.

" Juan is worried that you don't want to come in."

"I just don't want to track mud into the house." Tony replied as he poked at his shoe creases with a stick.

"I got news for you." I was barely able to suppress my laughter. "They have a dirt floor. You might be doing them a favor to track in mud."

"Shoot, I didn't even think of that."

Juan presided over the kitchen table as his diminutive wife, Ramona, and Ramón prepared coffee and then breakfast for us. Ramona hand-rolled tortillas on a makeshift countertop, while Ramón fed mesquite wood into the stove and the small fireplace opposite the table. Its flue drafted the smoke out an opening no more than eighteen inches off the dirt floor, and with heat emanating from both stove and fireplace, I found the kitchen toasty. Juan talked about his colorful life as a young man, and Ramona beamed as Juan noted that if it hadn't been for meeting her he would have drunk himself to death at a young age. While Ramón served us instant coffee, his mother heated skillets of beans and potatoes and browned the tortillas. Juan admitted to being wholly illiterate, remarking in Spanish, "I can't even write my own name."

He also bemoaned the fact that the family had few visitors. Even the two daughters seldom made the trip home. He chain-smoked as he talked, yet his breathing seemed remarkably clear for a heavy smoker nearing age seventy.

I asked many questions, and Juan seemed to thrive on the attention, while Ramona glowed after we praised her cooking. Juan mentioned having met a gringo couple who were canoeing the river below his ranch some years ago.

"Oh yeah, when was that?"

He thought for a moment, "Back when there was more water."

"About what year was it? Ten years ago? Twenty?"

"It was back when there was more water."

"When the children were small," Ramona added.

When I said Ramona's clarification of the timeline helped me to understand, Juan grinned. I sensed that illiteracy was his greatest regret in life, and he was determined not to handicap his children similarly. He had made great sacrifices to transport his children to a school well over a hundred miles upriver in El Porvenir, where they boarded with a cousin of Juan's for the length of the school year, leaving Juan and Ramona all alone at their modest ranch.

As Juan talked, I understood that his life resembled one in the nineteenth century more than one in the twenty-first. He and the boys brought their drinking water by mule from a spring high in the mountains. They cut all the firewood using a heavy, dull axe. For beans, lard, and tortilla flour, they traded their chickens and eggs. Juan also raised goats, and with the sale money, he bought cigarettes, coffee, and propane for his thirty-year-old pickup.

"Is it true you can make a hundred dollars a day in the U.S.?" Ramón asked.

"In many jobs you can."

"*Chingado,* life must be very easy with so much money! My brother works in Colorado. I want to go there, too, but my parents need me here."

Tony wanted to give the family a gift, so he and Ramón went out to the bikes. Juan reflected on the many changes in his *ejido* over his lifetime.

"Everybody wants to go to the U.S. When I was young, this was a thriving *ejido.* We had work. Everyone ate. We were happy. Now everyone is gone. Besides us, only one old man remains. They go to Texas and they never return, not even to visit. We used to be proud of our way of life, but now these young people are embarrassed. This way of life isn't good enough for them. They have to have televisions and cars and electricity. Now they laugh at us. When I die, this will all be lost. I can't write to keep the memory of it alive, and my boys don't want to write my story. I'm not a wise man, but I see the changes, and I see how the new ways take all of our sons and leave us here to die."

I wished I could volunteer to write his life story, not because I believed it could help to reverse the flow of rural Chihuahuans seeking prosperity in the U.S., but out of a profound gratitude for all that Juan and Ramona had shared with us.

Tony and Ramón came back babbling in their own mix of English and Spanish. I remembered what my friend Eric Clem, who knows no Spanish, had said one night in a Juárez bar years ago when

I found him in an animated conversation with a man who knew no English. "Jeez, Eric, how do you do it? You walk in this bar knowing no Spanish and now you're in the middle of a lively conversation with a guy who knows no English?"

"After eight beers," Eric said, "everyone is bilingual." I wondered if Tony and Ramón had shared our whiskey while they were outside.

Ramón gave me a fossilized snail that he had found high up in the sierra on a hike above the spring where the family got its drinking water. Tony then gave Juan a biking shirt emblazoned with the name *El Ganador* (The Winner) on its front. Juan stared at the words, mystified, until I read them to him. Then Tony produced two Christmas ornaments, one of a cowboy on a stallion, the second of a professor in a graduation cap, and offered them to Juan. Fascinated by the cowboy, Juan repeatedly turned it and studied each angle. I could see he was on the brink of tears, a proud man overwhelmed by Tony's generosity.

The next time I lampoon Tony for bringing so much gear along, I will remember this poignant moment.

We couldn't linger any longer at the Saucedos', although I suspect Juan and Ramona couldn't understand our need to keep to a schedule so that Tony could get back to Sacramento before he lost his job. We pressed on, exhilarated by our visit with the family, rejuvenated by the hot meal. I felt happy that Tony had been able to experience this world, and I sensed I had won back his confidence, not just because we had plenty of drinking water but because he'd seen firsthand how warm and giving the Mexican people are. Any preconceptions he carried about stereotypical Mexican bandits had died in the warmth of the Saucedo kitchen, and countless times over the next two days he recounted some tidbit from his conversations with Ramón.

I shot out ahead, and about two hours from Juan's house, I passed a small sign advertising cigarettes. I recognized this as the sign of a store, and as I braked to a halt, three young guys ran from the house toward my bike. I asked if this were indeed the Pilares store, and they waved me to come close, each eyeing my bicycle curiously.

I explained where I was going.

"Wow, so far? Are you alone?"

"No, my *amigo* is behind me, but maybe he's met a *muchacha* and she's delaying him."

They laughed, and watched with curiosity as I pulled out the walkie-talkie and radioed him.

By the time Tony had ridden up out of breath a couple of minutes later, the store's owner, Enrique, an affable man in his thirties, had come outside to invite us into the tiny room that served as the village store.

"What do you want to buy?" he asked. "But I must warn you I don't have much." His friends laughed. "It's not like those American stores in El Paso."

"Let me just see what you have in stock," I said.

"No, don't look. It embarrasses me."

"Do you have any beer?"

"No, sorry. I'm all out."

"Now I see why you're embarrassed!"

Since we had lost half the morning at Juan's, I had to refuse Enrique's offer to have his wife feed us lunch in his kitchen, so he insisted his wife wrap some burritos for us to take on the road.

For the burritos, Enrique refused payment, but his wife did accept money for the two soft drinks Tony had drunk during our short visit. Then she asked if we would like tamales, the traditional Christmas food in Mexico. I had almost forgotten it was Christmas Eve. We loaded up a dozen tamales with our bean burritos, and said our good-byes to this good-humored group of *muchachos*.

—◆◆◆—

The village of Pilares sits atop a mesa opposite crimson spires that form the Texas-side canyon wall of the Rio Grande. The view from town is stunning, although the squalor of the town itself seemed to defy its natural surroundings. For the first time all trip, despite his casual references to it several times a day ever since we crossed into Mexico, I could see that Tony felt far more fatigue than I did from biking. Carrying all his gear had to be part of it. But I was so thrilled to be in this environment that I wouldn't have acknowledged any fatigue even if I'd felt it. For me, everything was perfect, and I thrived. On the other hand, Tony spoke little Spanish, so he couldn't mix easily. Plus, there is a discomforting powerlessness when you are isolated by ignorance; this I knew well from my trips to Mexico as a young guy. And the biking was tough: mile after mile of poor surface, steep grades, and the continuing, enervating cold.

When we took a break, Tony said, "How the hell do you do it? I'm beat by lunchtime every day, but you seem to get stronger as the day goes on." I interpreted his comment as a plea to slow the pace.

Tony fell so far behind that the walkie-talkies were useless, so when I reached a hamlet named El Comedor ("The Dining Room"), I stopped near the one house that seemed to be inhabited to wait for him.

Some three thousand feet above the village, near the top of the rock face, a natural bridge formed a tablelike opening in the ridge. An immense flat rock extended across the gap in the ridge, and I saw why the natives had given the village its name: the rock looked like a giant kitchen table. For nearly a half hour, I marveled at this geologic wonder before Tony appeared, thoroughly exhausted. His face wore a pained expression of defeat.

"Tell you what, Tone," I said, trying to conceal just how energized I felt, "I'll go ahead a little ways and find camp and start collecting the firewood because we don't have much daylight left and we don't want to go much further. The road is going to leave the river pretty soon."

He groaned, knowing from our experience that unless the road hugged the riverbank, it was anything but flat. Our two really tough climbs so far had been when the road diverted inland, and a third detour waited ahead.

I found an arroyo for camp, and while Tony set up his tent, I searched for firewood. Within minutes I had uprooted two thick trunks of dead mesquite. With more firewood than we could burn, I roasted the dozen tamales in their cornhusks as we basked in our good fortune. Mexicans had treated us to a Christmas Eve bounty of enviable proportion, and we were grateful. As the campfire roared, we ate the tamales and sipped whiskey. Tony pulled out the Cuban cigars, and we smoked while watching a massive full moon light up our camp. When we retreated to our bedrolls, Tony fell asleep within seconds, his gentle snoring the reward for an impressive effort.

Christmas in Two Nations

Dec. 25

I awoke to an icy chill at first light, stoked the fire, and found our drinking water frozen solid into a two-gallon block of ice. I'd never experienced such cold along the Rio Grande. Having to thaw the frozen water supply gave me a ready excuse to huddle against the fire.

Tony emerged from his tent just as I had the coffee water thawed, and his bones creaked as he limped toward the warmth of the flames.

"Merry Christmas. *Feliz Navidad*," I called.

"Man, I'm feeling it this morning," he said, trying to stretch. "And Merry Christmas!"

The sun rose behind the mountain flank behind our camp an hour later, spilling warmth into the arroyo, thawing our chilled bodies enough to allow us to stray from the fire and break camp. Consulting the map, I saw that we had several hours to bike before reaching San Antonio del Bravo, the largest village we would visit on the Mexican side—large enough that it had two stores! More importantly, San Antonio del Bravo sits opposite Candelaria, Texas, and a dilapidated footbridge crosses the river there. Although signs erected by the U.S. Department of the Interior threaten prison terms and stiff fines for using the bridge, we planned to sneak into the U.S. over it.

The climb from our riverside camp to the pass above San Antonio del Bravo was gentle but long, each rise taking us further from the river as the route circumvented a mountain range that ran perpendicular to the river. Despite the long detour, the biking was pleasant as we rode in bright sunshine that warmed an otherwise brisk morning. Late in the morning we reached a summit and then had six miles of winding downhill road that delivered us to the edge of San Antonio.

There we found an obese man chopping firewood in his backyard, and I asked for directions to the store. He welcomed the breather from his work, and gave precise directions to the nearby *tienda,* where we found a crowd of people, many of them adolescents, in the dusty parking area. The youngsters gathered around our bikes, some asking questions in Spanish, others in English. These young people were a group of cousins spending Christmas together—half of them locals, the others visiting from New Mexico.

After the tiny shops of Lomas de Arena and Pilares, the San Antonio store seemed like Wal-Mart. It offered a full wall of canned goods, tobacco products, snacks, and sweets, and it had a refrigerator stocked with soft drinks and fruit juices. Tony downed two Cokes as I ordered Tecate, fruit juice, canned beans, and tortillas. The old lady attending the counter talked only to her bilingual grandchildren, pretending not to understand my Spanish. She appeared overwhelmed by our presence, and I was eager to depart. Tony was as eager to talk to the youngsters in English as he was to chug soft drinks. While we loaded the groceries, the kids swarmed around us.

On our way to the bridge, we saw three horsemen chatting on a rise above us. The instant they noticed us, one, a man dressed in black on a black mare, galloped toward us. He also wore a black eye patch over his left eye, and I joked to Tony, "I wonder what Juanito Cash wants."

"He's not looking too happy," Tony said.

As the rider reached us, he yanked the reins, forcing the horse into an abrupt change of gait, from full gallop to high-stepping trot, and the San Antonio Johnny Cash glared as he swung the horse uncomfortably close to the bikes.

"*Buenos días.* How's it going," I said. Mexicans use the English word "bluff" to describe encounters such as this one, and I wasn't backing down.

He nodded but did not speak, and I saw over my shoulder that he parked the horse in the road, glaring as we walked the bikes up a steep grade.

I whispered to Tony, "Let's get the hell out of here. Suddenly I don't like this place."

My decision to violate immigration law by using the footbridge was based on it being Christmas, and I thought only the most hardened Border Patrol agent would arrest us on that day. At the bridge we found several pickups parked on either side. Clearly, we weren't the only scofflaws. Family members residing in the U.S. drove to the unpaved parking area on the American side, crossed the bridge, and met their family members for the drive into San Antonio.

However, I still felt anxious about our use of the bridge. It had wide gaps capable of swallowing a bike tire, so I realized we'd need to carry the bikes across, and I waited for Tony to help me. Here the Rio Grande is only as wide as the average American living room, and the whole bridge could fit inside a tractor-trailer. In fact, you could stack a half dozen such bridges inside a trailer. It seemed incongruous that two large countries were connected by something so tiny. Under the bridge, the river hardly looked like North America's fifth-largest river, looking more like a narrow tributary in the Ozark Mountains— branches of salt cedar on one shore nearly kissing branches on the other. It seemed inconceivable that this diminutive brook was the mighty Rio Grande.

We worked in tandem to carry the bikes and then sprinted along the rutted road toward pavement. If we could clear the area before the Border Patrol saw us, we could plead that we had biked here on the

U.S. side to see the antiquated bridge. Given that my plastic storage basket brimmed with Tecate and foods whose labels were in Spanish, I hoped I wouldn't need my alibi. But we reached the pavement of Farm Road 170 at its terminus in the sleepy village of Candelaria, Texas, without seeing anyone.

Candelaria is likely the most remote town in Texas, sitting some fifty miles upriver from Presidio, itself a candidate for most remote. Although Candelaria once had a small schoolhouse and a thriving general store that supplied both sides of the border, it now has neither. Except for a few vehicles parked outside a row of trailer houses, this small settlement appeared deserted. In two previous visits, I had seen no one. I was, therefore, surprised to find a native of the town, Marcelino Lozano, walking idly next to the road as if killing time. We greeted each other in Spanish.

Marcelino had long since moved away for a career in the West Texas oil fields, but he and his wife returned at Christmas every year to visit family. Our trip interested him because his grandfather had lived his entire life in El Comedor, the site of our previous camp. His dark eyes twinkled as he recounted memories of his childhood visits there. I sensed he wished he could take a furlough from the oil fields and join me for the next thousand miles. I liked him immediately.

As with nearly every other encounter of the past week, we had to leave too soon. Tony's vacation was ending, and we were far behind schedule. With fifty miles left to reach Presidio, we couldn't afford to linger when we met new friends like Marcelino. As I apologized to him because we had to leave, he said, speaking English for the first time, "I'll see you all on the highway. I have to go into Presidio to get beer in a little while. The store here has been closed for a few years."

We pushed on, our pace now faster because of the pavement's traction, traveling more than double our previous speed. Grades we had had to walk on the unpaved road, we could now pedal up by shifting gears. In an hour we reached the tiny town of Ruidosa, and moments later, Marcelino arrived in his pickup. He offered to carry us to Presidio, an offer Tony was disappointed to hear me reject.

As we searched for camp, Marcelino returned and gave us a couple of cold beers. *¡Feliz Navidad!*

We found camp at the bottom of a steep grade where a wide arroyo crossed the pavement. We walked our bikes through the sandy wash until we reached the wall of nearly impenetrable salt cedar thicket that lines the river, and there we found a narrow gully beside a barbed-wire fence, a perfect campsite. Below camp, we heard the current of the river singing past twin riffles, small rocky drops that sounded more violent from our camp than our subsequent inspection of them revealed. Camping so close to the river piqued my interest in switching from the mountain bike to the canoe, as I would do in Presidio.

I had lugged a Danish canned ham for a week so that we could have a traditional meal on Christmas night, and once we had a bed of coals, I slid half of them out from under the fire to a makeshift grill we'd fashioned with sticks. With fresh tortillas from San Antonio, canned ranch beans, grilled ham, and cold Tecate, we feasted. Later, we sat close to the fire, finishing the beer, laughing about our luck, and congratulating ourselves on what had been one of the best weeks of our lives.

"Shoot," Tony said as he ate a dessert of beef jerky and dried fruit, "the only bad thing about this is that it has to end and I have to go back to the real world."

"Not to make you feel bad, but I'm sure glad this trip is just beginning for me. I couldn't face the end so soon."

Angry River

Dec. 26–28

I've watched, with a combination of incomprehension and mild re-pugnance, a number of friends who, after taking long backcountry trips, happily embrace their return to the comforts of civilization. Their routine is predictable: wastefully long showers; overeating; long phone calls home to loved ones they'll see, in some cases, later that same day; compulsive shopping; interminable sessions in front of the mirror; and an endless, almost hypnotic, attention to television.

Tony spared me all that. We agreed that if the comforts of civili-zation were all that gripping, we couldn't have had so much fun away from them. I was grateful that, when we entered our motel room at Presidio's only lodging, Tony didn't turn on the television.

I've never done well with the end of trips, and often I begin to miss the trip before I've even finished it, so it was refreshing to be at the end of our bike ride knowing that my long trip to the Gulf of Mexico had barely begun. I had months of adventure before me.

This temporary plunge into civilization would be mercifully brief. In fewer than twenty hours, I'd be on the river. And, having to do laundry, shop for the next leg of the trip, eat, shower, write a river report, and sleep in a bed for the last time until February, I didn't have enough time to tire of civilization.

My friend Louis Aulbach, author of three guidebooks on the Rio Grande, had suggested I send him letters from points along the way, which he would post on his website. The missives would serve a dual purpose: river lovers could learn about stretches no one floated, and my family and friends would know I had completed each leg safely. I spent hours sitting outside the motel room writing the first report to mail to Louis the next morning.

In Presidio, the news of that week's tsunami in Indonesia filled every television station, and I tried to avoid seeing the horrific images broadcast everywhere. By the time Tony saw me off at the riverbank in Presidio, I was eager to be far away from the media, automobiles, and the noise of our everyday world. It takes only a week in the wilderness to realize that we humans generate more noise than the rest of the natural world combined.

-◆◆▶-

The thing that had brought me to Presidio—the river—proved to be the most difficult to get information about. Tony and I asked many people where I might launch the canoe, but nobody knew; few residents of Presidio had ever wandered down to the riverbank. Frustrated, we rode out to Fort Leaton, a restored adobe fort constructed after the Mexican-American War by an Anglo settler, where a guide directed us to an access on the eastern edge of Presidio, a couple of miles downriver from the bridge to Ojinaga.

The border city of Ojinaga calls itself *la perla del desierto* ("the pearl of the desert"), but it seems highly ironic to attach to this arid town any name related to the sea. The average annual precipitation measures less than ten inches, and from April to October, Ojinaga bakes under an infernal desert sun, with temperatures in summer soaring above 110 degrees. The city of thirty thousand inhabitants is infamous as a drug-smuggling corridor. Its most famous resident was Pablo Acosta, a drug lord who in the 1980s shipped sixty tons of Colombian cocaine a month through Ojinaga. The *maquiladora* industries common to many border cities are absent here. A dusty city sitting on a hill overlooking the Rio Grande and the Rio Conchos, Ojinaga bills itself as the border city most like the interior of Mexico. Mexicans in the state of Chihuahua scoff at such a representation. One close friend from the capital city remarked, "Ojinaga is more like the interior of hell than the interior of Mexico. It's hot, dusty, and bleak."

The Rio Conchos, the principal tributary of the Rio Grande, enters the river just above Ojinaga and drains much of the immense state of Chihuahua. However, the drought in the Mexican mountains, coupled with the increased water demands of agricultural and population expansion in Chihuahua, has drastically reduced the flow of the Conchos, and on that day, it merely doubled the flow of the Rio Grande, turning a small stream into a larger one.

The Rio Bravo, as the Mexicans call the Rio Grande, is often mistakenly translated as "Brave River," but in Mexico *bravo* suggests "angry" rather than brave. "Brave" River, however, would be a more accurate translation than "Large" or "Great" River. Except during a flood, no single section of the Rio Grande as it forms the Texas-Mexico border is even moderately large. Brave, however, it is. Considering the systematic abuse man has delivered to this desert waterway through pollution, excessive irrigation, agricultural runoff, and the importation of salt cedar, the fact that the river remains as pristine as it does is a miracle of nature. For the Mexicans to name it "Angry River" seems to have inadvertently portended how the river feels about its mistreatment centuries later.

-◆◆▶-

From my put-in, I witnessed man's impact on the river. The current is nonexistent for miles due to the backup from a dam ten miles away. An elaborate levee system has been dredged into the floodplain on the American bank, obscuring any view of Presidio from the water;

and on the Mexican side, people had left all manner of trash along the shoreline—tires, automobile and tractor parts, fencing, and household litter. Had I thought the riparian environment would continue like that, I wouldn't have allowed Tony to leave without me. I struggled psychologically to adjust to Tony's absence. Although I'm a loner who's most comfortable on the river, I missed him and his cheerful presence immediately.

In spite of the trash on the riverbanks, I felt soothed to be drifting along in my fifteen-foot red canoe at a pace consistent with nature's pace, silent except for the soft splash of my paddle parting the water. I thought that of all the hundreds of transportation inventions man has made since Indians first introduced the canoe, none has approached its perfection. Noiseless, graceful, and utilitarian, the canoe offers the ideal access to the natural world. I negotiated turn after turn, grateful to leave the noisy world of Presidio and Ojinaga. Soon a blue heron appeared on the riverbank a hundred yards ahead, watching me until I came within thirty yards, then taking off with long majestic wing strokes, landing again two hundred yards later, only to repeat the exercise when I again drew near. We played this game of tag until I could no longer hear any suggestion of Presidio or Ojinaga.

Late in the afternoon, I reached a submerged weir—a kind of dam that reduces or diverts the flow of water but doesn't block it—called El Mulato and began to portage on the Mexican side, in view of an adobe village perched on a sandy hillside. A path led over uneven ground along the spillway to where the river narrowed again below the dam. I worked purposefully to move my gear from above the dam to the river's edge, each carry about one hundred yards.

Halfway through this process, I heard a vehicle. Looking up, I saw three well-dressed Mexican women and one teenage boy gazing at me. Bravely, one of the women approached.

"You have so many things," she said in Spanish. "Why so many?"

For the first time, it occurred to me that my small mountain of dry boxes, wet bags, and camping gear appeared excessive to anyone not familiar with river-tripping. People might conclude that I was in the smuggling business. Perhaps my haste to hustle the gear around the dam supported that suspicion. Plus, canoes, kayaks, or rafts almost never explored this stretch below Presidio. Probably this woman had never before seen a boater portage around the dam.

"I carry so much because I'm going a long way. All the way to the Gulf of Mexico."

She frowned. "You mean you're going all the way to the sea?"

"That's the plan," I said, "though whether or not I make it is another idea."

I smiled, then turned to cart more gear to the river shore. She lingered behind, pacing close to my canoe, awaiting my return. As I started back, the other two women now ambled toward my boat. As we all converged there, the woman said skeptically to her friends, "He says he's going all the way to the sea."

"So far? Do you sleep in the boat or travel all night?"

"I camp on the shore at night. It's too dangerous to boat in the dark."

I expected them to linger until I had finished the portage and launched the canoe, but when I returned for my next stage of the portage, they were already retreating to their truck. Apparently they had far more interesting people to visit.

The sun was setting, so I hurried downriver to find a camp. A mile later I saw a bare island that would serve nicely, its only shortcoming being a lack of firewood. I unloaded my gear, and carrying only my bow saw, paddled to the Mexican shore to cut mesquite limbs. Although there were many trees, I could find few limbs dead enough to harvest. I kept at it until I scarcely had light to cross back to camp. With the fire glowing, I opened a Tecate and listened to the sounds of the desert night: the river gurgling, the bats shrieking, the campfire crackling.

With island camps, I have no fear of interlopers, and my biggest concern—far more so in summer than in winter—is a rising river. During the monsoon season in summer, I wouldn't risk camping on an island because the river could flood in minutes. But in winter, the dry season, flooding is rare. With clear, starry skies in all directions, I felt at peace. I had worried that I might find the transition from camping with Tony to being alone difficult that first night. But I felt liberated from the need to converse, the responsibility to answer questions, and the demands of sharing an agenda. Through the darkness, I heard a coyote howling. It obviously wasn't enjoying its solitude nearly as quietly as I was.

◦◦◦

In the morning I passed, without any recognition of its presence, the small town of Redford, Texas, which had gained national attention in the late 1990s because our nation's government, desperate to take measures to stem the relentless tide of illegal immigration, allowed the U.S. Army to patrol sections of our border that were undermanned by the Border Patrol. Redford received one such patrol, and not too many weeks after the soldiers arrived, one zealous soldier gunned down an 18-year-old shepherd, an American citizen who tended the family flock in the thorny brush along the river. Although enraged locals disputed the testimony of the two soldiers present at the killing, one soldier alleged that the victim had attempted to flee when the soldiers demanded that he stop. For this disregard of orders, the teenage boy was executed. Apparently, the soldiers had no reasonable cause to suspect the boy had fled for any other reason than fright. They did not suspect he was involved in narcotics smuggling. Shortly after the incident, the Army patrols of the borders ceased.

A few miles below Redford, I experienced firsthand one of the justifications our government had used for the Army patrols. As I approached the Mexican town of El Mulato, a bleak collection of cinder-block homes on a cliff some fifty vertical feet above the river, an elderly man called to me to hike the steep trail into the village for a visit. The path was littered with tin cans and broken beer bottles. Apparently the residents disposed of their trash by dumping it down the steep embankment toward the river.

I found Ricardo Saenz to be a congenial man. As he hosed down a small pigsty on a dusty plot behind his house, he said he had spent most of his adult life working in West Texas at ranches along the river or in towns on the plains below the Texas panhandle. Despite living thirty-five years in Texas, he had learned little English. Hosing off an unhappy piglet, he proudly admitted he was fifty-three years old and the father of seven children, ages two to thirty, four of whom lived in the U.S. Ricardo expressed little curiosity about my trip, and he had no idea where the Gulf of Mexico was. I could see from his bloated face that he liked to drink, and I fought the urge to caution him about breaking beer bottles on the trail to the river, especially when his youngest son appeared barefoot a minute later. I asked Ricardo if I could take his picture, and he directed me to his front yard. As we turned the corner, I saw a handsome couple leaving the house next door in a late-model Ford pickup truck with Texas plates. Neither returned my wave.

Ricardo's wife emerged from the house, and her appearance seemed to perturb him. She asked him a question about lunch, and he dismissed her rudely; she seemed accustomed to such treatment. As Ricardo posed, I asked that his wife be included in the picture. Although she moved eagerly toward him, he ordered her to stand far behind. I felt uncomfortable witnessing such treatment and decided to leave. Just then, a surly-looking guy in his late twenties marched defiantly toward me from a house facing Ricardo's. Without breaking step, he grazed my shoulder as he passed, uttering in English that bore no trace of a second-language accent, "What's happening, man?"

I thanked Ricardo for his hospitality, though he had extended none–not even so much as a drink of water–and I wondered why he'd invited me up to visit. When we reached the trail to the river, I shook his hand, but as I began my descent, he called, "Hey amigo." I turned to see him making exaggerated sniffing sounds, his fingers held close to his nose. I gazed at him, unsure what he wished to communicate.

"*¿Qué te pasa?*" (What's up with you?), I said.

"*Coca.* Do you want to buy some cocaine?" he asked in Spanish.

"*No me interesa*" (It doesn't interest me).

"Come on, man. This is really good, really pure. You will never find anything this good over there."

I stood in disbelief as he made his pathetic sales pitch, his two-year-old son wandering thirty feet away in one direction, his nine-year-old son forty feet away in the other.

I felt vulnerable. Any man who openly peddled cocaine in front of his children was not a guy I could trust, and the whole of my brief visit in El Mulato had been unsettling in every way. Even several turns down the river, I felt paranoid. What was to prevent any of that sorry group from robbing me at gunpoint somewhere along the river?

I paddled vigorously, trying to put as many miles as I could between this distressing village and myself. When I believed I was far enough downriver to be beyond their reach, I pulled over on a Texas-side beach and opened a Tecate. At once, my attitude improved, and I laughed over how profoundly I'd allowed the experience to affect me. So some useless pest wanted to sell me cocaine? What was the big deal?

·◆◆◆·

A few bends later, I heard the telltale roar of a steep rapid up ahead. I knew I was approaching the rapid the Mexicans call La Boquita ("Little Mouth") because a horseman I had encountered before El Mulato had warned me of its danger. I pulled in to shore to scout the drop from the Mexican side, and saw a relatively straight drop where the river narrowed as it cascaded through a barely submerged bed of rocks washed in from the arroyo on the Mexican side. I decided to line the boat along the shore rather than run the rapid.

Lining a canoe involves leading the boat down through a rapid in order to avoid having to subject the boat—and yourself—to the dangers of running it. However, lining can present its own dangers, not the least of which are smashing or losing the craft. The idea is to walk the boat much as you'd walk a pet, leading it by a rope. Among many other potential problems is that the rushing water tries to carry the boat swiftly toward the bottom of the rapid while you guide it carefully at your pace. The river will try to sweep the unsecured end out from the bank, and you have to prevent it from doing so. Lining can be very tough with two people, each holding a rope tied to a different end of the canoe. By yourself, the job is much more difficult.

As I surveyed the drop, another realization came to mind. I wasn't an accomplished canoeist. Nearly all my river experience had been in my rafts. I've owned numerous inflatable rafts since I first became serious about boating a couple of years after my daughter's death, and although I had taken probably twenty canoe trips over the last twenty-five years, I had made all but one of those trips with another buddy in the canoe. When we lined, we lined together. When we ran rapids, we had two sets of paddles. As far as solo boating was concerned, I had as much experience as anybody—countless trips on countless rivers—but all except one of the trips had been in a raft.

The bottom line was this: Not only was I a less-than-accomplished canoeist, but I wasn't even very good. On my lone solo trip, I had spent five days canoeing eighty-four miles in the Lower Canyons, a couple of hundred miles downriver from where I now stood. On that trip, I had repeatedly made mistakes in the rapids because as soon as I entered them, my rafting habits dictated my actions. Time after time, I found myself in the harrowing position of turning the canoe sideways when I intended to straighten it. I'd spent well over a thousand days piloting my rafts, and those skills I'd developed to negotiate white water approaching Class V served only to put me in peril in simple Class I drops in the canoe.

I carefully lined the drop at La Boquita, though I feel certain an accomplished canoeist would have wondered what took me so long to do it. Ahead, I could see a gorgeous sandstone bowl, well over a hundred feet high, opening up on the Texas shoreline, and with a flat rock ledge leading from the bowl's wall to the river shore, it would offer an ideal camp. However, as the river made a bend, it dropped through yet another Class II drop, and I had to run it blind, as river men say. Although my run was hardly textbook, I cleared the last rock. But the river continued to bend, and moments later I entered a third drop blindly. I broadsided a rock I saw far too late, and barely avoided capsizing.

Adrenaline surged through me as I paddled to shore, just in time to beach on the end of the flat rock that served as the floor of this spectacular rock bowl. Usually, I'd scout a camp before unloading, but on this occasion I tossed my gear onto the safety of the rock, and opened a beer. The sports cliché "It's better to be lucky than good" shot through my mind. The campsite ranked as one of the most magnificent landscapes I had ever seen, let alone had for a private camp. Just above my boat, at the base of where the bowl curled back to the river's edge, sat two enormous rock spires, seemingly teetering as they towered above the rock floor. At once, it became obvious why the Mexicans called this amazing semicircle in the river La Boquita. The bowl formed the shape of a mouth, and the spires its teeth.

I gazed in awe at the surroundings for several minutes before I heard a man whistling nearby. Seconds later I saw a Mexican riding his horse through the shallow water downriver on the Mexican side in order to bypass a spot where the canyon wall rose directly out of the river. His song sounded faintly familiar, and I listened carefully, hoping to recognize it and surprise him by singing a verse. Before I could pinpoint the tune, he spotted me, and I waved.

"*Buenas tardes,*" I said.

"*Buenas,*" he replied. "*¿Watcha vacas?*"

"*¿Mande?*" (Come again?)

"*Watcha* cows," he said, pointing at his eyes to help me understand.

"*¿Si he visto vacas?*" (Have I seen cows?)

He nodded, smiling, and said in Spanish, "Who knows where they've gone? It seems they don't love me anymore."

I was disappointed that the declining daylight forced him to ride off in the direction of the arroyo at the top of the first rapid. I took comfort in having this innocent encounter at the end of my day displace the disagreeable experience I had had in El Mulato. Stretching out on the rock slab, I drifted off into a happy sleep filled with vivid dreams of idyllic dreamscapes only the subconscious can conjure.

Mistakes

Dec. 29–30

From my camp at La Boquita to the end of Colorado Canyon, the Rio Grande drops at a rate of over twenty feet a mile. My limited canoeing skills were about to be tested.

Around the very first river bend beyond camp, I entered a steep rapid that plunged some ten vertical feet before narrowing in a tight and violent lane. All the current squeezed into a ten-foot space between a massive boulder jutting out from the Mexican side and the Texas shore. Fortunately, I entered with the boat pointing straight ahead and kept it straight as I dropped through the V of the rapid. At the bottom, I saw that the river plunged out of view at the end of a short pool, and I frantically made for the Texas shore. Usually I like an easy beginning to the morning's paddling. This wasn't the start I wanted.

The next drop demanded canoeing skills I did not yet have. The river narrowed to a width of twelve feet, then dropped in a sharp dogleg left, the main flow pouring over a large boulder sitting mid-river at the turn. I studied the rapid nervously, still feeling the charge of adrenaline that had swept through me at the previous drop. I couldn't run this tight turn: capsizing was inevitable. After watching the water surge and boil madly as it rose over the submerged boulder, I decided I couldn't even line the canoe. The river's power was likely to sweep it to places I couldn't allow it to go. Unhappily, I began untying all the gear for the short portage to the base of the drop.

Because of the remoteness of the trip and the difficulty of replacing anything I might lose, I took every precaution to secure all of my gear in the boat each morning: tying, double tying, triple tying. Later in the trip, I would become adept at this, but I hadn't yet developed a pat system. I had a labyrinth of ropes and bungee cords, all woven differently each time I loaded, and undoing this intricate web often frustrated me. The job was even more difficult when I was charged with adrenaline. After a few exasperating minutes, I suddenly stopped, and told myself to slow down. "This is supposed to fun, you loser. Take your time and do it right."

But my frustration had only begun. Two miles later I ran another rapid that I entered blindly, and it required a tight right-hand turn in mid-drop. I failed to negotiate it properly, and my canoe slammed head-on into the embankment. With two feet of the bow on shore, the force of the rapid swept the stern around and tugged the bow free, and I finished the rapids going backwards. A few hundred yards later, I entered another drop that required a tight turn to avoid river cane overhanging the Mexican embankment. I started the turn a fraction of a second too late, causing my stern to sweep into the edge of the cane, and received a sharp smack in the cheek as I sped past.

I was confident the canoe could withstand a lot of abuse because it was a Dagger Reflection, constructed of Royalex, a tough, lightweight material consisting of multiple layers of plastic, closed-cell foam, and vinyl. However, because I was executing maneuvers so badly at each of the rapids, I knew I could smash the canoe if I continued making mistakes.

My follies continued. At the very next bend, I faced another turn in mid-drop; all the current constricted into a narrow lane and made a quick ninety-degree turn. Eager to avoid another mishap, I began the turn too soon, and nearly capsized the boat as the bow caught the eddy on the inside of the turn while the remainder of the canoe was thrust sideways by the rushing current. Disconcerted, I pulled in to the beach below the rapid. Ahead I could hear the thunder of yet another drop. Even on the flat stretches, the river appeared to be going precipitously downhill toward the depths of the canyon. I scolded myself, "You're not any good at this. And you'd better fix it real fast."

Instead, the river fixed me. At the very next drop, yet another tight dogleg right, I missed the turn; the current swept me broadside into a stand of river cane, and I capsized the boat. Feeling my body sink into the chilly river, I reacted with almost superhuman quickness, flailing for a handhold, then lunging for the shoreline with the overturned canoe in tow. Within seconds I was trembling with cold. I haphazardly tossed my gear onto the rocky beach and struggled to find a warm change of clothes in my wet bag.

What a perfect excuse for a pair of late-morning Tecates!

Now I boated in the depths of Colorado Canyon, which had been the site of my first canoe trip on the Rio Grande. To an accomplished canoeist, the rapids are not especially challenging at most water levels, but at the current water level, avoiding the many exposed rocks required adept steering. I did well turning sharply to the left, but in the opposite direction I often struggled.

Two rapids later I narrowly avoiding pinning the canoe in a narrow drop between two small boulders, and in my panic to avoid the breech, pushed off with my paddle and immediately lost hold of it. Again I completed the rapid backwards, and once at the bottom I had to go back upriver to retrieve the paddle, which had lodged between rocks. Further downriver, at Ledge Rock Rapids, I barely avoiding capsizing when I inadvertently turned the boat sideways and the river deposited me on a submerged rock in mid-drop.

When I finally located camp, a grassy bench on the Mexican side, I was amazed that I'd only capsized once; my lack of canoeing skill deserved numerous spills. My only consolation was that tomorrow I'd have only one marked rapid to run.

The following morning, as I tied my gear in the canoe, I saw a raft approach from upriver. The oar-propelled boat belonged to one of the four companies that run river trips in the Big Bend area. My brief conversation with the three people aboard was notable because the language of the river switched to English. Until this point, even in Presidio, I hadn't met a single person on the river who preferred speaking in English. I wouldn't need Spanish again for days.

Now, as I approached Big Bend National Park, the river scenery grew spectacular, the river cutting deep canyons as it coursed a path through the southern reaches of the Rocky Mountains. The scenic marvels of these canyons—Colorado Canyon just outside the park, Santa Elena, Mariscal, and Boquillas Canyons inside the park—draw thousands of tourists to the river each year. The Santa Elena Canyon river trip, as the outfitters run it, begins in the resort town of Lajitas, a sun-baked community that in the last decade has undergone a transformation from a dusty desert outpost centered around an old general store (the main attraction of which was a beer-guzzling goat who drunkenly lapped up dozens of beers daily) to a sort of Palm Springs golf-course community, with wildly excessive homesites perched on the arid slopes above the river. The contrast between Lajitas, Texas, and Lajitas, Chihuahua, immediately across the river, is shocking. I would guess that the population of Lajitas, Texas, ranks among the elite in wealth per capita of American resort communities, while that of Lajitas, Chihuahua–a community of maybe two dozen shacks–might be worth the value of the average resident's automobile.

Because of Big Bend National Park regulations, I had to secure a permit to boat the next two hundred fifty miles, which necessitated going two miles up the road to a visitors center. I calculated I'd lose close to two hours making the walk up and back. Also, I needed to buy provisions in town, for this would be my last chance for many weeks to restock.

When I pulled my boat up on the sandy beach, I found a young Hispanic couple and their two sons, taking pictures at the water's edge, and as I began my long walk to get the permit, the father inquired about my trip. He had grown up in El Paso and could appreciate what it would take to get this far.

"Wow, what you're doing is awfully brave."

"I don't know about that. The Mexican people are very helpful."

"Still, you must be a great man to travel so far on this river. I wouldn't have the courage to stay out even one night."

Victor Chabako then offered me a ride to the visitors center. He and his family climbed into the cab of their pickup truck, while I squeezed into the bed next to a mountain of camping gear and luggage. Victor insisted I drink the last beer in the cooler while we drove up the steep grade from the river into town and out the river road to the visitors center. While I went inside, Victor and his sons tossed a football.

Getting the permit proved something of a bureaucratic nightmare. The first person I spoke with grew perturbed when I asked for a river permit for the National Park section. This office oversees Big Bend Ranch State Park, and he angrily noted that he was beyond tired doing the work of the national park. I'd found him similarly unwilling the first time we had met, some months before. I had told him then what I planned to do—what I was now doing—and he had snorted, "That's impossible. You aren't allowed to float the river between Presidio and the state park."

On this visit, I could see we were both on the brink of losing our tempers, so I asked if I could speak to another ranger. He passed me on to David Long, an affable, pony-tailed man who picked up the phone to call the National Park Service to ask what to do about my permit. Within ten minutes, I was shaking hands with David and listening to his repeated wishes that I have a great trip.

I asked Victor and his family to leave me at the new general store, part of a long row of upscale shops, boutiques, and galleries built in the style of the Wild West. Victor insisted he would be happy to wait while I shopped and then drive me back to my canoe, but I felt I'd already overextended his kindness. As I said my good-byes, I committed a faux pas that I immediately regretted. My experience with the irascible park ranger had left me frustrated, and I said to this family of four Hispanics, "I often have a hard time in Whitey World. I hate to admit this, but sometimes I'm racist against my own race."

Victor's face clouded for a moment. Then he related that Anglo parents had adopted him, and had given him everything. "Some Whiteys are awfully nice people."

"I should never have said that. I'm just frustrated with that ranger up there. He seems determined to ruin people's day."

I felt undeserving of the Chabakos' generosity.

Like it or not, I was in Whitey World, and I knew I had to make a large adjustment, not just for the few minutes I'd be shopping, but for the remainder of my time in the National Park section of the river. I wouldn't be sharing the river with Mexican cowboys, cocaine dealers, or fishermen. Instead, I'd be sharing it with dozens of adventure vacationers, few of whom understood the culture on the south side of the river.

At the store, I loaded sixty-six dollars' worth of groceries into a large cardboard box and made the long, warm walk back to the canoe. Up ahead, I had to face Santa Elena Canyon with its Class IV Rock Slide Rapid, perhaps the single most dangerous obstacle on the entire run to the Gulf. And, given my ineptitude in the canoe the previous day, I was not eager for the challenge. Worse, portaging around it borders on the physically impossible. Even the National Park guide map describes the portage as "man-killer." But I would worry about all that tomorrow. This day I had a cooler full of cold beer, my food boxes brimmed with fresh supplies, and bright sunshine warmed the afternoon. As I paddled past the golf course, I popped open a beer and drifted toward the dramatic entrance to Santa Elena Canyon.

The Canyons of Big Bend
National Park

Dec. 31–Jan. 4

Had I been making this trip in a raft, I'd have awoken the next morning with a keen sense of anticipation, and I'd have hurried to the entrance to Santa Elena just so I could test myself in the pushy currents
and tricky rapids guarding the opening. Without the raft and facing
the limitations of my canoeing skills, I was nervous from the moment I opened my eyes. For the only time in many years of boating, I
wanted the day to be over before it had even begun. If there had been
a way to fast-forward this day to its conclusion, I might have opted to
use it.

About four hours below Lajitas, the river suddenly disappears
into a narrow cleft in a mountain face—the beginning of Santa Elena
Canyon, one of the scenic marvels of the American West. Inside the
entrance, the canyon walls are sheer, rising twelve hundred feet directly from the shoreline, and much of the canyon rim is as narrow
as the compressed river far below. During winter, sunshine reaches

the water at only a few short stretches in the canyon. The walls tower above, but the demands of navigating a canoe in the swirling currents leave little time to admire them.

If you're a fraction as claustrophobic as I am, it's tough feeling at ease inside this tight space. Adding to the anxiousness, the river appears highly agitated as it is constricted into this tight chasm, pushing its way to the nearest exit, seemingly every molecule fighting to beat the billions of others to the escape. When I think of the Mexicans naming our river the Angry River, I think of Santa Elena Canyon. One mile inside its menacing entrance, Santa Elena Canyon offers its biggest challenge: the Rock Slide.

The Rock Slide consists of a maze of monolithic boulders that tumbled from the abrupt canyon walls and landed in the constricted river. One Big Bend National Park publication notes: "The Rock Slide is not a rapid so much as it is a labyrinth of massive boulders blocking the river channel." You'd have to be splitting some very fine hairs not to call this obstacle a rapid. The water surges through very tight channels. The route is narrow, twisting, and tricky. To complicate the run, the hydraulics created by the enormous boulders magnify the slightest paddling error into a potentially boat-destroying disaster in any of the many constricted channels, most of which dead-end. And, reportedly, the boat-eating holes here do not suck the boat down only to spit it out ten feet away; they plunge it into the violent underwater world and trap it below for most of the remainder of the rapid. For at least one ill-fated river runner that I know of, the Rock Slide offered the ultimate punishment for boating mishaps: death.

A short two days after I had hit seemingly every obstacle on much tamer rapids, I now faced the terrifying prospect of navigating through the Rock Slide–which the park service rates as a Class IV–or, even worse, portaging around the house-sized fallen boulders that hadn't made it into the river. As I paddled from my camp to the canyon entrance, I tried a wide range of techniques to psych myself up for the challenge. No matter how much fleeting bravery I could muster, I kept hearing my inner voice say, "Oh, cut the b.s., will you? You couldn't even get this damn canoe through a Class I two days ago."

On the six-class scale of white water, with Class I referring to a straightforward drop easily navigable in a canoe and Class VI describing a violent and un-navigable rapid that could lead a river runner to death, the Rio Grande is primarily a Class II run, although the Park Service assigns a Class IV rating to its three biggest rapids. This is ostensibly due to the remoteness of the canyons and the impossibility for rescue in some of its less accessible reaches. In contrast, the Colorado River in the Grand Canyon offers, at certain flows, Class V water, which pushes the limits of navigability, and at all levels, strong Class IV white water, which, in addition to being quite capable of smashing boats into small splinters, has also been responsible for the loss of numerous lives over the 130-year history of river running in the Grand Canyon. The bottom line is that, on the scale of the great rivers of the American West, the Rio Grande is a relative lightweight. However, its dangers shouldn't be regarded lightly. With the exception of a few short stretches, the river is empty of people. Make one serious mistake, and you could wait a very long time—months in some cases—for the next boaters to arrive. The Rio Grande deserves as much respect as any other, mightier river. A small problem may quickly turn into a large one.

I had run the Rock Slide before, though not in a canoe, and my salient memory of the experience is that, in the moment after I had exited safely, I thought, "That wasn't *that* hard." It never is once you've already conquered it. I had landed on the Mexican side at the base of the first of the massive boulders; then, climbing to the top of one boulder, I had memorized a route through the maze. While I scouted, a single canoe, piloted by a man and a woman, had safely navigated the same channels. I had told myself that if they had done it, I could do it.

Now, a mile before the entrance to Santa Elena, I heard voices ahead and soon saw three brightly painted canoes pulled up on the beach. With my resolve waning the closer I came to the canyon entrance, I paddled over to shore to talk to these canoeists. One confident man, a New Yorker, separated himself from the group to answer my questions. I wanted to know if they intended to run Rock Slide soon because it might be wiser for me to tag along with a group rather than attempt the run alone. This gentleman mistook my question for a sign of ignorance about the river, and he then gave a detailed description of a minor drop right around the bend.

"You're either going to have to be very good in that canoe or very lucky to make it through that drop. I'm not telling you what to do, but we're going to line it."

I decided not to wait for the New Yorker and his party. I would run the Rock Slide alone because if this guy was so intimidated by the minor drop just around the bend, I couldn't count on him to help if I had problems a couple of miles later at the Rock Slide.

Approaching the entrance to Santa Elena Canyon, the current suddenly quickens and begins to pinball from one bank to the other, creating a succession of tight and tricky turns. I ran several of these, my heart already pounding as the river built a downhill momentum that made pulling into shore difficult. At one abrupt turn just outside the canyon entrance, I beached the canoe by ramming it into rocks in shallow water at the top of the drop. With the canoe wedged between rocks in the water, I inspected the tie lines. My stomach already knotted, I surveyed the sliver of the canyon opening downriver. If I hadn't known that the Rock Slide lay inside that dark opening, I'd have been eager to press on, keen to discover what beauties the canyon would reveal. Instead, I glanced at both shores, tempted to start looking for a campsite despite the fact that the day was scarcely half over. After several apprehensive moments, I recalled the words of a Laredo friend, Dr. Terry Tilton: "The hardest thing is to begin, to take that first step. Once you begin, you find that nothing was as difficult as the first step." But then Dr. Tilton had never run the Rock Slide.

Once inside the canyon, I found the river tamer, but knowing the Rock Slide waited, I let the canoe drift. In spite of my desire to postpone my arrival at the rapid, the river led me quickly toward it.

In my memory, at the top of the rapid, the Mexican side offered a gravel beach where I could land the canoe to scout a path through the obstacles. Instead, before I reached this beach, I heard the roar of cascading water, its sound magnified by the closeness of the canyon walls.

I beached on a narrow gravel bar extending from the Texas-side canyon wall to scout this unfamiliar rapid. Just below me, I saw the river dogleg hard left, the majority of the flow cascading over a boulder in mid-river right at the turn. I thought, "Where the hell did this come from?"

This tight turn took the river in a mad, surging boil thirty yards from the Mexican-side canyon wall to a collision with the Texas side. I couldn't run the turn without capsizing, but I couldn't portage either side because of the abruptness of the canyon walls. My only hope was to line the tight turn from the Texas-side gravel bar, and then race across the seething current before it piled me into the Texas-side wall. The margin for error was infinitesimal. Worse, I knew the boulders marking the Rock Slide awaited just below.

My fear of slamming the canyon wall produced a surge of adrenaline that made the crossing deceptively simple, and almost the instant I found myself clear of the wall, I saw the imposing sight of the entrance to the Rock Slide, twin house-sized boulders some ten feet apart, constricting the whole flow of the river between them.

I hurried to land on the gravel beach on the Mexican side before this gap, positioning the canoe parallel to the shore as the current pushed to sweep me toward the opening. Landing there, I cautiously set my right foot on shore. Instantly, the current swept the stern of the canoe out from the bank. I found myself in a hopeless predicament some river men call "the splits," one leg on shore, the other leg stretched painfully wide by the moving canoe.

My instincts were to stay with the canoe, though I believed doing so would capsize the boat as soon as I lifted my onshore leg. I pushed off from shore, and the momentum spun the canoe somewhere between sideways and backwards. In the same instant, I teetered desperately on my left leg, fluttering my arms as I tried to avert capsizing. Miraculously, I gained my balance.

From the seat of the canoe, I glanced over my shoulder to see the stern of the boat now close to smashing into the boulder on the Texas side of the opening of the Rock Slide.

I couldn't think of a worse beginning. The canoe was off-course and backwards, and I had missed my chance to scout a route through the maze. I knew immediately that only an act of God could save me. On the other hand, I had to fight while I waited for God's help.

With a desperate lunge, I jammed my paddle into the water and ruddered the canoe with all my strength. The canoe straightened, and with two short, powerful strokes, I cut for the opening between the boulders. My strokes drove the bow of the canoe swiftly across the violent current just in time to avoid being pinned against the Texas-side boulder, and my gunwale grazed the boulder as I cleared the opening. The second narrow turn between boulders sits on the Mexican side of the current twenty yards below the clearance of the first opening, and my inadvertent sideways entry put me in perfect position to enter it.

My new problem, though, was that I had no idea which way to go once I cleared the second opening. As I strained to scout beyond it, the powerful currents swept me out of position. Again, I thrust the paddle deep into the water, this time stopping the boat in mid-current as I straightened it for my run through the chute.

The bow of the canoe cleared the end of the boulders, but I still couldn't determine which way to go. An uneven line of boulders stretched across the river, inviting me to take any of three chutes. I paddled hard for the middle opening, which I barely had room to squeeze through. Once I got through, however, I saw the river open up. I'd reached the end of the Rock Slide!

People who are not spiritual might find it laughable that I raced my boat to the first landing and collapsed to my knees in prayer. I talk to God often on the river, but signs that he is listening are seldom so obvious. A canoeist who runs Colorado Canyon as sloppily as I had two days before—with one capsize and six near misses—doesn't ace the Rock Slide two days later after a backwards, off-course entry and no planned route. Somehow I had pulled it off, and I was sure God had pulled me through.

◆◆◆

Once my heart had stopped pounding, I felt the chill of the canyons and longed to be in the desert sunshine. Six miles of Santa Elena remained, and despite the grandeur of the scenery, I raced toward the end.

I met a guided party of four canoeists lining their boats around a little drop that fed into the canyon wall. It seemed improbable that anyone who would line such a small hazard had just navigated the mighty Rock Slide, but I didn't ask the guide of the foursome how he had passed the two boats through. We chatted for a few minutes, but I was too cold to linger.

A mile later, I saw a flotilla of canoes launching after a hiking stop at Fern Canyon, an impressive tributary that enters from the Mexican side. This picturesque canyon is a mandatory stop on Santa Elena trips, but I passed it, valuing warm sunshine more than scenery. All the way to the canyon mouth an hour downriver, canoes surrounded me. If any of them stopped paddling for a minute, I'd overtake them. If both paddlers worked, they easily passed me. As badly as I wished to be free of them, my desire to bask in the sunshine at the canyon's end made me press on.

At the mouth of Santa Elena Canyon, a trail enters, leading from a parking area to a dead end just inside the canyon. There I saw dozens of tourists. Most of them eyed me with interest. Because a dozen or more canoes trailed close behind me, it took me a couple of minutes to understand why my canoe attracted all the attention. My mountain of gear acted as a magnet, and several of the onlookers descended to the shore to take pictures. I tried to be gracious, but I wanted to hurry another half mile to where I knew sunshine would spill over the Mexican-side canyon wall. Tourists waved timidly, even trailing me along the shore to take more pictures. I calmly but methodically paddled, trying to appear as if I were lazily moving downriver, but I gave each paddle stroke a push that I tried to hide. Finally, I felt the sun pouring over the Sierra Ponce, the Mexican-side formation that now angled southeast away from the river. I let the boat drift and opened a beer. It was time to celebrate.

My relief at passing the Rock Slide was nearly matched by my elation at being alone again. It helped that the Great Unknown section I now entered—fifty miles of open desert—offered no dangerous

THE TECATE JOURNALS

rapids or obstructions. Since few people ever wander out into this vast wilderness, I had my pick of campsites, nearly all of them on pristine beaches that had no footprints other than those of coyotes, blue herons, or ducks. I had to make good time because I was on a tight schedule to meet my close friend Hayesy—who was driving all the way from Massachusetts—on the other side of Big Bend National Park, more than a hundred miles away, four days later.

—◆◆◆—

Mariscal Canyon is the most remote of the three river canyons in Big Bend National Park and, for my tastes, the most spectacular. The rock walls here rise 1,600 feet above the river.

Mariscal contains two rapids, neither comparing in difficulty to Santa Elena's Rock Slide. The first, called Mini-Rock Slide because it too was formed by the fall of boulders from the canyon wall, forces canoeists to make two close turns, the first a ninety-degree right turn as the river bends away from the Texas-side wall, the second a similar left turn as the current collides with the Mexican-side wall sixty yards later. Shortly after Mini-Rock Slide, the current is pushed through a very narrow opening, ten feet or less, where a massive flat rock blocks the channel. Appropriately, this rapid is called Tight Squeeze. The "squeeze" itself is wide enough for a canoe, but potential problems exist both before and after it. Leading into the squeeze, a canoeist must navigate around several exposed rocks that dot the main channel. Below it, another exposed rock necessitates a sharp left-hand turn just as the canoe's bow clears the squeeze. Coming off my difficulties at the Rock Slide, I entered Mariscal Canyon with apprehension. I resolved to take every precaution at the two rapids, even lining the boat through each hazard if need be.

I reached the opening of Mariscal, at the southernmost point of the Big Bend, late in the afternoon of January 2, after a hard day's paddling in bright sunshine. Immediately, the canyon's coolness refreshed me. Within moments, I could hear the dull roar of the first rapid ahead. Almost too quickly, the current pushed me toward it.

88

Mini-Rock Slide offered no landing for a scouting stop, forcing me to enter blindly where the main channel squirreled around the boulders. I hugged the inside of the current as it surged around a tight right-hand turn between the boulders, but then found myself on the wrong side of the main flow as it barreled toward the nearby Mexican wall. Thanks to a rush of adrenaline, I powered the canoe across the swift lane to set up for the second turn and, within seconds, glided safely around the last of the boulders. It was almost too easy, I thought.

Before Tight Squeeze, I landed on a beach to look at the rapid. At first glance, I questioned whether I could navigate around the half dozen rocks that were scattered above the entry. Realizing that my options were limited to running the rapid or making a wearisome portage along the Mexican shore, I decided to chance a run. I easily guided the boat through the rock-strewn channel leading to Tight Squeeze and then cut hard to the left as my bow cleared the narrow opening. In fact, I cut the turn so hard that I found the dead water immediately behind the massive boulder that caused the squeeze, and I sat there out of the current, drinking a Tecate in the canoe as I marveled at the rock's enormity.

"Not bad," I told myself. "You're finally getting the hang of this."

I pressed on, hurrying to emerge from the wintry interior of the gorge before dark. By the time I left the canyon, an hour and a half later, it was the hour when I ordinarily would've been in camp already. However, I charged around turn after turn but couldn't find a campsite. One possible site lacked firewood, the next was too muddy. When I found a third possibility a mile later, I was scared off by the cries of hundreds of goats grazing nearby. Few things in camp are more bothersome than the sound of baby goats braying all night. Finally, when I'd nearly escaped the sound of the goats, I landed on the Mexican side. I didn't like the site at all, but it was now twilight and I still had to collect firewood. With bow saw in hand, I plunged through a salt cedar thicket in the direction of a stand of mesquite trees a hundred yards back upriver.

I found a well-worn trail running parallel to shore. From the downriver direction of the trail, the sight of a man approaching on a burro, a hundred feet or so away, startled me. I surmised that he was tending the goats I'd heard. As he drew near, I could see his dark eyes beneath the wide brim of his sombrero. Nothing about my sudden appearance seemed to surprise or interest him. As the burro plodded lazily along, I called out a greeting, and told him I was searching for firewood. I didn't expect his complete indifference.

"There's wood everywhere," he stated in Spanish in a matter-of-fact manner as he steered the burro around me and continued down the trail. I noted that his eyes were glassy, suggesting that perhaps he'd been drinking, but I didn't smell alcohol as he brushed past.

I walked behind the burro toward the firewood, but before I reached the mesquite, I saw a few fat sticks of dead salt cedar above the trail, and these I collected and carried back to my camp. Returning to the trail, I found the Mexican–a short man, about forty years old, dressed in a poncho and khakis–tying his burro to a salt cedar tree in a clearing a hundred yards from my camp.

"Cut all the wood you want," he said, pointing to the live mesquite trees lining the trail.

I watched him tie his burro and asked, "Are you camping here?"

For the first time, he looked at me squarely, and his gaze seemed to say, "Man, you gringos really are as stupid as they say you are!" Then he turned back to the animal and said, "No, this is where the burro is staying."

It dawned on me that he had a home tucked up over the hill in the direction of the goats. He began lopping off large reeds of river cane with a rusted machete and feeding them to the hungry animal. "This is beef steak for my burro."

I laughed. "Your burro eats better than the *chilangos*."

(*Chilangos* are natives of Mexico City, who are almost universally disrespected because of their arrogance. To call someone a *chilango* in Mexico is akin to calling someone a Yankee in Texas; it implies that the person thinks he is better than you because of where he comes from. I compare *chilangos* to New Yorkers in the U.S., many of whom have a superior air that suggests that the rest of us are unsophisticated, so provincial. *Chilangos* are also reviled because Mexicans in the north feel that for decades they paid an unfair share of taxes in order to finance a better life for the residents of the capital city.)

For the first time, the man warmed up to me. I added, "And he looks a lot better than they do."

I struggled to find dead wood, and five minutes later I passed by him and the burro. Despite my effort, I had only a small armful of puny mesquite branches, not enough to do more than heat a can of soup. He saw my meager load.

"Cut that live mesquite. It burns."

"No thanks. I only burn dead wood."

He rolled his eyes, giving me another one of those looks that suggested he thought we gringos were too difficult. Already I could feel the chill of the evening, portending a very cold night, and I needed a lot more wood. Examining my armful of wood, he said, "Well, that ought to be enough to cook your supper."

Now it was my turn to give him a look. I realized that he had no idea how I'd arrived or what I was doing on that path along the river shore.

"Man, it's going to be a long cold night. I'm not going to sit in the dark and freeze."

Perplexed, he asked, "How did you arrive?"

"*Por chalupa*" (By canoe).

For the first time, he seemed to understand what I was doing there.

"You can find dead wood a little further up the trail, beyond where you first saw me. You'll find enough there for the whole night."

I thanked him, and as I was about to hurry off, he stopped me.

"Where are you from?"

"Laredo, Texas," I answered, using the Spanish pronunciation of each place.

He switched to flawless English. "Man, you sure speak good Spanish."

From his accent it was obvious he had spoken English his entire life. Probably he'd attended the National Park school in Rio Grande Village as a youngster.

In the morning, I heard him yelling angrily at his goats, and whatever had made his eyes glass over had long since worn off. I kept expecting him to drop by my camp, but he didn't.

━●●●━

Once I'd rounded the big bend at Mariscal Canyon, I was moving northeast, and the Mexican state of Coahuila, rather than Chihuahua, now lay on the right shoreline. Knowing that the river bordered only four Mexican states between El Paso and the Gulf, I felt some measure of accomplishment at having passed the largest of them. That day I hoped to make the Big Bend National Park campground of Rio Grande Village by midafternoon. There I could walk to a small camp store, buy supplies, and use the phone.

A couple of miles before Rio Grande Village is Langford Hot Springs, a principal attraction for park visitors. The springs are enclosed by a stone wall that forms a square pool large enough for a dozen bathers. I hadn't planned to stop there because I knew the springs would be crowded with park visitors. As I entered the long, shallow rapid that leads past the bathing pool, a National Park Service helicopter hovered over the springs at a height of only several hundred feet. Just as I came into view of the stone wall surrounding the pool, the helicopter circled, then flew back upriver directly overhead. I worried that someone had drowned in the springs. At the bottom of the rapid, I could see a dozen or more shirtless bathers standing at the periphery of the hot springs. The tricky rapid that leads past the hot springs demanded all my attention, and I couldn't look again until I was almost on top of the small crowd. What I saw astonished me.

Two angry park rangers were writing citations for each of the bathers, and the group mood was sullen. The younger members— college-age kids—appeared stunned, while their middle-aged companions seemed eager to appease the rangers but were having no luck. No one acknowledged my presence as I passed only a few feet from them. I resisted the temptation to pull in below the springs to investigate, since nothing in the mood of the group suggested I'd be welcome. Then I noticed an elaborate camp set up on the sandy beach of the Mexican side, immediately adjacent to the hot springs. I concluded that the group I'd seen had been wading across the shallow river to the hot springs whenever they wanted to soak, and the rangers were fining them for illegally entering the U.S.

Within the hour I landed below the Rio Grande Village campground and walked up to the store. As I passed the primitive campground, I saw a family of five javelinas roaming among the picnic tables, while tired campers lounged next to their hanging stockpiles of food. Javelinas, or collared peccaries, are among the least attractive of all wild animals. They look like a cross between a domestic pig and a wild boar, with grayish black, bristly hair and a long snout, but are smaller than both, growing to sixty pounds and standing about two feet tall at maturity. Neither the javelinas nor the campers paid me any attention.

At the store I was able to use the pay phone to leave a message for Hayesy, telling him when to expect me in La Linda.

Back on the river, I passed beneath the Mexican village of Boquillas, which sits high on a hill some two hundred feet above the river, and looks like the sort of settlement you might see in *The Treasure of the Sierra Madre*. Boquillas had formerly been, for my tastes, the single most interesting attraction on any trip to Big Bend, but about a year after the September 11 attacks, the Border Patrol and the National Park Service had closed the informal crossing to the dusty village, with the excuse that terrorists could enter the U.S. through this desolate outpost. For decades, many park visitors had hiked to the river's edge below Rio Grande Village, where a flatboat from the Mexican side crossed the river to ferry them across, and then they rented burros for a fifteen-minute ride up the rutted road into the village. Once there, they found a small souvenir shop and a fly-infested cantina for their Third World amusement. Outside of town, another half mile into the desert, sit massive sand dunes formed by winds howling up nearby Boquillas Canyon. The magnificent Sierra del Carmen forms a stunning backdrop, rising to heights in excess of eight thousand feet—six thousand feet higher than the elevation of the windswept village. I resisted the temptation to hike up the steep trail into Boquillas on this warm afternoon. Instead, I approached the entrance to Boquillas Canyon, the longest of the three great canyons of the Big Bend.

Boquillas is the oldest and, therefore, the widest of the three canyons, as the force of the river has had who knows how many more millions of years to erode the canyon walls. Although its walls are not as dramatic as those of Santa Elena or Mariscal, the surrounding countryside makes this canyon equally spectacular, especially in the first stages of the run. Because it is wider, sunshine floods in every day, and the canyon is much warmer in winter than its upstream counterparts. I felt no eeriness or claustrophobia here, as I had in the previous two canyons. Less than a mile into the canyon, I pulled over on a gravel beach along the Mexican side and set up camp.

From this camp, I had twenty-nine river miles before La Linda and eight hundred and five miles to the Gulf of Mexico. Already I was more than a third of the way to the sea—at least measured by river miles—yet I was only sixteen days into the trip. But the trip hadn't developed a clear "personality." Although I was happy with everything about the journey, I realized I was racing down the river at a terrific rate, and I hadn't settled into whatever it was I expected to settle into by this point. One problem was the fact that I had allowed other people's schedules to dictate the pace of my travels—not that I blamed them. On the bikes, Tony and I had hurried from beginning to end. Then, once Tony left, I'd been hurrying in order to meet Hayesy a hundred and ninety miles downriver in La Linda. As a result, the trip seemed less like an adventure and more like a race. I needed to slow down, if only to redirect the considerable energies I expended on the water to use for adventures on land. I worried that I might race to the Gulf in far less time than I expected and then feel I'd missed the entire trip. I resolved to slow down.

I had left two rafts at Heath Canyon Ranch, opposite La Linda, with the ranch's owner, Andy Kurie. Because of the heavy demands of the white water in the Lower Canyons section, which begins there, I planned to switch from canoe to raft for that stretch. This switch would enable Hayesy and me to run all the rapids and to carry enough gear to go for weeks between supply points without having to resort to dried food.

The next morning I lazily broke camp, lingering beside the fire, cooking quesadillas and boiling water for tea. When I did get into the canoe, I paddled leisurely and spent far more time admiring the surrounding rock formations than I had in the previous two canyons. When I wanted to stretch my legs, I didn't hurry back into the canoe, often wandering away from shore to scout for animal tracks.

Early in the afternoon I heard the sound of people's voices ahead of me, and around the next bend I saw a group of six canoes. For the next hour and a half I trailed them. I expected them to pull over, and I would then pass and have the river to myself again. But they stayed in the boats, paddling steadily enough, two paddles to a boat, that I was unable to close the gap between us. Just as I was about to give up and allow them time to separate themselves further downriver, Rabbit Ears—two large rock columns rising out of the Texas-side talus slope—came into view. From a distance, this formation looks like a thirty-story-high cattle prod made of stone. Apparently, an early river traveler saw the ears of a rabbit instead. Here, the canoeists pulled into shore.

I had planned to greet this party and then put some distance between us so that I could claim a good camp without having to take their plans into account. As they all greeted me, I could tell from their accents that they were Canadians. I pulled in to visit with them and learned that they had come all the way from Edmonton, Alberta. We enjoyed an animated conversation with much laughter. They told a curious story about how they practice canoeing and kayaking during the winter at a watercourse inside a shopping mall.

A couple of hours later, the walls of the canyon disappeared and the river widened. I passed camping opportunity after camping opportunity, pushing late into the afternoon before settling for an island outside the boundary of the National Park. I felt both elated and disappointed to be so close to La Linda, only seven miles downriver. As excited as I would be to see Hayesy, that excitement was tempered by the undeniable reality that I preferred the solitude of a solo trip.

.

El Despoblado

Jan. 5–8

When I rounded the last bend before La Linda and came into view of the Gerstacker Bridge—the barricaded span connecting the abandoned mining town with the paved road on the U.S. side—I felt giddy. For one thing, I knew that just below that bridge awaited my close friend Hayesy—my favorite river partner—and that the spirit of the trip would turn festive over the next few weeks. Hayesy is a fun-loving Irish Catholic, with far more emphasis on the Irish than the Catholic, and his capacity for silliness and good times equaled my own. I could count on one thing: no matter how adverse the conditions—whether those conditions included freezing weather, incessant head winds, icy precipitation, or dust storms—Hayesy and I would find a way to think we were having the time of our lives. Whether the situation called for a prolonged struggle against the elements or an assault on our beer supply, he was equal to the task. Hayesy is the kind of never-say-never guy you want on your side for every endeavor. He's part trench warrior and part Good Time Charlie. Also, he would come equipped with three weeks' worth of supplies that included such luxuries as steak, fresh fruit, and Tecate.

My eagerness to see Hayesy was temporarily eclipsed by my excitement at the prospect of visiting Andy Kurie, the retired geologist who owns Heath Canyon Ranch. For me, Andy serves as a father figure, a mentor in the ways of the Chihuahua desert. He had spent much of his life there, working the mines in Mexico for Dow Chemical and Dupont. Upon retirement, he purchased the company guest quarters on the U.S. side and had spent the last decade running a guest ranch there. Except for occasional visits from his family, Andy lived alone in the main house, which sits a hundred vertical feet above the river just upstream from the bridge.

Andy describes himself as "an old hermit," and he's a man who has lived so long in remote areas that he, like the mountain men of the Old West, feels overwhelmed when he has to go into town for anything more than a shopping trip or an evening with his wife. Seven or eight years ago he suffered from prostate cancer and had to spend several months in Houston undergoing treatment. Afterwards he remarked, "I don't know which was worse, that damned chemotherapy or that damned city."

Another time he told me the story of watching a flood surge under the bridge below his home. Suddenly, an entire house came floating down the river, and as it passed, Andy saw a man sitting calmly atop the roof. Andy called to offer help, but the man said he preferred to stay with his home until the end. Andy said, "I bet he was scared to death of having to move into town."

When I used to play baseball for the mine team, my teammates referred to Andy as *el gringo amable* ("the kind gringo"), but I didn't meet him until he bought the company ranch after the mine closed. When I finally got to know him, I felt as if I were in the presence of a living legend, a man who knew the backcountry of Mexico south of the Big Bend better than any person. If you ask any Mexican in a wide area surrounding La Linda about Andy, it's certain that person will break into a grin and say, *"Es buena gente"* (He's good people).

I arrived at Andy's river access a couple of hundred yards below the Gerstacker Bridge around lunchtime of my eighteenth day on the river. Far above, on the hill, I could barely make out the figures of Hayesy and Fred, the ranch's security man, sitting in the bright sunshine next to a trailer. I made several exaggerated waves in the air with my paddle, and then hauled my gear and canoe up the steep embankment to the beach. Minutes after I finished the job, the Edmonton contingent arrived, and I helped as the large group emptied its six canoes, forming a sort of bucket brigade to move the mountain of gear from water's edge to beach. Amidst all this activity, Andy arrived in his pickup, and we enjoyed a cheerful reunion. Hayesy followed him a few minutes later. I left Hayesy on the beach with the Canadians while I accompanied Andy up to his home, where we would visit while I did laundry and used Andy's computer to write another river report to send to Louis in Houston.

"How's everything been here?" I asked Andy as we drove the road up from the river.

"As usual, there have been all kinds of things going at the river, most of them at night. You know how it is. I keep hoping the bridge will open and we'll have Customs down here to keep an eye on things."

"What are the chances of that?"

"Pretty good, I hope. I'm getting too damn old to look after this corner of the world by myself. Fred is a big help, and I don't know how I would manage without him. But the Mexicans are running all kinds of contraband. And who knows what sort of help they have on this side of the border?"

The next day Hayesy and I loaded the two rafts for the next leg of the trip to Langtry, Texas.

"You know one thing I like about this trip?" Hayesy said as we stood above the loaded rafts. "Not only did I get to see Andy at the beginning, but I'll also get to see him when we come back to get the canoe."

"He is quite a guy," I said.

"The best."

—◆◆◆—

The Lower Canyons of the Rio Grande extend from La Linda, Mexico, to Langtry, Texas, a distance of one hundred thirty-seven river miles, and the combined population on both sides of the river for the entire distance is zero. It's a pretty safe bet that you can make this run at most times of the year and not see another person. This stretch of river is so remote that not even undocumented workers sneak across the border here. And two U.S. survey teams abandoned the effort to map it. The Lower Canyons remained the last great unexplored wilderness of the contiguous United States for more than three decades after John Wesley Powell descended the Grand Canyon. Legends about the area's canyons and rapids grew. Many believed the Lower Canyons were as deep as seven thousand feet, and stories about bandits and boat-eating rapids proliferated.

In 1899 a U.S. Geological Service survey team led by Robert Hill finally completed the charting of the Lower Canyons. Hill enlisted the help of James McMahon, a trapper who knew the river well and served as his boatman. When Hill's survey team reported that the canyons were only two thousand feet deep, interest in the mysterious area evaporated. Until white-water boating became a popular recreation in the 1970s, the Lower Canyons were ignored.

—◆◆◆—

After ten days in the canoe, I found the overloaded raft as hard to maneuver as a barge. In the canoe each paddle stroke had lunged the boat through the current; in the raft each paddle stroke accomplished little. In the canoe I'd traveled four to five miles an hour; in the rafts Hayesy and I traveled exactly five miles the first afternoon. We made camp on the grassy floodplain at a narrow straightaway in the river beneath a towering spire on the Texas side. It was a camp I used often because of its easy access, its reserves of mesquite wood, and its scenic beauty. Downriver, the narrow opening of Temple Canyon swallows the Rio Grande, the twin canyon walls rising six hundred feet. And if we could keep the noise down, this camp would afford a great chance to see wildlife. In the past, I'd often seen a horde of javelinas rumble across the beach, and bobcats lived in the mesquite immediately across the river.

Our mood in camp was light, and we drank Tecate and grilled steaks over the mesquite coals. However, the next morning, as we loaded the rafts for departure, the feeling changed abruptly. I heard the unlikely sound of voices moving through the mesquite growth above the opposite shore. A moment later I spotted two heads, and I called out a friendly greeting in Spanish. Suddenly ten or twelve men, all outfitted with bale-sized backpacks, scattered for cover. Even as they hurried to hide, I could tell that not one had seen me, although I was only a hundred feet away on the other side of the river. I noticed that all of the backpacks were identical—yellow and waterproof, similar to the wet bags Hayesy and I use to keep our gear dry while running white water.

It would be difficult to overstate how pervasive marijuana trafficking is along the Rio Grande, but even I found it surprising that smugglers had chosen this remote route. By river, La Linda sat only five miles away; by land, because of the need to circumvent two impassable canyons, the distance was more than double. Furthermore, the next access on the Texas side, via the rough road network of the Black Gap Wildlife Management Area, was six river miles away, but two more canyons required long walks around.

Rumors abounded—many passed along by very trustworthy sources—that the business of drug trafficking had infiltrated all levels of the Border Patrol, the National Park Service, and local law enforcement agencies in the Big Bend region. The most publicized case involved the bust of Presidio County Sheriff Rick Thompson, a twenty-year Marine Corps veteran, who was arrested in December 1991 after federal agents found a ton of 94% pure Colombian cocaine in his horse trailer at the fairground outside of Marfa, Texas. Thompson pled guilty and initially received a life sentence, which was later reduced to twenty-two years on the grounds that he had "cooperated." Reputedly, the ex-sheriff was part of an intricate smuggling network, originating with the legendary Pablo Acosta, that stretched through many of the backcountry ranches of the Big Bend area and included the cooperation of ranch owners and Park Service officials.

In the vast desert triangle formed by Highway 90, Highway 385, and the Rio Grande—an area of roughly four thousand square miles—an extensive network of seldom-traveled ranching and wildlife management roads crisscrosses the terrain. Rarely visited by the Border Patrol or any other law enforcement agency, these roads offer smugglers routes to circumvent the B. P. checkpoints on all the area's paved highways leading from the river to the state's interior. Apparently, this group of a dozen "mules" who carried the backpacks in the mesquite grove adjacent to our camp was headed—or at least their cargo was headed—for this isolated network.

Hayesy grew nervous at once, but it became clear that the mules were more disturbed by our presence than we were by theirs. A moment later, two of the men emerged in a clearing downriver, and one insisted on conversing in his limited English.

"Hey man, what you doing?" he asked.

"We're going downriver to Acuña."

"Really, man. This is your work?"

"No, this is our vacation," I said.

"That's cool, man. *Que le vaya bien*" (Have a good trip).

Hayesy and I spoke in hushed tones as we tried to assess the situation.

"What are the chances these guys are going to give us problems?" Hayesy said.

"What kind of problems are you talking about?"

"Murder."

"Zero chance," I said. "I'm sure they're more worried about us than we are about them."

"There's no chance they would try to get rid of us?"

"Why would they do that?"

"So we can't rat on them to the Border Patrol."

"Hayesy, where the hell are we going to find the Border Patrol way out here? These guys just want to ferry the drugs across the river and get paid. They're not in this to murder."

I decided that our best course would be to move downriver, where we almost surely would find the smugglers waiting for us to pass.

Sure enough, we boated only three hundred yards further when we found the group huddled in the shade of a catclaw acacia tree twenty vertical feet above the shore. I whispered to Hayesy to paddle past while I angled toward shore to chat with them. The men ranged in age from late teens to mid-forties, most of them anxious about my approach. The yellow bale-sized backpacks were nowhere in view. One of the men asked for cigarettes. As Hayesy paddled by, I took an exaggerated amount of time to retrieve the cigarettes. Once I saw that Hayesy was well beyond me, I tossed the pack of cigarettes onto shore. Three men sprinted to retrieve it, and I saw that they were more relieved to have cigarettes than they had been to learn I was not a drug agent. I asked in Spanish, "So just what are you guys doing out here?"

"Fishing."

—◆◆◆—

Nine miles out of camp the next morning, we came to a narrowing of the river where Big Canyon—a wide drainage—enters from the Texas side, and suddenly the canyon walls along the river soar to heights in excess of a thousand feet. This marks the beginning of Reagan Canyon, also known as Bullis Canyon, one of the more majestic enclaves on our planet. For the next forty miles, the river courses below dramatic canyon walls rising as high as two thousand feet, offering striking geologic wonders that have been carved over millions of years as the river has scored the limestone substrata. While the Grand Canyon is no doubt more spectacular, you cannot, as I have done on the majority of my trips through the Lower Canyons, have the whole thing to yourself. No matter how many times I enter this canyon, my pulse inevitably quickens when I turn the sharp bend at Big Canyon and plunge with the narrowing river into the first mile of Reagan Canyon. If the sight of the mighty rock walls doesn't humble you, certainly the challenges of navigating your craft through the surging currents will. You sense immediately that you are in a new ballgame.

A river guidebook published by the Big Bend Natural History Association warns: "Because of the remote and wild nature of this run, ALL PRECAUTIONS MUST BE EXERCISED TO INSURE THE PERSONAL SAFETY OF ALL MEMBERS OF THE PARTY!!" The same book says, "This trip is for properly prepared and experienced river runners only! It would be a very arduous and miserable trip for the careless or ignorant adventurer. You should not attempt this run unless the overall experience level of your party is very high. Help is, at the least, several hours, and possibly days, away."

Once you enter Reagan Canyon, there are few places where help is as close as "several hours" away. In fact, for the next forty miles, exactly two such places await: one where a Mexican ranch sits twelve miles up a side canyon, and the other where an American ranch sits seven miles up an impassable road. Few river runners know the location of either.

During my twenty-eight trips through the Lower Canyons, I'd already experienced my share of dangerous confrontations, injurious accidents, and boating mishaps. In late June of 2003, for example, while boating the flooded river alone on a wild run from La Linda to Langtry, with the river flowing forty percent above the legal limit for rafting it in the size craft I piloted, I ran the three major rapids of the canyon flawlessly. However, that same evening in camp, while I was kicking at a two-inch-diameter black-brush acacia stump I intended to harvest for the campfire, the stump failed to snap despite my most powerful kick; my tennis shoe slid up the two-foot-high stump, and I fell into its pointed tip. The sickening consequence of my fall—I learned after I painfully extracted myself from the prickly pear cactus in which I had landed—was that the tip of the stump impaled my leg just below my calf, boring a neat but hideous two-inch hole in my flesh directly to the bone. As I stared at my exposed tibia, a yellowish fluid flooded out with each heartbeat. I realized immediately that I was in big trouble.

By the time I reached a hospital five days later, my leg was so swollen that doctors worried aloud that they might not be able to save it. The irony of the Lower Canyons is that you can meet all the obvious dangers the river offers and then be undone by something as routine as collecting firewood. One key to making a successful trip in such a remote area is to never let your guard down, to be aware at all times that if you can't get out by yourself you're not getting out.

When Hayesy and I entered Reagan Canyon on a balmy afternoon in January, my excitement at being back was not the edgy and anxious nervousness of battling the pushy river in a remote and intimidating setting, but rather the happy familiarity at being home again after a long absence.

Oasis

Jan. 9–10

Over three years had elapsed since Hayesy had last accompanied me on a Lower Canyons adventure. Health problems had forced him to miss several trips. Clearly, he seemed less than the invincible young man who'd been such an integral part of my first decade of Lower Canyons experiences—his back now bent from a lifetime of blue-collar labor, the skin around his eyes leathery, his hair now silver. Still, there remained something unmistakably youthful about Hayesy: his high-pitched laugh, his adolescent quality of exhibiting so much excitement over beautiful scenery, his crystalline blue eyes, which seemed forever childlike.

Hayesy and I work together as a team as well as any two people. Although my stubbornness may have riled him a few times in our dozen trips together in the Lower Canyons, he never let on that I was anything but a model partner. If his propensity for small talk about his hometown of Beverly, Massachusetts, ever drove me to the brink of rudeness, I never uttered a word. Together we had endured just about every conceivable hardship the river could throw at us, and I felt confident in Hayesy's abilities as a boatman, a camper, and a decision maker. His strength, capacity for silly fun, and dedication to comfort and good eating helped to counter my endurance, my tendency toward reserve and silence, and my austere eating habits. Hayesy's presence ensures that I have a lot more fun; my presence ensures that he has a lot more discipline.

Four days after leaving Andy's, we arrived at a major drop named Hot Springs Rapids, a river runner's oasis where clear warm pools of mineral water spring from the earth near the Mexican bank. The rapid re-forms itself often, as violent washouts entering from San Rosendo Canyon compete with floods roaring down the main channel of the river. On one trip, in July of 1999, I found the steep Class III+ drop in the river had been completely flattened by a surge of water through the canyon. In the ensuing years, the steep drop formed anew, the submerged boulders now creating two tiers to the drop in place of the one that had existed previously.

We pulled in to scout the rapid, and I could see that Hayesy's long layoff from rafting had robbed him of much of his confidence. Not wanting to show him up or force him to think he had to run the rapid, I offered him alternatives. We could line the boats close to the Mexican shore. Or we could portage, a short carry through the dry wash of the canyon.

Hayesy didn't seem comfortable with running the rapid, so I suggested we move the boats right to the beginning of the drop by hugging the Mexican shore. There, I suggested, we'd have a shorter carry if he elected not to run.

"How about this?" I said. "I take my boat out into mid-river and look at it from there?"

"Are you high? What happens if the current sweeps you over the rapid?"

"Well, then I run it."

I didn't even give him a chance to voice his objections. After running the Rock Slide in a canoe without a scout, there was no way I was walking this one. I wanted to respect Hayesy's wishes and save his dignity, but not at the expense of having to lug two weeks' worth of supplies over slippery rocks to avoid a Class III drop. The run, I knew from countless times through, always looked more foreboding from shore, and the secret was to scout quickly before your mind had time to make the relatively small obstacles in the channel into boulders. The minute I walked back to the boat, I knew I would run the rapids.

Once I reached the bottom, Hayesy asked if I wanted to run his raft through. I remembered a time years before when he had asked me to run his raft and had then spent the next year regretting not having done the run himself.

"Hayesy, you know you'll regret it if you don't run it. It's a lot easier than it looks from here."

Still, he lacked confidence. A long layoff from rafting will do that. When you're running good rapids all the time, it seems you can always find a lane through. When you're rusty, even the smallest rapids seem really dangerous.

"Okay, all you have to do is line up off that triangular rock about forty percent of the way across the river, the one that is just two inches above the water line, and make sure your boat is going straight when you begin the drop. The river will do the rest for you. And if you hit anything when you're lining up, just make sure you straighten the boat."

Hayesy nodded, his countenance still flushed with nerves. He turned tentatively toward his raft, and repeated the exact directions.

"Hayesy," I said, "You'll ace this one. I know it."

"The first one is always the hardest," he replied. "But I'm just going to follow your directions, and then I'll meet you down at the cooler."

—◆◆◆—

The sense of relief and exuberance boaters feel about ending their day with a perfectly executed run of a challenging rapid is one of the most seductive elements of the sport. Experiencing that exuberance at Hot Springs amplifies the high manyfold. There you have warm bathing pools, an inexhaustible supply of firewood, a hard-packed sandy beach for camping, and the soothing roar of the falling water. We bathed, and I washed my clothes and sleeping bag at the base of the runoff from the springs. Warmed by the sun, we lounged on the rocks in camp, organizing our gear, drinking beer, and talking. Hayesy asked numerous questions about my trip thus far, and later we talked about the different directions our lives would take once we reached our goal of Amistad Dam a couple of weeks downriver. When darkness fell, we built a glowing fire in a sand hole against the base of a boulder, and I told the story of meeting Antonio at this same camp several years before.

Antonio was one of the most remarkable men I've ever met. He had walked into my camp at Hot Springs one December afternoon. The water had been very low, and I had struggled to reach this site, having had to drag my loaded raft through many of the shallows in the river. The rapids had been even more demanding; because all of them lacked sufficient water for a run, I had had to muscle the boat over one rock after another. By the time I reached Hot Springs after five grueling days, I was physically spent. I was worried about my body, and, frankly, I was feeling sorry for myself.

Realizing I had to lighten the load, I'd left some of my provisions, including a case of beer, on the trail leading from the river to the rough canyon road by which Mexicans accessed the area from the interior. Atop this small pile of foodstuffs and beer, I'd left a note in Spanish, explaining that I'd had to abandon them because I was oversupplied.

Carrying only a small plastic grocery bag filled with seven tins of sardines and about twenty key limes in one hand and a one-gallon water jug in the other, Antonio arrived at my campsite on his long walk to Fort Stockton, Texas, where he worked as a welder on a ranch. He had left his home in Múzquiz, 180 miles to the southeast, three days before. First he had hitched a ride with an acquaintance who made deliveries to the outlying ranches. When the friend left him fifty miles south of the river, Antonio walked.

"Me gusta caminar siempre solo" (I always like to walk alone), he said often.

He would walk day and night for the next six days to reach his workplace, sleeping only when he grew too tired to walk another step. Because he did not carry a blanket or a sleeping bag, he usually awoke due to the cold after only a short sleep. Then he would walk again. Antonio planned his walks around a full moon so that he could walk all night. He seemed to think no more of the 200-mile walk than we would think of our morning commute into the city to our jobs. This was his eleventh trip via the paths that led past Hot Springs. He had made another half dozen trips via La Linda.

"Why did you go home this time? Did you miss your family?"

"I had a toothache. The dentists in the U.S. are very expensive."

I convinced him to camp with me that night, and I promised to ferry him across the river in the morning. I asked him many questions about his family, which included a wife and six children, all of them living in Múzquiz.

"I work for the youngest, a girl. She's nine years old and she's very intelligent. I did not go to school, not even for one day. My daughter attends three schools. She's already much smarter than I am."

"How long have you been married, Antonio?"

"Twenty-five years."

"How old is your wife?"

"Thirty-two."

"Thirty-two? And you've been married twenty-five years? How old was she when you married her?"

"Fourteen."

I learned he couldn't read either. After we had eaten a meal together, I wanted him to proofread the short note I'd left with the supplies I'd abandoned, so I walked back up the trail and retrieved it. He crouched down above the note for several minutes, but his eyes never moved. Finally, I realized that he not only couldn't read but was too embarrassed to admit it.

"*Se ve bien ¿no?*" (It looks okay, right?), I said.

"*Sí, pero no me pegan las palabras*" (Yes, but the words don't stick to me).

Around the campfire, we talked about our fears. I told him the story of the mountain lion charging into my camp.

"Aren't you afraid of *pumas?*" I asked.

"I fear only three things. I hate rattlesnakes, and that's why I walk in the winter when they're sleeping. And buffalos give me much fear. There is a ranch in the mountains on my way to Fort Stockton, and there they keep buffalos. I walk many hours to avoid them."

"What's the third?"

"*La onza.*"

"*La onza?* What's that?"

"It's a wildcat, smaller and darker than a mountain lion, but much more deadly. It eats people. It stalks you for hours, waiting on the edge of the camp while you sleep. At dawn, when it is satisfied a larger onza isn't going to kill you, it charges in. This is the fiercest of all animals. I do not camp because of it."

"I've never heard of this animal."

"You don't have them in the U.S. For that you are lucky."

I learned later that only three *onzas* have been spotted since 1970, all of them on the Pacific side of the Sierra Madre. Andy Kurie explained Antonio's fear of them as "the result of Indian myths."

"How is it, Antonio, that you can walk all the way to Fort Stockton with so few provisions?"

"I eat very little because eating slows me down. Every day when the sun is high, I eat one can of sardines. That's all. When I tire, I suck on a lime."

"And you have so little water."

"I find water at the ranches along the way. The ranchers know me now, and most are very helpful."

In the morning, after a restless night in which Antonio repeatedly chased a skunk from our camp, I ferried him across the river, where he began the next six days of his walk by ascending a steep drainage up the thousand-foot canyon wall.

Another half day on the river brought Hayesy and me eight more miles to an island camp, and on the way we ran two more marked rapids and explored Cañon del Caballo Blanco, or White Horse

Canyon. Almost five years before, Eric Clem and I had paddled this same stretch in March, and near the canyon's opening, we found two horses feeding in the grass of a thin beach along the canyon wall. Eric had grown up around horses on a Nova Scotia farm, and as we passed one of the two horses, a white mare, he noticed that it still wore a bit and bridle. The crude rope dangling from the bit suggested that the mare had recently broken free from a ranch, probably the ranch up San Rosendo Canyon. Eric surmised that the mare might slowly starve to death because the bit hampered her ability to eat. Immediately, I pulled hard for shore, telling Eric I was determined to remove the bit and bridle. "OK," Eric conceded, "but it might not be nearly as easy as you think."

In the last couple of years of my daughter's life, her love for animals became one of the principal sustaining forces in her life. In fact, for her Make A Wish Foundation trip, she chose a trip to the San Diego Zoo and a visit with Joan Embery, the zookeeper who often brought animals onto a popular late-night TV show. Eric's suggestion that the white mare could starve to death, or even struggle to eat, instantly made me think of my daughter, and I had to rescue the horse.

Two hours of chasing the two horses back and forth across the powerful but shallow current finally yielded results. The mare allowed us to stand within three feet of her, and I lunged for the crude rope. I held the fidgety horse while Eric deftly removed the rudimentary bit and bridle, a souvenir I still hang in my kitchen. The white mare and her coffee-colored mate then spent the next four years grazing in the immediate area of White Horse Canyon, and each trip through I'd call a gentle greeting to the pair as I paddled by. This year, however, the horses had gone, perhaps reclaimed by the ranchers from whom they escaped.

Our island camp offered an opportunity to repack all the gear because the following day we planned to run the two biggest rapids of the Lower Canyons: Upper Madison Falls, a long, violent Class IV, and Lower Madison Falls, a steep Class III. Upper Madison would be the biggest challenge since I had run the Rock Slide back in Santa

Elena Canyon. And less than a mile out of camp, we would descend a drop called Rodeo Rapids, so named because the interference wave at the bottom of the six-foot drop bucked rafts nearly out of the water, much as a bull or bronco rider is thrown by its high-kicking and reluctant carrier. Upper Madison, because of its length and technical difficulty, offered the greater number of potential problems, but I worried more about the shorter, steeper and faster Lower Madison, which kicked as violently as Rodeo Rapids but included an additional hazard: two tiers of barely submerged boulders, which the river surged over as it charged toward the bottom of the twenty-foot drop. We spent the afternoon packing and tying our gear so that we wouldn't lose anything if we capsized in the rapids. We could worry about the rest the following day.

Some boaters prefer to end a day by running a major rapid and camping below it, secure in the knowledge that the obstacle is behind them. Others prefer to meet the challenges of a major rapid when they are fresh in the early part the day, the one drawback being that anxiety over the obstacle ahead often interferes with a restful night's sleep. For me, neither of the Madisons constituted a major threat, and I could probably have slept soundly on a barrel tethered to a post in the middle of either one. Hayesy, however, showed signs of pre-rapid nerves as we broke camp the following morning. I did not ask him how he had slept. I could already guess what his answer would've been.

I didn't worry about Hayesy's ability to negotiate any of the rapids on the Rio Grande, instead interpreting his nerves as a healthy sign of his respect for the dangers of our isolation. People who regularly boat the Lower Canyons often stress the warning "You can never let your guard down." I think the most trying four days I ever spent on the river were the result of a tiny cut in the pinky toe of one of my feet. Because the cut was so small, I neglected to administer first aid, ignoring the increasing soreness until swelling due to infection made walking very painful. My difficulty walking narrowed the parameters of what I could do to such a degree that I suddenly felt overwhelmed by my inability to perform even the most basic chores like gathering firewood, loading and unloading the boat, and setting up the tent. Finally I realized the cut wouldn't heal itself, and within twelve hours of treating it, I had full mobility.

But that's the way it often goes in the canyons. You match the obvious challenges with determination, concentration, and caution. Then, with your confidence increasing to the point where you have begun to think you are invincible, one false step into a cactus gives you painful notice of your vulnerability. And virtually every plant and tree in the canyons is armed with barbed thorns, daggerlike spines, or sharp spikes. Even river cane, the one notable exception in the spiny plant world of the desert terrain, grows razor-sharp leaves capable of slicing skin to dangerous depths. When I impaled my leg on a black brush stump, the wound stopped secreting fluid within fifteen minutes, but I've had river cane cuts spill out an hour's worth of blood.

Hayesy understood the dangers, small and not so small, that we confronted the moment our guards dropped. His long absence from boating, however, seemed to inflate his respect for the potential problems that could occur at the major rapids. When a day of successes had bolstered our confidence to the level of complacency, we always reminded ourselves: "We haven't accomplished anything yet. Let's wait until we're safely off the river before we start the congratulations."

Fasten Your Life Jackets

Jan. 11

If you study a map of Texas and follow the Rio Grande as it moves northeast after turning the Big Bend, you'll notice—just before it turns back to the east, and then southeast—a little nipple where the river makes an abrupt 180-degree turn in a space of two miles. This nipple marks the location of Burro Bluff, which rises above Upper Madison Falls. After this point, the river flows twelve miles almost due north before resuming its long-detoured course toward the Gulf of Mexico. The impenetrable barrier of the Sierra del Carmen, which forces the river to seek easier passage along its western flank, causes the 140-mile detour.

Hayesy and I crept around the bend at the base of Burro Bluff in close formation, his boat nearly grazing mine as we boat-scouted the first drop.

"It's a simple diagonal slot, from center to Mexican side," I reminded him. "Just make sure you paddle below the boat as you cross;

otherwise the current will sweep you into the rocks. See you at the bottom."

I never worried about the first drop. Even a novice couldn't get into too much trouble there, not in a raft anyway. Sure, you could pin the boat against the many rocks and perhaps even tip it in doing so, but below the drop you had a relatively calm sixty-yard stretch to recover before you had to worry about lining up for the toughest part of the rapids—the second, or main, drop. Hayesy trailed me right through the diagonal lane to the Mexican shore, and we landed on a grassy beach at the base of the portage trail. Several years had passed since he had run the falls, so I sent him up to scout the rapids.

On my first trip in the Lower Canyons, Rob Boushel and I had attempted to run Upper Madison Falls only because we weren't able to find a path to portage around it. At the main drop, we capsized the canoe, losing nearly all of our food. For the next three days, we worried whether we'd make it out alive. Ever since then, I've had a lot of respect for the potential dangers here.

The problem with Upper Madison Falls is that you have to find, and hit, a chute just above the drop. This chute is only inches wider than the raft, and the water drops violently through it, plunging ten feet within ten yards between Winnebago-sized boulders. Worse, you have to go diagonally to the current as you enter, creating the danger that you can pin the boat sideways at the top of the drop. Another problem is that if you graze either rock marking the entry to the chute, the impact immediately tosses you off course, and you have exactly ten feet in hard-charging and fast-falling water to correct the boat. No matter how many times I run this part of the rapid, I am surprised on each new run how small the margin for error is.

My run went as smoothly as I could hope, and I paddled hard for the rocky shore of the island just below the drop to photograph Hayesy's run. With the water thundering around the island, I felt a strange calm. I saw, as if in slow motion, Hayesy's raft come into view above the chute. After he cleared the rock at the top of the chute, he overcorrected and hit the right side of the chute with the front of his raft. For an agonizing moment, the raft squeezed sideways into an opening too narrow to accept the width of the boat. His next move would either save the run or bury the boat in the tight wedges of the monstrous Texas-side boulders, trapped there by a force of falling water he'd never be able to outmuscle or outwit.

One reason my trust in Hayesy borders on absolute is that he has exceptional rafting instincts when he gets into trouble. Only one maneuver could extricate that raft from the clenches of the chute, and in a fraction of a second, Hayesy executed it. With two powerful strokes he righted the raft, and the river thrust him cleanly into the chute and safely to the bottom of the drop. He paddled into an eddy to allow me to get back into my raft so he could follow me through the third drop, a hundred yards further downriver.

I didn't like to get too complacent about our clean run of Upper Madison when we still faced Lower Madison two miles downriver, but I'd have to have been a spoilsport not to celebrate at the bottom of the rapid with Hayesy in the warm January sunshine.

◆◆◆

Lower Madison, also known as Horseshoe Falls, is the single steepest natural drop on the entire Texas–Mexico section of the Rio Grande. On your approach, the rapid is first recognizable by the utter disappearance of the river. The abruptness of the falls also serves to muffle the roar of the rapid. It's possible a novice could be committed to running it before he even knew it was there.

Running Lower Madison turned out to be anticlimactic—a simple matter of good entry yielding a good run. We landed on the limestone ledge below the rapids for another beer. Just below the end of the ledge sits a natural spring, where we filled our water jugs, fourteen gallons in all, for the next leg of the trip.

At Panther Canyon, three miles further, sits another rapid, a Class II at most water levels, one of the few in the Lower Canyons that grows progressively more difficult with increased flows. We had fought stout head winds in the dead water leading to the rapid and, with twelve miles and two major rapids behind us, decided to pull in for camp. After unloading the boats, we set out to gather firewood up Panther Canyon, one of the most picturesque of the hundreds of side canyons that enter the Rio Grande. Lovely canyon walls layered in striking shades of orange rise six hundred feet above the narrow wash. The canyon floor offered a myriad of *tinajas*, or natural rock pools, some the size of birdbaths, others as large as backyard swimming pools.

I could see that Hayesy's energy level was waning, and once we had the wood piled in camp, I asked him if he felt okay.

"It's been a tough day physically," he said. "You're more used to it because you've been out here close to a month now. The paddling, the wood collecting, the loading and unloading, it's all starting to catch up with me."

Before Tony had left from Presidio, he had asked me to tell Hayesy, "Keith is going to run you into the ground."

I'd delivered that message to Hayesy, who scoffed upon hearing it. "Hey, I've done river trips with you so many times. I know exactly what I'm getting into."

Still, I had decided to schedule our itinerary by alternating what I called full days with half days, typically two of each. On full days, we would raft all day. On half days, we'd rest in camp either all morning or all afternoon. Seeing Hayesy's fatigue, I felt bad because our schedule allowed for no rest days. My idea of resting included collecting hundreds of pounds of firewood, walking steep canyon trails to take photographs, or following animal tracks. I never stopped moving because I never felt a need to rest. Each day in the canyons, I thrived more and more, my energy building, my excitement increasing. Whatever mechanism Hayesy had in his body to signal fatigue, I didn't have it. I could go, go, go, and the only evidence I felt of the terrific physical demands of the trip was morning soreness. But I quickly worked past that, jumping into the physical demands of another river day. Fueled by a growing sense that time was running out—I was, after all, approaching fifty years old—and the joy of being in the depths of the Lower Canyons, my energy was practically limitless.

Even more frustrating to Tony, and later to Hayesy, was my diet, spare by any standards. Much of the time I felt too excited to eat, and when I did get hungry, I didn't want to experience the lethargy of overeating. Eating represented work, and unlike the gathering of firewood or the running of rapids, I didn't enjoy it. You could spend an hour chained to a smoky campfire to produce one meal, and the payoff, in my mind, didn't merit the effort involved. I was happier eating a slab of cheese or nibbling a handful of almonds to ward off hunger.

When we were on the bikes, Tony had said in complete exasperation, "You have to eat more. The way you're working, you need five thousand calories a day!"

Hayesy often seemed uninterested in cooking, but I learned later that he was too tired to do it. The small reserve of canned food that we carried for emergencies vanished quickly as night after night Hayesy would heat a can at the rim of the fire.

At Panther Canyon that night, I cooked a double portion of tortellini so that Hayesy could eat to his heart's content. He ate ravenously, set his dirty dish and utensil in the sand, and retired to the tent. Within moments, I could hear his soft snoring. The poor guy was worn out.

The Border Patrol Strikes Out at Home Run or Nothin' Camp

Jan. 12–17

Six miles below Panther Canyon Rapid, San Francisco Canyon Rapid sits at the end of a long, lakelike stretch of river where often the wind blows upstream with gale force. At least part of the reason for the absence of current in this stretch goes back to the flood of 1978, when a surge of water blasted down San Francisco Canyon with such force that the Rio Grande reportedly flowed backwards for the next three days. This backwards flow silted in the two miles between San Francisco Canyon and the next upriver canyon that enters from the Mexican side to such a degree that, even twenty-seven years later, the lake is essentially flat and the current, even on a windless morning, imperceptible. Generally, the afternoon winds blow fiercely, and I suggested to Hayesy that it might be wise to rush out of camp and try to reach the lake before the winds built around lunchtime. Having battled this stretch in howling winds many times in the past, Hayesy agreed, saying in a resigned tone, "Whatever it takes."

San Francisco Canyon marks the geographical end of the Big Bend in southwest Texas. It is further north than Presidio, even though it's two hundred fifty miles downriver. From this point on, the Rio Grande moves in its predominant direction—southeast— toward the Gulf.

After San Francisco Canyon Rapid, the stark walls of Reagan Canyon begin to recede as the river turns east, having finally passed the easternmost foothills of the Rocky Mountains. Immediately the current quickens, playfully twisting through bend after bend, as if finally liberated from its confinement inside the close, towering walls of Reagan Canyon. In the eleven miles to our next camp, the canyon walls shrank from seven hundred feet high down to fifty, and the river shore came alive with wildlife. Skunks, raccoons, and ringtail cats crept on narrow rocky paths below the canyon rim. Javelinas foraged in the dense willow thickets along the shores. White-winged doves sang as if orphaned. Blue herons or green-winged teal led our way downriver, the herons by air, the teal by water. Beavers glided below, only their heads breaking the surface. Suddenly, the entire natural world seemed to be on the move.

Thanks to a fickle wind, we fought at times to make any progress, and then one turn later, found ourselves being blown downriver by gusts. Immense canyon walls no longer blocked the sunshine. We bathed right in mid-river, cupping the water with our hands to splash it under our arms. I washed my hair by dunking my head over the edge of the raft, then lathering in soap for an indulgent length of time. Hayesy's fatigue evaporated. At our next camp, a concave slab of smooth rock ringed by boulders, we bounced like young kids from boulder top to boulder top.

Not far out of camp the following day, the canyon walls disappeared altogether for a few miles, and we could, for the first time in a week, see the surrounding countryside, now dotted with barren, conical mesas rather than the craggy buttes to the west. Our boat-loads now considerably lighter, we had little difficulty darting around obstacles at the remaining rapids. In the afternoon, we entered a new canyon—Martin Canyon to the Texans, Indio Canyon to the

Mexicans—and each time we found an access to the canyon rim, we landed the boats and hiked up to the highest point to snap pictures.

Late in the afternoon we reached the final rapid Hayesy would have to run, a steep rocky drop that fed directly into the canyon wall on the Texas side. We called it "Buck Naked" because it is the last rapid on the La Linda–to–Langtry run, and years before we had begun the dubious practice of running the drop naked. At the base of the rapid sits a fine campsite above a fishing hole teeming with catfish, and this site is one we seldom pass. Furthermore, a cave the size of a living room is located in the canyon face above the campsite, and mature mesquite trees abound in the side canyon extending into Mexico. On past trips, we'd often stay two or three nights at this site, exploring the country above the canyon wall, doing our laundry in the rapids, and resting. Also, we had a tradition of cooking a big pot of kidney-bean stew here while we rested, flavoring it with a Danish canned ham, garlic, onion, cumin, and a generous dose of hot sauce.

I caught a catfish for Hayesy and grilled it while making the beans the following morning. Hayesy poked at it, and I sensed he didn't believe my claims that its taste would compare favorably to that of any freshwater fish caught in his part of the country. Once he had his first taste, though, he made quick work of the fish.

After a lazy morning tending the beans, we packed everything into the boats and left for the deepest and most scenic part of Martin Canyon. About four miles below the rapid, we landed to explore a Mexican rock house built into the canyon wall three hundred feet above the river. The builders had constructed the home by stacking and cementing nearby stones to form a wall from the floor of the talus slope to a rock overhang, and in this wall they had built a crude window frame out of two-by-four lumber. Until the elements weathered it to a degree that it would no longer stand the weight of man, a wooden makeshift ladder hung from where the house sits to a part of the slope accessible from the river. The rock house blends into the canyon face so well that, from the river, it is next to impossible to spot unless you know exactly where it is. Hayesy was delighted with the diversion of exploring the rock house, even though reaching it required a difficult walk along a prickly wildlife path. We were extracting cactus needles from our legs for days afterward.

Howling head winds forced us into camp at an island not far past the rock house. By this point in the trip, our camping had settled into a routine that required little conversation or direction. We'd each unload our boat and trudge the gear up to a campsite close to the water's edge. I'd pitch my tent on the hardest ground at the site while Hayesy looker for softer bedding.

While Hayesy set up his tent, I'd write in my river journal in the declining daylight. Hayesy, meanwhile, would chatter to himself, using different accents, one an Irish brogue, another the hard-edged inflection of an Italian mafioso. When I allowed my attention to stray from my writing, I was entertained by his ongoing dialogue. One minute, when the wind lifted an end of his tent, he would mutter at the tent in the mafioso persona, "Get down on the ground or I'll tattoo your face with a baseball bat." The next minute, while zipping the tent door, he'd sing an old Irish folk song, carefully imitating the inflection of the Emerald Isle: "I'm a rambler and a gambler, and I'm a long way from home." If I missed his previous utterance, it mattered little. I could always follow the next line since there appeared to be little connection between them.

The next day we departed Martin Canyon and entered a long winding section we called "the Badlands," twenty-five miles devoid of canyon walls, where the river passed through lakelike stretches two and three miles long before dropping through a piss-pot set of riffles only to enter yet another long lakelike stretch. During this stretch, you begin to see regular signs of human existence: barbed-wire fences, occasional ranch trailers, rough roads terminating at the river's edge. Few people would appraise the landscape as scenic, at least not after having passed the grandeur of Reagan and Martin Canyons, but this stretch rated among my favorites of the entire run.

Hayesy and I stopped in at a cabin that belonged to some rancher friends to top off our water jugs, and then took advantage of favorable wind conditions to make the most miles we would make on any day in the rafts, arriving at a ledge camp that we called "Millennium Ledge" because he and I had stayed there on New Year's Eve, 1999.

One more purposeful day in the river brought us past the weir dam, seventeen miles from Langtry, that marks the beginning of the Painted Canyon stretch of river. Here we left the Wild and Scenic Area of the Rio Grande, a designation bestowed upon over two hundred miles of river by the federal government in an attempt to preserve it from commercial and industrial development. The weir dam also marks the end of the National Park Service's jurisdiction over the river. Below the dam, the rangers of the Amistad National Recreation Area preside. The line is, for the most part, arbitrary. The reality is that much of the river receives little attention from either agency. The NPS sends its river ranger down a seventy-two-mile section of the Lower Canyons four times a year. I've never, in all my trips down the river, seen an NRA ranger.

A couple of days later we approached the most impressive camp on the entire border, a large rock bowl some one hundred feet high that we call "Home Run or Nothin'." We decided to hike across the desert to the rim of the bowl and, once there, take photographs from above. To do this, we landed the rafts a mile upriver. This long hike took hours because we had to circumvent two canyons, and just as we got back on the river, a Border Patrol vehicle arrived. We ignored it and paddled down to set up camp in the bowl.

An hour after dark we were startled by the sudden appearance of bright light flooding over the canyon rim, lighting up the walls of our bowl far more than the campfire had. A gruff voice identified himself as "United States Border Patrol."

"How many of you are down there?"

"Just two."

"Where are the other guys?"

"What other guys?"

"Come on. We know from tracking your footprints that there are more than two."

"No, there are just two of us."

"Read me your shoeprint!" a second officer said to Hayesy.

"My what?"

"What kind of footprint does your shoe make?"

Hayesy paused for a long moment, as if he weren't sure whether to answer or remove his boot, and he said, "Uh, I think it makes a V."

After several contentious minutes, the officers left, but nothing had been resolved during the interrogation. We hadn't convinced them of our story, but the bowl blocked their access to us. At any other campsite on the river, these guys could have burst into camp, rifled through our gear, and left us to enjoy the remainder of the night. Our unlikely campsite in the rock bowl served only to pique their suspicion. I sensed we hadn't seen the last of them, and I half expected to hear the sound of a B. P. fan boat racing upriver.

Hayesy and I talked in hushed voices, trying to keep the sounds of our giggles from rising to the rim of the rock bowl. For all we knew, the two guys could be kneeling directly above us, listening, waiting for our conversation to implicate us in a smuggling operation.

Thirty minutes later the flashlights flooded the campsite once again, and now the two agents were really hot. They insisted that our trail indicated at least three sets of footprints.

"Take off your shoe and read me the exact print," one agent told me.

With the aid of a flashlight, I did as I was told.

"Listen," I said, "Do you know Gus Fernández?" Gus worked out of the same office these agents worked out of.

"Yeah, why?"

"You can ask him about me. I'm out here all the time, and he can tell you as much."

"How do you know him?" the agent said, his voice softening.

"He took a couple of my classes years ago when he was a student at the college in Laredo."

"You're a professor?"

"Yeah, when I'm not on the river."

"OK, we'll talk to him. Have a good night."

As the flashlights retreated, Hayesy took a deep breath and said, "Wow."

"I bet that's likely just the beginning of that kind of harassment for me. I'll be dealing with those guys often from here on out."

West of the Pecos

Jan. 18–20

Langtry, Texas, population fewer than twenty, sits high on a bluff above the Rio Grande at a point where the lake waters created by Amistad Dam begin to back up the flow of the river, reducing the current to a snail's crawl. The river is invisible from the town proper, and the thousands of tourists who make their way from the Judge Roy Bean Visitor Center to the river viewpoint are disappointed to find a thick growth of willow and salt cedar trees obscuring the Rio Grande.

Langtry clings to the embellished legend of Judge Roy Bean, the self-described "law west of the Pecos," who in the late nineteenth century ran the local saloon and dispensed a dubious form of frontier justice. The old judge, who apparently drank himself to an early grave, brought international attention to Langtry by hosting a world championship boxing match on a ring constructed on a platform in the middle of the Rio Grande. Originally called Eagle's Nest, Langtry was renamed for Southern Pacific boss George Langtry, but Judge Bean claimed to have named it for British actress Lillie Langtry. He had fallen hopelessly in love with her even though he knew her only from photographs.

I have a special friend in Langtry named Nelson "Pete" Billings, now eighty-eight years old and one of the town's few remaining denizens. I first met him when he worked as a railroad engineer, in a twist of fate that now seems divinely determined. One night in 1982, I rode the Southern Pacific hobo-style across West Texas. The railroad workers' union had called a strike for midnight that day, and I asked brakemen in the yard at Sanderson what would happen come midnight. "They'll dump the train," one warned, an expression that means the crew disconnects the engines from the freight cars at the first siding it reaches after midnight and then rides into the division stop—in that case, Del Rio—leaving the remainder of the train sitting for the duration of the strike or until management finds time to move it. Fearing I might get dumped far from the highway, I hopped a boxcar, and when the strike call came, I pleaded with the conductor to carry me into Del Rio with the rest of the crew. Fatefully, Pete Billings, then sixty-five years old, was the engineer of the locomotive that delivered me to Del Rio.

Some thirteen years later, having just finished an eighteen-day Lower Canyons trip, I met Pete for a second time. He eyed me from a craggy perch atop the bluff at Langtry, watching as I struggled to tote my rolled-up hypalon raft up the rugged trail. Although boaters were not welcome to use the trail, Pete let me do it dozens of times.

Through the next decade, Pete and I became close friends, bonding over our mutual love for the river and the surrounding country. As old age began to sap Pete's considerable energy, I inherited the job of maintaining the long trail. Brief visits at the end of a river trip turned into long visits before and after the trip. Short chats on his veranda evolved into meals in the kitchen. Over the decade, I came to count Pete as one of my most valued friends. His wealth of river experience dated all the way back to his boyhood growing up in Langtry, when he used to help the fur trapper James McMahon, the same boatman who had guided Robert Hill on the first successful survey mission in the Lower Canyons.

Pete and I spoke a language together that no one else could penetrate. He might say, "You know that stand of mesquite just after that rock face below El Soldado. Well, the boys and I were fishing right below there years ago."

I would interrupt, "At the pool right below the mesquite or the next one down where the dagger cacti sit on that sandy rise?"

Pete would smile and say, "At that first one, right by the mesquite." Then he would continue with his story of big catfish caught or black-tailed rattlesnakes killed.

I was not surprised to see, when I looked at an old photo Pete showed me of himself, that in his younger years he bore a stunning resemblance to a man I had seen thousands of times—every time I looked into a mirror.

When Hayesy and I paddled the homestretch into Langtry, I looked forward to seeing Pete more than almost any thing else all trip. But I didn't want to show up empty-handed. While Hayesy docked and unloaded his raft at the base of the trail, I anchored along the Mexican-side ledge and tried to catch a big catfish. However, when Hayesy had all his gear up the bank and began rolling the deflated raft into a tight bundle, I still didn't have Pete's fish. I had to cross the river and begin unloading my raft. I kept my line in the water until I had all the gear up the bank, and just as I began to drag my raft from the river, my line grew taut: I had a white bass. Proudly, I walked the long mile uphill to Pete's, and together we returned to the river's edge. I had left the boat inflated in the water, with the fishing line tied to it. Pete deftly removed the hook, but I saw he had little interest in the small fish. Instead, he gazed at my raft.

"Shoot, that's a really nice boat. Where can I get one of those?"

"You can have it, Pete."

"No, I don't want to take your raft. You need that raft, as much as you go down this river. But I'll give you the money to buy me one just like it."

"The raft is yours, Pete. I have two more I can use. This one is just going to get in the way at home."

I couldn't have accepted a cent from Pete. He had already paid for the raft tenfold in all he had done for me. I knew I would receive far more pleasure from knowing Pete had that raft than keeping it ever could have given me.

—◆◆◆—

We had to drive back to Heath Canyon to get Hayesy's truck and my canoe, so that night we camped on Andy Kurie's beach, arriving with just enough daylight to cut our firewood. As the campfire flames leaped into the blackness of the night, Hayesy remarked, "Man, this is special. I get to see both Pete and Andy on the very same day."

I grabbed a couple of beers from the cooler and we toasted the two men, one at each end of the Lower Canyons, almost as if no one else on the planet deserved to be in such revered company. In one sense, they lived next door to each other, since there were no other houses in between that were always occupied.

After restful nights at Andy's and at a Del Rio motel, we drove out to the headquarters of Amistad Dam to ask permission to leave our truck in the parking lot there while we canoed from Langtry across the lake to the immense dam. The project manager, Ken Breitlin, a lean and graying man, listened to our request with raised eyebrows, and then turned his gaze toward the window and the choppy lake waters. He asked grimly, "Do you have any idea how rough that lake is going to be in a canoe? I don't know if you have much chance of making it across there."

I assured him that my resolve was strong. A silence fell heavily in the office. Ken continued gazing out the window. Just as I expected to hear his words of rejection, he turned and met my eyes for the first time. "Sure, you can leave the truck here, but you'd better leave me some contact information, just in case. I think you'll understand why I'm asking once you get out on that lake.

"By the way, once you do get here, how are you planning to get around the dam? The mile and a half below the dam is closed to the public because the Feds worry a terrorist will blow up the dam."

"I'm going to ask the Mexicans to let me put in over there."

He chuckled disbelievingly at the delusional idea that I could convince the Mexican authorities to allow me to launch over there. "If it's not possible," I said, "I'll figure something else out."

I had met some form of resistance from nearly everyone else— aside from Pete Billings and Andy Kurie—I had talked to about my river-trip plans, so Ken's incredulity was nothing new, and I had long since learned to deflect it. Besides, if traveling the entire length of the border by mountain bike, raft, and canoe had been something less than a colossal challenge, I would have found the trip far less appealing. I felt I could deal with the river, the lakes, the dams, the natural elements, the dangers that intimidated those who hadn't spent a lot of time alone on the river. Only people, and particularly government people, presented obstacles and restrictions I couldn't easily overcome.

We went back to Pete's, and he drove us to the bluff and helped us unload our gear. Hayesy and I began the arduous job of carrying it all to the river's edge. After nearly two days of rest, I felt renewed, strong. Hayesy and I worked purposefully, both of us eager to be back on the water, paddling toward a new camp.

"This is going to be very interesting," he remarked as I secured our load with ropes and bungee cords. "I knew I would like the La Linda–to–Langtry stretch. It's always a great trip, but going past the Pecos River confluence is the reason I came. I've really been looking forward to going past the furthest point we've been on this river."

Four days later and sixty-six miles below Langtry, I think it safe to assume that Hayesy had resolved never again to get in a canoe with me.

The Fury of the Lake

Jan. 20–24

Amistad Dam, completed in 1969, backs up not only the Rio Grande but the Pecos and Devils Rivers as well, forming a reservoir covering 89,000 acres in both Texas and Coahuila, Mexico. The Rio Grande had periodic catastrophic floods. One in 1954 knocked out the international bridge in Eagle Pass, carrying it 135 miles to Laredo, where it toppled both the railroad bridge and the highway bridge; it also inundated the entire downtown area of both Laredos, with the banks of the river extending more than a mile inland from its normal shoreline. Hundreds died. Thousands of homes were destroyed. Civic and business leaders wanted to harness the river for agricultural, hydropower, and recreational benefits. By creating the reservoir and controlling its releases, the government was able to ensure regular flows for irrigation and power generation, and the reservoir has become something of a fisherman's paradise. The dam would tame the Rio Grande and maintain the international boundary. One landowner told me, "I was sick of waking up some mornings to find twenty-five acres of my land now on the Mexican side of the river."

The reservoir's level had recently rebounded after a decade of drought, during the worst of which it had dropped enough that the river reclaimed forty miles of the outer reaches of the lake, cutting a narrow channel in the silted canyon floor. As the lake water receded, salt cedar, willow, mesquite, and native plants like agave and prickly pear flourished on the silted shores of the river. Where salt cedar dominated, it formed a nearly impenetrable thicket of saplings, home to thousands of beaver and nutria, as well as lesser populations of skunks, ring-tailed cats, raccoons, and feral hogs. Closer to the main part of the receding lake, native trees like mesquite, *huisache,* and willow prospered. As the drought eased in the two years preceding our trip, the lake had filled, gaining close to fifty feet and rising to within three feet of conservation level, leaving the ten-year growth of trees and cacti either fully or partly submerged and creating a prickly and wooded barrier between the waterway and the shore. In short, for much of the way from Langtry to Amistad, getting to shore for everything from camping to peeing had become close to impossible.

For twenty-three miles below Langtry, the river winds between impressive painted canyons, streaked with earthy color: smoky grays, oily blacks, tawny browns, clay reds. When the lake backs up and the current ceases, the river offers a glassy mirror, reflecting the multihued canyon walls. The bow of our canoe sliced through these sublime waterscapes, leaving rippled distortions of those liquid images in our wake. We had a windless day, mid-sixties temperatures, and bright sunshine to enjoy the river.

Hayesy settled into the bow and watched as our tandem strokes propelled us quickly down one straightaway after another. "I can live with this. We're really flying." Then he chuckled under his breath and asked, "Do you know what Pete said about you while you were loading the gear in his truck? He said you were tougher than cold shoe leather. Yep, cold shoe leather. I never heard that before, but I think it's a compliment."

"It's amazing the good things a guy will say about you when you give him a raft."

We pulled over for a shade break under the overhang of a cave on the Mexican side, one I had camped in before. Thousands of bats cling to its ceiling all day, then fly in a frenzy in and out all night. I told Hayesy about the time I had taken a similar break one scorching summer afternoon, and had awakened a bat, which had promptly grazed my ear and then, after hovering in midair directly in front of me, dive-bombed my head. My sudden dive to the ground kept me from a head-on collision with the ornery bat.

"What would you have done if the thing was rabid?"

I had no answer for him, and we fell silent.

Around midafternoon we came to one of the few places where the shore offered us a clear place to land and set up camp, and sensing it might be the last such place for hours, we decided to stop for the night. Someone had burned the growth on the floodplain, and the hard-packed silt was littered with charred willow trunks. After we had set up our tents, I calculated that I had traveled exactly half the distance from El Paso to the Gulf of Mexico.

The riparian environment below Langtry is somewhat oppressive because of the closeness of the canyon walls and the thickness of the non-native growth, which teems with frogs and insects. Beavers patrol the river just off the banks and periodically deliver thunderous blasts with their tails on the surface, trying to scare off interlopers such as beer-drinking canoeists. Occasionally, Hayesy would respond to the beavers' aggression by muttering in his mafioso voice: "How would you like it if I smashed your face with the canoe and then ripped your heart out with my teeth?" The beavers were not intimidated.

On the following unseasonably warm winter day, we reached the confluence with the Pecos, where we encountered the first in a series of motorized fishing boats. From the confluence, or "the Y," as the powerboaters refer to it, you can see the "high bridge" a mile up the Pecos. Below this bridge, Texas's highest, lies a boat ramp that powerboaters use to access the upper reaches of the lake. The first boaters who saw us were sensitive enough to kill their motors promptly to spare us their wake as they approached. They looked genuinely surprised to find a canoe navigating the deep water. One pair of old gentlemen reacted enthusiastically when we told them how far we had come; the second boat's occupants asked if we needed anything.

The river widened out to fill the entire basin between the three-hundred-foot-high canyon walls. A third boat sped by and sent a rolling wake of two-foot waves. We turned into the wake to avoid being sideswept, and I swore at the pilot's lack of boating etiquette. With sheer canyon walls defining each shoreline, a capsize here would put us in big trouble; losing the canoe and suffering from hypothermia were distinct possibilities. Just as my anger began to subside, a second powerboat blasted past, and again we spun the canoe into the rolling wake. As far as we could see, a mile or more, the shoreline offered no place to land, so now our paddling took on a sense of urgency I had never expected. Moments later, yet another powerboat sped past, followed closely by a fourth. Clearly, the lowly canoe ranked at the bottom of the totem pole on Amistad Reservoir.

Hayesy listened as I vented my frustration and anger, while both of us paddled for all we were worth. As we rounded the bend at the end of the first straightaway after the Y, we had traveled two miles without seeing a single place to land the canoe. With the sun casting a long shadow to our east as we turned north, we raced ahead—that is, whenever we had an opening between the wakes of passing boats. As far as we could see on this new straightaway, there were only the canyon walls.

Suddenly a narrow cove came into view on the Mexican side, and we angled for it, slicing across the wake of yet another powerboat. The cove dead-ended at a partially submerged mesquite tree that guarded the rocky landing, and there we set up camp in a ravine barely wide enough for the canoe and a sleeping bag. In order to get the canoe to shore, we had to trim the tree. Hayesy sighed as we finished the chore and said, "That was interesting."

He looked both relieved and concerned. In two days of

sometimes-frantic paddling, we hadn't reached the halfway point to the dam, despite nearly ideal weather—warm sun and no wind.

Three days below Langtry, we got our first harrowing taste of the infamous Amistad winds. From the moment we broke camp, we fought rolling surf; the lake's surface felt more like an ocean than fresh water. The winds ushered in cool temperatures, but the powerboats, it being Saturday, came in droves. As the winds pushed the swelling waters in one direction, stern to bow, the passing powerboats bombarded us from the side, and we often found ourselves precariously tacking a dangerous diagonal course between competing waves. A few times waves crashed over the stern, soaking my back.

As we turned back to the southeast, the lake widened, and the canyon walls receded, a mixed blessing for us: although we had more chances to get ashore, the waves built to greater heights. Despite our determination to make many miles that day, by midafternoon we limped into a camp above a rocky point, feeling defeated by the surf and saturated from the waves that broke over both bow and stern.

An hour after we had set up camp, a powerboat trawled into our cove. The two middle-aged fishermen waved tentatively as they cast their lines. A few minutes later, the younger of the two, a heavy-set, bearded man in a windbreaker and blue jeans, called out, "You sure as hell didn't come in here on that canoe!"

"We sure as hell did."

He called back, "Well, then you all are a lot tougher than we are."

"Hey, can you all spare some ice?" I figured Hayesy needed some cold beer as a reward for what I had subjected him to out on the rolling lake.

The older of the two, a fit man with a salt-and-pepper beard and a blue jean jacket, said, "No, our ice has mostly turned to water."

I muttered a Spanish phrase attacking the man's mother, and decided to ignore them for the remainder of our time as lake neighbors. Hayesy crept over to me and said in a voice barely above a whisper, "How much ice do you think they have stashed on that boat? I mean, they're fishing and drinking, and they're miles from the nearest dock."

Almost as if Hayesy had called their bluff, a moment later, they trawled the boat into the rocky shore and introduced themselves, one a self-described "outdoors writer," the other a hunting guide. The guide leaped off the bow of the bass boat and delivered us a plastic grocery sack filled with ice and two Miller Lites. The burly outdoors writer asked if he could snap our picture with the intent of publishing it along with an article he wanted to write about our trip. I took the ice and beer as a down payment on the story, and Hayesy and I eagerly dumped the ice into the cooler and opened the two Millers. Neither of us was exactly overwhelmed with gratitude.

The writer stuffed a big pinch of Copenhagen into his lower lip and tried to intimidate us with horror stories about the rest of the lake.

"Men, you have some very rough going ahead of you. It can get so bad further down that I don't even like taking my boat out there. A canoe would be suicide."

"We'll be okay."

"You say that now. But when the lake gets really wide, the wind howls, and the surf is nasty! I'm talking six-foot swells."

"He ain't lying," his partner said.

"How much further do we have to reach the dam?" I asked.

"It's a strong thirty miles. But you'll have to paddle twice that many miles because you'll have to stay so close to shore due to the size of the waves."

"That far? I was thinking we were only about twenty miles out," I said.

"Hell, no. Let's see. Today is Saturday. You might make it by Wednesday or Thursday, at the earliest."

When the two men shoved off to return to the Pecos River boat dock, Hayesy was disheartened. He grew pensive. "What are the chances those guys know what they're talking about?"

"Oh, I don't know. On one hand, I see them as just two more of the 'You can't' crowd. On the other hand, they seem to know the lake pretty well."

I was beginning to think Hayesy wished he hadn't agreed to accompany me on this leg of the trip. For one thing, he had now been away from home and his girlfriend for three weeks, and that's a long time for most people to stay content while sleeping on the ground and picking cactus spines out of their bodies. But worse were the conditions we had faced on the lake all day; if, as our new friends promised, those conditions became more extreme as the lake grew wider, we faced a very demanding test on the following day. I had often had to remind myself that this trip was supposed to be fun, but I suspected Hayesy wasn't having much of it.

Moments later a Border Patrol trawler eased into the cove and made for the shore directly below our camp. The two young agents, handsome Anglo guys well over six feet tall, their faces not yet weathered by the desert sun, greeted us warmly, and I caught the boat's throw line. They both came forward and chatted with us amicably. Already they knew about our encounter with their fellow agents several nights before at Home Run or Nothin'—a story they appeared to find far more amusing than their fellow agents had.

They disagreed with our two powerboaters' assessment of the distance to Amistad, and the captain retreated to the pilot's chair to consult the map, returning to say that the precise distance to the dam was twenty miles. They warned us, however, that the two fishermen had not overstated the dangers of the lake, especially where it grew really wide about five miles further on. I could see from their expressions that neither of them would attempt to navigate the lake in a canoe, and they were quick to offer their help, saying they would tow us to the dam that night if we wished. I said I believed we would find a way to navigate, no matter what conditions the lake threw at us, to which the captain replied, "Well, if you change your mind, we'll be out here every night. Just flag us down and we'll be happy to help you get out safely."

Then darkness descended, and with clouds blowing in just as the sun disappeared, the night seemed to press into our camp; even the fire had difficulty cutting through the blackness. Hayesy spoke in hushed tones, and I had to lean close to hear him. The wind whistled and tossed the fire mischievously, sending horizontal flames along the ground and forcing us to shift positions often, reminding me of old

Western movies when the villain makes the coward dance by spraying the ground with gunfire. Hayesy voiced his concerns: we didn't have much food, we wouldn't last long in the lake if we capsized the canoe, and the powerboaters couldn't care less about our welfare.

In the morning we awoke to a wintry chill, but the stout winds of the night before had subsided, offering us some hope that we could race toward the dam. We broke camp early and paddled hard, taking every possible shortcut. About an hour from camp, we came to the first of the buoys that mark the main channel to the dam, some thirty in all, each a half mile apart. Another hour of steady paddling brought us to a very wide section of the lake, where everyone had warned us that the going would border on the impossible from there on. Indeed, despite light breezes, the waves were already building, and unlike the day before, those waves now rolled directly against us. Little by little, the winds increased and the swells now began to whitecap.

We proceeded point to point. Every time we reached a spit of land jutting out into the lake, we would stop for a break, have a drink, and then set out across the choppy water for the next spit and the next rest stop. Sometimes the next spit would be a mere half mile, sometimes several harrowing miles, away. The chill of the day made the threat of hypothermia more pressing, and as the winds built Hayesy voiced more and more reluctance to stay in the canoe. About midafternoon, we saw a cluster of trailer homes on a rise above the lake, and we paddled hard along the shore towards them. With the winds now kicking the waters angrily, we were forced to stop several times to bail water out of the boat. By the time we reached the boat ramp below the cluster of trailers, we were thoroughly chilled, and the waves thrashed the rocky shoreline on either side of the ramp.

With our shoulders bent against the cold and our feet numb and wooden, we trudged up the long ramp to the first of the trailer homes, but there we could rouse no one. We proceeded to the next and then several more; no one would answer the door. Finally, an elderly man welcomed us inside his house.

"Canoeing on the lake?" he said. "That must be a rough trip."

"Can you tell us how far it is to the dam?"

"Not far. As soon as you round that next point of land below town, you'll see it just across the lake, and then you'll only be two or three miles away."

Feeling elated, we hurried back to the boat and poured a celebratory round of merlot into our tin coffee cups. We could camp at the point and do the last two or three miles in the windless conditions of morning. Hayesy regained his Irish good humor, and the guilt I had harbored for putting him through this test disappeared. Despite the fact that the waves were bigger than we had seen them all trip, we shoved off and paddled hard for the point. Warmed by the wine and the vigorous paddling, we crossed the undulating waters in high spirits, landing in a shallow cove on the leeward side of the point. Once we hiked to higher ground in search of firewood, we could see the massive Amistad Dam far across the lake. But my heart sank when I noticed how small it looked against the broad expanse of water that separated us from it.

We built a roaring fire to match our hopes. I said nothing to Hayesy about the incongruity of the elderly man's estimate of "two to three miles" and the visual evidence that suggested the dam was more like eight or ten miles away. Hayesy, I could see, was elated that tomorrow he would be starting for home and sleeping in warm motel beds en route. And I felt equally content in the knowledge that tomorrow I would have river current beneath my boat, and Amistad Lake's rolling waves would play havoc with some other craft. I felt sure we could count on a calm morning and a placid lake surface for our last hours of paddling to the edge of the dam. Regret about losing my best partner was tempered by my sense that his heart was no longer in the trip.

The next morning we found the lake was not as eager to release us as we were to be free of it. When I awoke in the gray light of dawn, Hayesy already had his gear ready to load in the canoe after a restless night in which he had managed only a couple of hours of sleep. I hurried through my morning rituals—the coffee, the drinking of a half gallon of water, the packing of my gear and the boat—and we were on the water early, but not early enough to beat the wind, a persistent cross-breeze that furled the surface of the lake in a direction that spelled trouble for us. In big waves, you must either canoe with the waves at your back or plunge directly into them. To our dismay, the swells rolled perpendicular to the direction we needed to go. We had paddled only as far as the opposite side of the cove where we had camped when the surf forced us to retreat to shore, not a hundred yards from where we'd slept.

"How the hell are we going to get across now?" Hayesy asked as the waves crashed the canoe into the prickly pear cacti guarding the shore. I did not have an answer. Our next spit of land lay a half mile away, but in order to reach it we would first have to go deep into the cove in order to achieve the necessary angle to tack into the waves. The best way to get the canoe into the cove was to line it, which meant walking through the chilly water and the submerged cacti for hundreds of yards, until we had reached a point far enough into the cove to allow us to take the hard charge of the surf head-on. Even then, with waves crashing into Hayesy's lap, we hardly felt safe. After a vexed crossing to the next point, we hurried to shore, nervous that the rising waves would capsize us at any moment. Gaining shore challenged us most of all: after plunging into wave after wave, we had to execute a sharp turn in between charging waves, and then ride the charge into the prickly undergrowth at the edge of the rocky shore.

From this point we gazed out across the roiling lake to the next point, a third of a mile distant. Again we lined deep into the cove and again battled the agitated water, until we were forced to execute a harrowing turn in the tight depression between oncoming waves. Cove by cove, point by point, we proceeded, each step presenting higher waves.

After a dozen coves, I said, "Sorry, but I have a feeling this is going to take all day."

Hayesy gazed out across the lake. "The dam doesn't seem to be getting any closer."

Three coves later, we spotted some houses perched on hills, and Hayesy began what became a series of suggestions of alternative ways to get out. "Go ahead," I told him, "I'm listening."

Every plan he voiced involved his walking from the homes to the dam, retrieving his truck, and then meeting me when I canoed across to the end. Each time I nixed the plan by reminding him that walking out would require him to go many miles around the lake's perimeter, and–assuming he made the walk without getting lost–that he wouldn't know where to find me once he did reach his truck.

"Why can't I just meet you at the highway bridge?" he asked.

"What makes you think I'm going to be able to get there? What if I'm stuck out here two days? How are you going to know I'm okay? You could be sitting there thinking I've drowned while I'm sitting in a cove trapped by the wind."

"Well, why can't we just walk everything to the highway?"

"Because it's a long way. The highway is miles from here. We'd spend days walking all our gear."

We battled on, lining deep into each cove, plunging into the waves until we reached the next point, executing our hair-raising turn in the depression between swells, crashing into the prickly, sub-merged growth offshore.

At midafternoon, with the winds showing no signs of abating, we spied, some two miles in the distance, a ribbon of Highway 90. Between it and the lakeshore we could see two small shacks, which offered our first real hope of reaching the highway by a land route. When I suggested that we canoe far into the cove to scout the shacks, Hayesy declined, opting instead to walk the long way around.

Above the shore, we found a ranch road that appeared to lead to the highway. We decided to abort the canoeing, and I was to walk to Hayesy's truck while he portaged all our gear up to the ranch road. Accordingly, I changed into tennis shoes, ate a quick snack, and set off in the direction of the highway. Three hundred yards later, the road dead-ended at the water's edge, and we were forced to retreat to the lake.

Hayesy refused to get back in the canoe, insisting that the cross-ing was "too dangerous," so I set out alone for the next point while he again walked around the long shoreline. When he arrived, we spent several long minutes trying to agree on how to proceed. Clearly, waiting for him to walk each of the many coves between points would take three times longer than any other approach, and we were now close enough to the dam that it appeared we had a reasonable chance of reaching it before dark. But convincing him to get back in the canoe posed no small challenge. Ultimately, our diminishing food reserves persuaded him: we had planned to reach the lake in four days from Langtry, and now, well into the fifth day, our rations allowed for only one more meal.

With Hayesy back in the bow, we struggled on, crossing several more points, gaining confidence with each successful leg, until late in the afternoon, we reached the final point, one mile from the dam. Here the lake offered two options. We could head directly into the two-foot swells and cross to the dam; however, in addition to fighting the swells, we would have to cross the most heavily traveled powerboat channel, which meant navigating the boat wakes and tacking into the predominant current of the swells. The other option involved slicing sideways through the waves toward the highway bridge, also a mile distant, but this choice bordered on the impossible, since we'd almost certainly capsize. We paused a long time, gazing at the surf that separated us from the dam. Finally, I asked Hayesy what he wanted to do.

"I can do the direct crossing. What is it, about a mile?"

I didn't answer. The more I looked at the waves and measured them against the competing wake of the passing powerboats, the less confidence I had in our ability to cross upright. Worse, if we did capsize, the prevailing current would push us toward the bridge, meaning that we would be in the water for a mile, plenty of time for the boat to fill with water and sink.

"There's a third option," I said. "We can wait for someone to come along to help."

"What are that chances of that?" Almost the instant Hayesy spoke, a powerboat appeared just off the point, and I waved toward it while I hurried to the water's edge. The powerboat cut its engine and circled once, both gentlemen aboard eyeing us carefully. Then the driver trawled the boat in toward us. I plunged into thigh-deep water to meet with them.

"I know this sounds strange, but can you help us get across to the dam? The waves are just too big for the canoe."

"Well, George," the older of the two said to his companion, "It's your boat. What do you think? Can we help these two young men?"

"I don't see why not. I'm just trying to think how we might do it."

Bob Young, the older man, suggested we tie the canoe to the back of the bass boat, and George Keesling would try to tow it across to the Air Force boat dock one mile distant. Although I doubted the canoe would stay upright in such choppy waters, something about Bob's demeanor assured me; he had the air of a corporate executive, someone who knew only success, never failure. George deferred to Bob's judgment so completely that I too trusted Bob implicitly. Hayesy and I tied on the canoe, climbed aboard, and settled onto the Astroturf that covered the flat bow of the boat.

The canoe dipped and rocked as George eased the boat into the wide channel, but it appeared stable enough that I fell into conversation with Bob, who expressed a keen interest in my trip, and prefaced each new question by addressing me as "young man." I failed to notice that the canoe had capsized until suddenly all four of us struggled to right the boat. Hayesy and I tore off the gear lines and passed our things to Bob and George, who, while driving the craft, simultaneously managed to move our heavy gear to the bow. Then I held the bow of the canoe high above the water while Hayesy steadied the stern, and in this fashion, we emptied the canoe of most of the water it had taken on during the capsize. We continued across the lake, with me holding the bow three feet above the lake, George holding the midsection with his right hand while steering the bass boat with his left, and Hayesy holding the stern flat against the water. In that manner, we crossed the main channel and trawled up to the Air Force boat dock.

I suspect George and Bob got the idea that we were grateful, but neither of them will know the depths of our gratitude. After they had left, Hayesy smiled for the first time in days.

A Clear but Disappearing River

Jan. 25–27

After the terrorist attacks of September 11, the U.S. government fenced off a mile and a half of the Rio Grande below Amistad Dam. The reasoning was that terrorists could blow up the dam and send a torrent of water downriver, which would level the city of Ciudad Acuña, the Mexican city opposite Del Rio, Texas. In the months leading up to my trip, I made several efforts to gain access, but each agency I contacted—U.S. Customs, the International Boundary and Water Commission, and the National Park Service—asked me to consult with one of the other two agencies. I decided to enter the river below the dam on the Mexican side, so I had procured a letter from the Mexican Consulate near my home in Laredo giving me a blanket pass on the river. I hoped the letter would convince Mexican authorities at the dam and other places along the way to allow me to access the river. If the Mexican officials denied my request, I had no backup plan other than to skip the thirteen miles of river between the dam and downtown Acuña, a stretch that I knew from my research contained two weir dams I would have to portage.

On our final day together, Hayesy and I crossed the six-mile-long causeway above the dam in his truck, cleared Mexican customs, and from high atop the dam scouted my intended put-in. I could see far below that the access road for the hydroelectric plant did not reach the river, passing at least fifty vertical feet above it. There, at a tight turn in the road, I would have to unload and carry everything down a steep rock incline. I didn't like the look of the job.

Hayesy and I had to drive all the way into Acuña to find a store where I could restock, but although the city's population is 150,000, we could not locate a *supermercado*. I shopped at a corner store, with two small shelves and a beer cooler, buying every can of beans the young owner had, two stacks of tortillas, peanuts, canned tuna, and fruit juice. Laredo sat two hundred fifteen river miles away, and I figured this cache would last me until I reached there.

Ciudad Acuña is the most friendly of all Mexican border cities, and my history there is long. One of two Spanish nicknames I have was given to me in a barroom there in the summer of 2002. I was in town watching a former student, Hiram Franco, a Chihuahua native, play baseball for the Acuña Athletics. Hiram, or *el Indio*, has more charisma than any person I've ever met, and that night, in the post-game revelry, we were in the middle of the ever-adoring crowds that he attracts. Hiram enjoys showing off my knowledge of Mexican culture, and he likes to sing the first line of a classic Mexican song and have me sing the next line. Together, we are able to sing many of the great Mexican standards. On this night, every person in the crowded barroom circled us, roaring at Hiram's jokes, marveling at my reservoir of Mexican lyrics, and fighting to buy us the next round of beer. Suddenly, Hiram commanded the crowd: "I need one of you guys to give my friend Keith a nickname in Spanish. 'Keith' is too hard for us to pronounce."

Several volunteers offered their help, but Hiram turned to a shy man on the outside of the circle, and told him to choose my nickname. The entire bar grew silent, all eyes on the timid young man. He blurted out, "*¡El guerrillero de Acuña!*"

Everyone broke into a raucous applause, and the nickname stuck.

So the "warrior from Acuña" was back in town, looking for a place to put in. Seemingly, the entire city wished to assist. Man after man gave me detailed instructions about places to access the river.

On the advice of several guys, I directed Hayesy to a park beneath the international bridge to Del Rio, where we found an access road leading to within seventy yards of the river. As Hayesy and I began to unload the gear, two men approached on foot from the park gate we had passed upon entering. Neither appeared happy as I greeted them. One, a bookish-looking man in an ill-fitting brown suit, said in Spanish, "What the hell are you doing here? This is a private park."

"I'm sorry. Everyone in town told me this was the place to launch a canoe."

He peered over his glasses, his face rigid. Then he pointed across the river to a Border Patrol boat ramp reaching the water. "Why aren't you over there?"

"The government doesn't allow it. I thought you Mexicans would be much more understanding."

"But you're on private property. You have no permission to be here."

"I have a letter from the Mexican authorities that explains what I am doing."

"Let's see it."

A group of onlookers gathered nearby, youths who had been playing soccer until they realized this man was about to back down two gringos. The man read the letter, and softened.

"I'm going to make a phone call to see what the owner says. I'll need to take this letter to read it to him. You wait here."

"Can I keep unloading?"

"Continue with your business. I think it's going to be okay. You should have shown me the letter first. This isn't your country, and the park is private."

Next to the put-in, the Mexican government has erected a sign to discourage people from illegally entering the U.S., one of hundreds of signs I would see in the weeks ahead. The sign reads in Spanish, "Don't expose yourself to the elements," and it features six symbols of the hazards travelers face, among them a rattlesnake, a blazing sun, and a saguaro cactus. I wondered about the effectiveness of the sign.

I was about to embark on a section of river unlike the nearly seven hundred miles I had traveled so far. From Fort Hancock to Amistad Dam, there is exactly one bridge not closed to border crossings, and aside from Ojinaga and Presidio, there are no villages large enough to have even a small schoolhouse. Now, I would pass through a series of cities, giving my trip an urban element I feared. As I gazed at the sign, I thought how different my trip would be from the experiences the government warned undocumented workers against. Rather than fearing snakes, dehydration, sun exposure, cacti, or wildlife, I feared people.

Hayesy and I said a brief good-bye. In one sense, I had already lost him on the lake, and facing the remainder of the trip alone gave me no new concerns. Still, it was tough to see him go.

Then one of the guys who had interrogated me returned from the park office to tell me I was free to put in there. This fellow, Arturo Serrano, the park's groundskeeper, returned my letter and told me proudly that he owned a small ranch an hour downriver.

Soon many others in the park ventured nearer. A group of young teenagers in school uniforms crowded around my canoe as I tied the gear. Then ten happy fishermen gathered, most of them with tackle consisting only of a ball of fishing line wrapped around a soft-drink can. The soccer players joined at the fringes of the crowd. Just as I was sliding the boat into the river, a family of four appeared. When I boarded the canoe, the crowd of onlookers numbered nearly fifty, and many in the group trailed me downriver by walking the riverbank, shouting encouragement, whistling, and hollering good-byes.

Before I left, Arturo Serrano had pointed to the muck between the dry ground and the edge of the river and warned me that the river, because of fluctuations in dam releases, rose every night. The change in water level was impressive, and I could see that the river swelled to more than double its daytime size with the increased flows. I made a mental note to scout my future campsites carefully.

Below Amistad Dam the Rio Grande is clear, and except in the deepest pools, you can see everything: populations of catfish, gar, and carp; turtles; and manmade debris, such as cement blocks, beer cans, and hundreds of automobile tires. At every drop in the river, the submerged tires stand like river rocks in the channel. Onshore, the signs of Acuña quickly fade; the cinder-block houses are replaced by stands of trees, primarily mesquite and catclaw acacia above the floodplain, and ash and willow on the riverbanks. Small, forlorn ranch shacks appear in openings. On the American side, river cane blocks all view of the outskirts of Del Rio. Aside from the distant noise of the bridge, I had no sense of being between cities.

The day was warm and the beer cold. I floated more than paddled, nursing a beer during the calmer stretches, steering through many quick drops, always watching the river bottom for tires. The afternoon had the lazy feel of summer—honeybees buzzing around the canoe, birds flitting in and out of shadows. I fell into a dreamy reverie while floating the crystalline pools between the drops.

Suddenly, the loud roar of an engine startled me, and moments later, a Border Patrol fan boat slid around the river bend. The agents noticed me in time to kill the engine and spare me the brunt of the boat's wake.

The two agents appeared suspicious at first, but as they drew near, they relaxed. I asked for permission to cling to the side of their craft as we chatted. One agent, a young Arabic-looking guy with dark, bushy eyebrows, told me he too was from Laredo, and we talked about mutual acquaintances. Neither agent seemed interested in my trip, treating me more like a welcome diversion from the tedium of patrolling the same stretch of river every day than a lawbreaker. I knew of one small dam somewhere between there and Eagle Pass, and I asked if they could give me a distance to it. One guy replied, "It's not far. Maybe a mile or two."

When we had drifted for ten minutes and the river was about to carry their boat into the Mexican shore, they wished me luck and fired up the huge fan, some six feet in diameter, sending out a sweeping wake that splashed either shore in seconds.

A few miles downriver, I found an island across from a water pump on the Mexican side, and since the island sat high in the river, I decided to camp there. Above the Mexican shore, three men were working on the pump motor, and I boated over to chat with them and collect firewood. I asked the foreman if I could saw firewood. He smiled, and said in Spanish, "Cut the whole goddamned ranch if you wish. It's not mine."

I sawed five thick sections of dead mesquite, each about five feet in length and a foot in diameter, and hauled them to shore through a tight path with numerous overhangs of thorny mesquite branches. Once I had loaded them in the canoe, I glanced over at my island and found all the gear I had unloaded now partially submerged in water. The river had risen a full two feet in twenty minutes! And it would rise more in the next two hours, halving the size of my island by nightfall.

My plan was to camp on islands all the way to the Gulf of Mexico. That way I wouldn't be surprised by Border Patrol officers while I slept, nor would I leave myself open to Mexican smugglers or *coyotes*. On a metaphorical level, I felt most at home in mid-river, part of neither the U.S. nor Mexico, a citizen of the river rather than of a particular country. On the islands, I was far less likely to encounter scavenging animals such as raccoons or coyotes. Feeling secure on my island, I lit the campfire and wrote a long entry in my journal, listening to the festive sounds coming from a village above the river. After so many nights of camping in remote sections of the river, it would take some getting used to the noise—endless *cumbia* songs blaring from cheap stereos, drunken laughter, yodeling of roosters, gunning of truck motors—but separated from land by the river channel, I felt no danger or vulnerability.

◆◆◆

In the morning the river had receded again, leaving me a mucky path from camp to the water's edge. I wanted to start early to make many miles after a relatively lazy effort the day before. As I loaded the boat, the B. P. fan boat approached from upriver, and I greeted the two surprised agents. These two were unusually friendly and more curious about my trip than their counterparts of the previous day, and they asked dozens of questions about camping, wildlife, Mexicans, and weather. When they said they had better be on their way, I asked how far to the dam.

"Not far. Only a mile or two." I had already heard that answer three or four miles back upriver.

Four miles downriver I saw them again below "the movie set," a village of fake façades constructed by a Hollywood production company for filming Westerns. It sits high up on the Texas bank at a sharp bend in the river. Just before the bend, a long narrow island divides the main channel. I took the Mexican channel as the fan boat sped past in the Texas channel and disappeared around the bend in the river, throwing up a cloud of mist in its wake. Another four miles downriver, the current slowed, a telltale sign that the dam was near, and as I rounded a turgid bend, I spotted the fan boat parked in mid-river, where the river seemed to disappear altogether. As I approached, the two officers waved.

"We've been waiting for you," one said with a smile. "We wanted to make sure you got around the dam safely. There are some dangerous people in this area."

"Hey, I really appreciate it. How's the river below the dam?"

"It's just a trickle. They divert all the water off for power in Eagle Pass. I don't know if you're going to be able to get through."

After the officers' erroneous distance assessment, I didn't take much stock in this warning. I paddled to the Mexican shore right at the edge of the concrete diversion dam, a fifteen-foot-high wall that crossed the width of the river. The diversion canal was out of sight, hidden by an island dividing the river. The portage went quickly. All I had to do was carry fifty yards from the top of the dam to the river shore below, some five trips in all, and once I had loaded the canoe again, I scaled the portage trail to say good-bye to the agents.

For the first time, I saw the river below the Maverick County Diversion Dam. Because nearly all the water above it was diverted into a canal feeding a power plant twenty miles downriver, only a trickle of water formed what remained of the Rio Grande. The river, sixty yards wide above the dam, narrowed to twenty feet below it, and the flow of 800 cubic feet per second (CFS) was reduced to 10 to 20. For comparison's sake, the National Park Service lists 250 CFS as the minimum flow for canoeing.

For the next mile, I dragged the canoe much of the way, at times lifting it over rocks, at other times forcing it violently through shallow channels less than half the width of the boat. The work exhausted me, yet I had no choice but to battle forward. Gradually more water entered the river, likely through springs under the surface, for aside from one small creek entering from the Mexican side, I saw no inflows. The pattern of much of the Rio Grande is similar to what river runners refer to as a "pool drop," meaning that the river backs up in long pools with little current before dropping through a small rapid or series of rapids, and then slows in another long pool before yet another drop. On the Rio Grande, the pools are wide and long, often more than a mile, and the banks are often lined with river cane. At the drops, the river narrows and squeezes over a rock ledge, and typically at least one bank of the river is bare rock. I found the drops almost impossible to run cleanly because of insufficient water. Some I lined along the rock shore; others I ran partway and then lined in mid-rapid. At one, I came around a blind corner, and the tight channel forced me to go hard against the Texas bank, where an overhanging tree limb smashed me in the cheek, causing a bruise I would have for weeks.

About midafternoon, I met a Mexican man fishing in his underwear in mid-channel. He raised his bushy eyebrows when he saw me approach, giving me a look that seemed to say, "What in the world are you doing here?" He was about thirty, with a medium build and olive skin; his features bore no suggestion of *mestizo* blood, and he looked more Italian than Mexican. He seemed to view my arrival as an intrusion, so I kept a steady paddle as I approached.

"Can you tell me more or less where I am?"

"You're arriving at Jímenez," he said in Spanish, "but you might have trouble getting there because of the rocks. About a mile ahead, the river fills with rocks. I don't think you can get your boat by them."

"What do you mean? Is it a dam?"

"There are rocks in the riverbed that block the river so much you can walk from one shore to the other and barely get wet. They're flat and the ones that are underwater are just barely underwater."

Twenty minutes later the current filled with slabs of limestone, some visible above water, some hidden beneath the slow current. I had to steer carefully to snake the canoe through constricted channels, at times scraping the bottom of my boat over the coarse limestone, at other times having to get out of the canoe and lift it over rocks that blocked the channel. For two miles, this labyrinth continued, and my progress was slow and difficult, yet the challenge of picking a path through the web of tight channels provided some of the trip's most entertaining boating.

During much of the afternoon my thoughts had drifted to a trip planned by "Pecos" Jack Richardson, whom I had met a couple of years before. Something of a living legend among those who boat the Pecos and the Rio Grande, Jack was the coauthor of a guidebook for running the Lower Pecos. He had rigged his thirty-four-foot canoe with a massive sail, and he spent many weekends sailing it up the canyons of the lakelike Pecos. Jack and his friends had recently hatched a plan to travel the length of the Rio Grande as it forms the Texas-Mexico border, the exact route I was now undertaking, except that they were going to do it in reverse, upriver, against the current! They planned to sail Jack's canoe/sailboat, counting on the prevailing southeast winds to carry them upriver against the current at a pace roughly equivalent to the pace I achieved going downriver in a canoe less than half the length. Jack had devised a mile-by-mile, day-by-day itinerary, and I had copied it from his website to use it for my map, since aside from the Joint Operations graphic map I had used when Tony and I biked, I had no other guide to the river. Jack's itinerary had served me well by giving me a close idea of how far it was by river to the next town. On the other hand, the idea of his going in reverse for over twelve hundred miles of river had made such an impression on me—albeit a dubious one—that I had spent much of my own trip wondering how Jack and his crew would push the boat upriver through formidable obstacles.

Until this day, I had felt their mission would be extraordinarily difficult, but not impossible. Once I found myself dragging the boat below the dam and then picking my way through and over labyrinthine channels, I reassessed Jack's chances. He isn't a young man, probably sixty years old. As I struggled over or around the rocks, I imagined the spectacle of Jack and his crew trying to push the large boat. Certainly, the sails would be useless here.

When I had passed the worst of the rocks I entered a long pool, and near its end, the roar of a rapid filled the afternoon. I came to a mucky island on which I decided to make camp rather than run the noisy drop. The day was warm and humid, and I sweated as I gathered driftwood mired in the river cane. I had been very lucky with weather for most of the thirty-nine days of the trip to that point, and as I slid around the grimy surface of the island, setting up camp, I wondered if I had seen all I was going to see of winter. I guessed we were already in the early stages of spring, with February only a couple of days away. The moon had been full the night before, usually a sure recipe for a crisp, cold January night. But the opposite had occurred. The night had never cooled, and the morning air had been warm and thick. On this evening, just as I brought the fire to a blaze, it began to rain—only droplets at first, then a steady shower, which persisted much of the night and kept me tent-bound half the next morning.

—◆◆◆—

When the rain quit, the rapid below camp gave me trouble: the ledges beneath the surface ran in different directions, creating a fury of competing currents, all dead-ending into a slab of rock one more rung down the rapid. Midway down the drop, I beached the canoe on a ledge in mid-river, lifted it over the same ledge, then got back in the boat for a wild, rocky ride to the bottom.

An hour later, I ran an even trickier drop with the same sort of competing crosscurrents and the same rock-slab obstructions blocking the river at angles all the way down. Although the river had taken on more water since the diversion dam, it still had a flow of probably only 150 CFS, below the minimum necessary for a clean run through the drops. At the same time, the drops were steep enough that once I entered, the decline pushed me precipitously toward the bottom and made it hard to navigate the sharp turns between the barely submerged flutes of limestone. Just after the second drop, the river backed up because of the presence of another dam. I portaged on the Mexican side.

I found a wonderful camp on a high island and pulled in early, lured by the impressiveness of the site. Moreover, my sleeping gear had been saturated in the previous night's showers, proving that the waterproofing I had applied to my tent before the trip had failed. Once I had set up camp, I paddled the empty canoe to the Mexican shore to harvest firewood.

By my rough calculations, the island sat fifteen miles outside of Eagle Pass, and I figured I could reach there the following day after four hours of paddling. The river flow had improved all day, and I now had nearly as much water as I had lost at the diversion dam. With a sustained effort, I could now start to paddle good distances each day, twenty miles or more, and the following day I expected to paddle twenty-five as I tried to get far below Eagle Pass. Feeling confident that I would be in Laredo within a week, I began a small celebration, with beer, canned beans, and tortillas heated on the grill. I dried my sleeping bag by the fire in the declining daylight. Just as I completed the job, it began to rain anew, and all evening I listened to heavy raindrops sizzle in the campfire.

Gringo Wetback

Jan. 28–31

"Beware the back side of a full moon" is an adage I coined after living in South and West Texas for most of the last twenty years. During that time I noted a winter pattern of clear, warm days leading to a full moon, followed by the arrival of northers after the moon began to wane. The one constant in winter weather along the border seemed to be that if you were going to get really inclement weather in December, January, or February, it nearly always came after a full moon.

When I awoke at my island camp, the morning was breezy and cold, but not unlike the majority of winter mornings. I felt the cold more because I had enjoyed three unseasonably warm mornings in a row. The nighttime rains had left the air fresh, and the birds were cheerful as the sun shone brilliantly through the leafless trees lining the banks. A pair of cardinals flitted in the river cane across the narrow channel on the Texas side of the island, seemingly invigorated by the brisk wintry breeze. In contrast, white-winged doves on the Mexican shore sang lonesome, dirgelike melodies. A rare green jay squawked as it fought for territory with a sparrow.

I hit the water early, despite the cold, and paddled hard, two powerful strokes on one side of the canoe alternating with two strokes on the opposite side. The river wound through a valley, the arid terrain of the semidesert forming the valley's borders hundreds of yards off either bank. Along the water grew tall stands of deciduous trees, most of which I struggled to identify. I navigated turn after turn, straightaway after straightaway, passing lonely ranch shacks on the Mexican side, cattle, a solitary coyote, a dozen wild turkeys, a small family of javelinas—but nothing on either bank suggested that I was approaching Eagle Pass or Piedras Negras. I grew more determined, increasing the pace and power of my paddling, working hard even when the swift river current offered me an opportunity to rest. One tricky drop with a tight dogleg left turn nearly capsized my boat, but for the most part, the river offered ideal conditions for making mileage: fast current, easy drops, and favorable winds.

After five hours of relentless paddling, I turned a bend and suddenly the water diverted by the Maverick County Diversion Dam reentered the river, instantly producing a powerful current, a much bigger river than I had known to that point. Immediately, I felt the smallness of my canoe. I paddled a sweeping bend and saw an old truck parked Mexican-side, close enough to the river that I was certain its owner had to be nearby. I found a diminutive, bearded fisherman, wearing a backwards baseball cap, huddled on shore, watching his line. Angling the canoe toward him, I called out a greeting. As I drew closer, I could see he was about thirty, and he seemed nervous about my approach.

"Do you have any idea where the bridge is?"

On the border, we always refer to an international bridge as "the bridge;" any other bridge receives a modifier, such as "the railroad bridge" or "the freeway bridge."

"It's a long way," he answered, sweeping his arm in the downriver direction, as if to suggest I had half a continent yet to travel.

"Hours away or days away? Can I get there today or tomorrow or when?"

He glanced at his wristwatch, and said with great concentration, "It's five minutes before two right now. You'll get there at five o'clock."

It didn't seem possible that I had pushed so hard all day and still faced three hours in the canoe before reaching Eagle Pass. I expected each new bend in the river to lead me within sight of downtown, but bend after bend revealed nothing but a tree-lined or river cane-lined embankment stretching as far as I could see. Only the Border Patrol surveillance towers, one every mile or two, gave me hope that I was drawing near. I had expected to see signs of Piedras Negras far in advance of the bridge, since it's a city of 200,000 inhabitants that sprawls for miles along the hills above the river. But I saw nothing.

Finally, late in the afternoon, I negotiated a powerful but gradual drop, turned a sharp bend in the river, and there before me, basking in a wintry sun, sat the homes of the north side of Eagle Pass, stacked on the hillside. Moments later, the B. P. fan boat roared upriver, its two agents waving as it speeded past, sending a rolling wake that had me scrambling to keep the canoe upright. Swearing under my breath, I landed on a low-lying island in mid-river to have a quick beer. Moments after I got back in the canoe, the same fan boat came by even faster, and it sent huge swells. It was as if, having failed to tip me the first time, the agents had decided to make a more concerted effort. This time we did not exchange waves. I entertained thoughts of extending a different sort of hand signal.

Around the next bend, I found three international bridges—two for cars and one for trains—and before them, on the littered banks of the Mexican shore, a family stood waving at me. Above them, in the background, stood the downtown area of Piedras Negras: a cathedral tower, two billboards, a cluster of customs buildings, and palm trees. On the American side, fishermen—rumored to be watchmen for *coyotes* smuggling undocumented workers across the river—fiddled with their tackle, pretending not to notice my passing. Up ahead loomed the first of the three bridges spanning high above the water line.

Finally, after the longest and most physically demanding day I had had on the river so far, I was about to pass under my first bridge in exactly two hundred eighty miles.

When I passed the clock above the bridge in Piedras Negras and saw that it read two minutes until five, I laughed, thinking of the fisherman who had predicted my arrival time. It would be the only light moment I'd have in Eagle Pass.

—◆◆▶—

Eagle Pass and Piedras Negras are relative newcomers in the history of settlements along the Rio Grande. A year after the signing of the Treaty of Guadalupe Hidalgo, which ended the Mexican-American War, the U.S. established Fort Duncan along the banks of the river to protect the newly defined American border. The following year, 1850, the Mexican government reciprocated by building its own fort. Because of fierce Indian raids in the area in subsequent years, the two towns developed close to the walls of their respective forts. Eagle Pass became an important port during the Civil War, when Union forces imposed a shipping embargo on the Texas coastline, and it was the last town to surrender the Confederate flag at the conclusion of the war.

Eagle Pass/Piedras Negras is currently the fifth largest of the *cuates* (twins) on the Rio Grande, and, with the exception of Laredo, Eagle Pass is the most Mexican of the Texas cities. Its population is almost ninety-five percent Hispanic, and the majority of its residents speak Spanish as their first language. Like Laredo, Eagle Pass is geographically isolated from cities other than its neighbor, Piedras Negras. San Antonio sits a hundred and forty-five miles to the northeast; Del Rio is fifty-five miles upriver; and Laredo is a hundred and twenty miles, by highway, downriver. In between, the thorn-scrub countryside is sparsely populated. Like all cities on the border, Eagle Pass suffers from poverty. Roughly a quarter of its residents fall below the national poverty line, and the city's per capita income ranks among the lowest in the U.S. However, compared to its sister city, Eagle Pass is affluent.

-◆◆◆-

Just below the bridges, on a dusty hillside above the Mexican shore, I saw astonishing squalor: an encampment of impoverished men who apparently had been deported by the Border Patrol and lacked the funds to return to their hometowns in the interior of Mexico. Temporary hovels, constructed with fraying blankets supported by string and wire, swayed in the breeze. I could see wisps of smoke rising from an underfed campfire below the shelters. Men with woolly, unkempt beards stood in a loose circle and cheered as I paddled below. They appeared cold, hungry, dirty, and—remarkably—happy. I wondered how, in such deplorable conditions, they could maintain high spirits, and then concluded, perhaps wrongly, that they had spent the afternoon sharing dirt-cheap tequila, brandy, or *aguardiente*. Several called down, asking for a ferry ride across the river, pleading with me to stop to help them out. With the sun already near the horizon, I pushed on, now growing worried about where I would camp.

The American side of the river was thick with river cane. I studied each opening for a possible campsite, but each was littered with deflated inner tubes, discarded clothing, and empty plastic water jugs—all sure signs of a trailhead for undocumented workers crossing the river. On the Mexican side, the bank had been cleared of vegetation but was strewn with trash, with empty quart beer bottles everywhere. I could see the modest homes of Piedras Negras above the bank, many surrounded by dilapidated pickup trucks or rundown American-model cars. Due to the cold, few people were outside their homes, though those who were paused to watch me, some walking toward the river for a closer look. Everybody waved.

Below the bridges, the river enters a very long straightaway, two miles at least, and in the declining light, I worried that I wouldn't make the end of it with enough time left to find a suitable camp. I worried that if I raced to the end of the straightaway, I might round the bend to find another long straightaway with even more homes along the river. Hugging the American shore, I paddled furiously, the noises of the two cities almost deafening after my four days away from people. Nearing the end of the straightaway, I found on the U.S. side an opening in the cane, divided by a fallen tree, and landed the canoe. As a camp, it was a dismal site, too narrow to harbor both my tent and the canoe, and in plain view of the homes opposite above the Mexican bank. Above the camp, a bulldozer had recently cleared the hillside, pushing all the dirt toward the river, putting me in plain view of the Border Patrol or anyone who looked down at the river from above. I could hear the nearby cars accelerating in the streets of Eagle Pass. As woeful as this site was—noisy, muddy, claustrophobic, and public—I decided to set up camp. I began sawing at the limbs of the downed tree in order to clear enough space to erect my tent.

Across the river, a man approached along the bank, and when he was directly across the water from my camp, he cast a fishing line and then expertly started a fire with a hastily gathered micro-pile of sticks. His hair, long and matted, appeared frozen, likely owing to having passed weeks without a wash. He wore a pair of cheap tennis shoes that were ripped, and the front of one shoe flopped when he walked. Seeing him start the fire so effortlessly, I decided to start my own before darkness fell. My first flames made the green wood sizzle before the fire sputtered and died. I sensed that my friend across the river felt he had won a small victory.

For a long moment I resigned myself to a fireless camp. I imagined myself sitting in blackness, listening to the deafening noise, sipping a can of beer I could barely see, miserably cold. Then I thrashed through the river cane until I found dry wood, a large armful of it, and returned in near-blackness to camp. Within minutes, I had the flames leaping into the darkness. Meanwhile, my friend across the river grew agitated and began firing rocks into the river. I could no longer see him well—just a faint outline defined by the shy light of his tiny fire—but he flung rocks violently into the river at the very spot where he had dropped his fishing line. It made for a grotesque sight, yet I couldn't tear my eyes away.

Only two things saved me from plunging into a profound funk. One, I had built an impressive fire, burning a mix of green wood and dry wood. Two, I treated myself to generous amounts of Tecate. As woeful as my campsite was, I was determined to rescue the night, and once I had downed half a dozen beers, the claustrophobic site was feeling downright homey.

-•-•-•-

On April 4, 2004, on a night in which no rain fell in Piedras Negras, the Rio Escondido, a tributary of the Rio Grande, rose from a depth of eighteen inches to twenty-five feet in a matter of half an hour, due to localized downpours further up the normally tranquil riverbed. The surge of water destroyed six hundred homes in the *colonia* of Villa del Fuente, on the south side of Piedras Negras, and killed somewhere between thirty-five and sixty people, depending on sources. At eight o'clock the following morning, the Rio Escondido still flowed at over 31,000 CFS. For comparison's sake, in seventy-three years of river monitoring, the second-highest flow ever measured on the Rio Escondido was 13,100 CFS. Even during the deadly flood of June 1954, the Rio Escondido's flow didn't reach 5,000 CFS.

The flood left its mark on the Rio Grande in a peculiar and unsightly fashion, effectively covering every tree on both sides of the river with trash, giving the impression that Mother Nature had hosted a tree-decorating party of grotesque, Ripleyesque proportions. For at least fifteen miles below the confluence with the Rio Escondido, every branch of every tree within the floodplain of the Rio Grande had trapped the litter from that flood, and thanks to the pricked or stickled branches of that riparian growth, no amount of subsequent wind or rain has been able to free the unsightly trash. Furthermore, a wide swath of riverbank on both sides of the Rio Grande hosts a coating of litter carried in by the flood: debris from shattered homes, lawn furniture, automobile tires, children's toys, and anything else too heavy or slippery to be trapped by tree limbs. At one beach where I pulled in to stretch my legs, I found the small pocketbook, adorned with a drawing of Snoopy, of a preadolescent girl, and when I opened it I found a tube of imitation lipstick.

It occurred to me as I paddled through this section that if I were to explore the floodplain on either side of the river, I would likely find the skeletons of cattle, fowl, and perhaps even humans. However, I found the river eerie enough already. In one tree, I spotted a soiled disposable diaper some twelve feet above the river. In another I noticed a feminine napkin. Mile after mile, the otherwise pristine riparian environment was adorned with the considerable refuse of the Rio Escondido basin. I could only guess at the vast amount of trash on the river bottom.

━●◆●━

Below Eagle Pass, the river is powerful, the current pushy, the drops frequent, and the waves large. In particular, violent crosscurrents present a formidable challenge to the canoeist. On a warmer day, I would have considered the challenges of the bigger river fun, but this day brought a chill out of the north that stoked my fear of hypothermia in the event of a tip. At every drop, I had to navigate through large cross-waves, some splashing water in my face, all of them slapping the canoe and tossing it as if it were merely Styrofoam.

By the time I reached Las Islitas—or Kingsbury Falls, as Texans call it—I was nearly overwhelmed by the elements. In addition to the trash, the cold, and the power of the river, my body struggled to meet the demands of the pace I had been keeping. At least when Hayesy was present, I had paced the trip to accommodate him. Alone, I went all out every day from sunup to sundown, seldom stopping the canoe, skipping lunch breaks, paddling ceaselessly. Now finishing my seventh week, I had lost a significant amount of weight, and whatever fat stores I had begun with were long since burned away, replaced by sinewy muscle, especially in my stomach and upper back. Still, I wasn't consuming sufficient calories to fuel the incessant activity, and with the cold now entrenched, I often felt listless, driving myself more on the adrenaline rushes the tough canoeing conditions dealt than on a hearty diet.

I stopped atop Las Islitas, which, as its name suggests, is a rapid clogged with small islands of rock, many barely above the water level. The maze of channels leading down the long rapids is complex but not especially difficult if you have good command of your boat. In the nineteenth century, Las Islitas posed a barrier to riverboats. No channel is wide enough to allow the passage of a boat wider than eight feet, and with a strong current swirling in the tight lanes, any boat wider than five feet would likely pinball between the rocks. I looked at the drop for a long time, more to stretch my legs and imagine the nineteenth-century boats struggling to negotiate it than out of need to study it carefully. The rapid offered three channels to run and wasn't technically difficult if I entered well and didn't lose my read. Another similar rapids, with rocky islands congesting the drop in the river, followed an hour later, and numerous tight and choppy lesser rapids punctuated the end of every long pool.

This section of the river also offered profuse collections of birds, more birds than I've ever seen on any river anywhere. In addition to blue and white herons, the river was thick with ducks, white pelicans, Canada geese, barn owls, kiskadees, and ravens. I found the owls and pelicans especially interesting. The pelicans would perch on rocks at the tops of rapids, typically two or three birds when I first sighted them, and as I drew to within forty yards, they would take off, seemingly too heavy to fly, propelling themselves by pushing their webbed feet against the water as their monstrous wings flapped the air. At the next rapid, I would find that the group had grown to four or five, but this time they would alight at the bottom of the drop. Just as I reached the bottom, now closer than they had allowed me to get when they sat above the rapid, the small flock would fly in a horizontal formation, perfectly spaced, landing below the next rapid. When I would arrive there, I would find the flock had increased in number again, and this process would repeat itself for miles. One flock grew to seventeen before it allowed me to pass, and another reached thirteen.

The barn owls slept in the river cane and would awaken, groggy and disoriented, upon hearing my paddle strokes just below their roost. Invariably, their fear of me would result in their dropping whitish feces in the general direction of my canoe as they struggled to flee, sometimes downriver, sometimes upriver. The ones that fled downriver typically fled three or four times before they would figure out that the only sure escape was to fly inland.

The river was always replete with birds, and teals or other ducks led me the entire way. I knew from my research that Bentsen Rio Grande State Park far downriver had gained national attention as a birders' paradise, but the section of river below Kingsbury Falls had dozens of times more birds than Bentsen offered later.

The birds, the absence of human signs other than the trash, the vibrant fall colors of the forested hillsides above the river, and the challenging currents all helped keep my mind off the physical discomfort that the cold and my lack of energy were causing me. Rain fell intermittently, and I kept my rain jacket on all the time now because it was the warmest garment I had. Late in the day, I plunged the paddle into the water for yet another hard draw and suddenly felt completely drained. Realizing I needed a rest, I stopped Mexican-side at the bottom of the next rapid, where I found a grassy access used by the local ranch for riverside picnics and fishing, and there I sawed firewood to carry to a high island I could see mid-river half a mile away. The late-afternoon light reminded me of November in Canada; on such a raw day, Canadians would hustle home to a warm fireplace or woodstove, hot tea, and a good book. For the first time all trip, I felt a hint of loneliness.

Ironically, despite having left a campsite very close to downtown Eagle Pass that morning, I had seen no one the entire day; but not long after I started my campfire on the island, I saw large lights flashing on the ranch upriver where I had sawed firewood. These lights flashed in series of three, every couple of minutes. Half an hour later, a light on the Texas side answered with two short flashes. Then I saw the headlights of a pickup descending Mexican-side to the river. On the Texas side, a group of three handheld flashlights appeared. Out of paranoia, I tried to shield the light of my campfire by standing on the upriver side of it, but all that accomplished was to send out a gigantic shadow of my body over the river. The apparent smuggling operation proceeded over the next half hour. Whether the traffic was human or narcotics, I couldn't know, but it was the first sighting I had had of smuggling since Hayesy and I had talked with the drug mules more than three hundred miles back upriver.

An hour later, all the lights disappeared. The pickup retreated inland, and a truck on the Texas side carried the cargo back in the direction of Eagle Pass. I was left to contemplate the carp that, drawn by the light of my campfire, hovered in the shallow water next to the island, occasionally splashing the water with powerful thrusts when my moving shadow alarmed them.

The rain fell ceaselessly, swirling in the cold wind, and I took comfort only in the idea that the smugglers in the river would likely find the weather too inclement to investigate me. I tried to stay up late, but fatigue made my eyes heavy. With the rain sliding off my rain jacket in rivulets and saturating my jeans, it seemed far more work to stay warm by the fire than inside the tent. With a sigh, I uttered a brief prayer for better weather in the morning and crawled into my tent, falling into a deep sleep almost the instant I lay down.

—◆◆◆—

The sound of rain pattering on my tent awoke me the following morning, and the cold stung my cheeks as I tried to will my aching muscles up off the ground. Outside, a thick mist rose off the river, the result of nearly freezing rain mixing with the much warmer river water. I hustled over to the fire, found coals deep beneath the sodden ashes on top, and worked to ignite the saturated kindling I had left uncovered nearby. While huddling over the first reluctant flames of the fire, I thought it unlikely that I would be getting into the canoe that day. With temperatures barely above freezing, rain falling, and my body sapped and aching, I decided the wisest thing to do was paddle across the river, saw more firewood, and spend the day cooking a pot of dried beans. Even the birds weren't moving.

Feeling hungry, I reached into a wet bag in which I carried the canned beans and found it empty. Thinking I must have stored some of them in the plastic Rubbermaid box in which I also carried dried food and first aid supplies, I searched there, but found none. I checked the cooler and found I had but a handful of tortillas and a small wedge of cheese, just enough to cook two quesadillas. I emptied a barrel I used to store food and found only spices and seasoning.

Returning to my plastic box, I did an inventory of my food supplies and discovered that aside from the dried beans and a canned ham, I had only six small packages of instant oatmeal. If I cooked the dried beans and the canned ham, I would have enough food to last as long as two days, but the downside of the equation was that I would lose all day cooking. Despite the raw cold, I had to move!

Just then I glanced upriver and saw a boat sitting midstream about a third of a mile away. Initially, I questioned my own senses, and I peered at it for several minutes to reassure myself that it was really there. Expecting that the powerful current would quickly push it in my direction, I waited for it to arrive. I needed directions, or even a ride, to the nearest store. Assuming I had traveled twenty-five river miles the day before, I still had a hundred and ten miles before I would reach Laredo, and I was undersupplied. The problem had occurred because when I had shopped in Acuña the day was quite warm and my belly was full, and the tiny store offered very little. Knowing that I ate far less in warm weather than in cold, I had gambled that the cache of canned beans, tuna, and tortillas I bought would last until Laredo. The cold weather, however, had sharpened my hunger, and I was consuming twice the rations I would consume on warm days.

The boat did not move—a logical impossibility, I thought, in all that current. I began to distrust my senses again, and for several minutes I looked for signs of movement from what appeared to be two men inside the craft. Finally, I slid the canoe into the water and paddled out of the current, along the Mexican shore, in the direction of the boat.

Two Mexican men shivered as they fished. The younger seemed afraid of me. He had mongoloid features: squinty eyes, an expansive forehead, and a small, downturned mouth. The older man, about forty, sat in the stern and eyed me as I approached from the Mexican shoreline. Only the older of the two spoke as I greeted them and asked about nearby stores. The man said two stores near the river had gone out of business and that I would have no opportunity to buy food until Guerrero. When I asked how far it was, he replied, "Not very far. You can make it there tonight or tomorrow."

"Listen," I said in Spanish, "I'm very short of food, and I'm worried that I don't have enough to last nearly as far as I'm going. If you were in my position and you had to buy food today, what would you do?"

He thought for a long minute, and suddenly his face showed the faintest suggestion of a smile. "If you are willing to walk for a while, you can find a store downriver in San Vicente."

Then he proceeded to detail directions in a curious fashion: "Go to a wide spot in the river and you will see a water pump on the Mexican side. Leave your boat there and walk up above the pump. There you will see a small ranch road. Follow it until you come to some horses. Keep going straight past the horses and then you will come to some cows. Keep going straight and then you will go up a hill. At the top of the hill, you will see three houses, and the store is in the last house on the left."

The river had so many wide spots and so many water pumps that I thought it unlikely I would find the store. In case I started exploring at each pump, I needed to have a rough idea how much time my walk would consume.

"How many kilometers from the river to the store?"

The man shot me a quizzical look, and if I had had less confidence in my Spanish, I would have guessed I had used the wrong word for kilometers. I asked him, "Well, how far is it?"

Patiently, he began to repeat the exact directions, getting as far as the horses, before I told him I understood. I thanked him and paddled downriver to my island, already so cold that I needed to huddle by the fire for several minutes to get warm. Even during the activity of taking down camp and loading the canoe, I frequently retreated to the campfire to warm my numbed hands or feet. At least the rain abated, changing from a steady shower to a silvery mist.

I had zero confidence that I would find the store, but several miles downriver, I came to a wide spot where a water pipe reached the shore on the Mexican side, and there I docked. Above, I found a narrow ranch road—a promising beginning—so I walked along it for several hundred yards, sidestepping horse dung as I went. A half mile later I reached an opening in the mesquite grove, revealing a damp pasture, the grass of which had been gnawed to nubs. There I found six horses. Maybe the meeting with the fishermen was going to pay off, I thought hopefully, as I walked toward a hill about a mile away.

Several hundred yards later I heard the loud thumping of a steel tool striking wood, and I saw a long-haired man splitting mesquite with a chisel and a mallet. I called a greeting, but he neither acknowledged nor returned the greeting. Watching him angrily strike the mesquite log, I hesitated out of fear. Figuring that in the worst-case scenario I could outrun him, I approached, calling from a distance of thirty feet, "Can you tell me if the store is nearby?"

Again he did not reply. He continued pounding the mesquite with forceful swings, his eyes fixed on the log. I gazed toward the distant hill, wondering if it was wise to face this standoffish woodsman again. I decided to continue on, and a short while later, I reached the cows.

At the base of the hill, the road twisted left and then right, leading me past a warehouselike barn where I could hear a man working, but I continued to the top of the hill. There I found three small homes, separated by scraggly growths of cactus and dwarfed mesquite. At the third house, I found a small sign advertising cigarettes, and, without knocking, I entered.

Immediately, I was overcome by two sensations: an almost palpable warmth and a dizzying array of color from the bright hues of packaged goods—potato chips, chewing gums, canned beans, soft drinks, fruit juices, and cigarettes. A woman emerged from behind a narrow curtain at the corner of the room, and I greeted her self-consciously, knowing I hadn't bathed or groomed myself in days. She seemed not to notice. I piled goods on the counter, first some beans, then packages of tortillas, then potato chips. When I turned to peer at the shelves, she asked me if she could help me find something.

"I would like some cheese," I said in Spanish. She pointed to an old refrigerator standing near the door.

"Do you sell beer?"

"No, you have to go up to the highway for that, but it's not far, only about ten minutes."

"On foot?"

"You're on foot?" she said. "Where are you coming from on foot?"

"I'm canoeing the river."

"Oh God," she said smiling, "You're a gringo wetback. I always knew that if I lived long enough I would meet one." We both laughed. "But, no, the store is ten minutes by truck."

Sensing my disappointment, she lowered her voice: "My husband has some beer in the bottom of the refrigerator. I'll sell it to you if he doesn't come out. He's not going to like it, but you'll be back on the river by the time he learns the beer is gone. Besides, he can drive to the other store. I need some things anyway."

As I was leaving, I asked her if she knew the man splitting wood. I was nervous about passing him on my way back, since I wouldn't be able to outrun him while I carried my new supplies.

"Oh, don't worry about him," she said. "He's deaf and dumb. That's why he didn't talk to you. And he can barely see, so he didn't even know you were there."

Several hours later the current suddenly died, a sign I knew meant that either a large rapid or a dam waited downriver. Now having to propel the canoe solely with paddling power, much as if I were on a lake, I labored ahead, my arms weary and rubbery. Around the next bend, I saw a crowd of a dozen Mexicans onshore next to a flat-bottomed boat, and several of the group were boarding just as they came into view. During my slow approach, the boat crossed the wide river, left four young men on the Texas bank, and returned to pick up more. Both the ferry and I arrived simultaneously. I was surprised that the remaining eight guys eagerly came to the shore to talk to me. Two held shotguns.

I asked them if they could tell me where I was. One sarcastic man wearing a New York Yankees baseball cap responded, "Yeah, you're on the Rio Bravo. This side is Mexico. That side is Texas. You probably are looking for that side."

Everyone laughed, and they laughed harder when I replied, *"No mames, güey"* (very roughly: Don't suck [your mother's breast], man).

I asked if a dam or a rapid waited up ahead, and they confirmed that a dam *followed* by a rapid sat around the next bend. They assured me the location was dangerous and that I should carry around the dam on the Mexican side. As I was thanking them, four more of the young crowd piled into the flatboat and took off for the American shore.

The dam, Los Cortines, extended across a wide section of river. Near the Texas shore, a very steep chute released water down a drop of twenty feet. At the base of the drop the river exploded into a long, bouncy Class II rapids. I pulled my canoe to the wall of the dam near this chute. There I climbed onto the cement wall, and while holding the canoe tight to the wall with one hand, I untied and unloaded with the other. On the dam wall I immediately ran into dangers. In order to reach the ground below, I had to descend a steep cement grade slick with rain and a mossy growth. My only option was to slide all the gear down and then drop the canoe by rope. My barrel tumbled into a pool of water below the base. My sleeping bag rolled right off the edge of the cement and joined it. While I shimmied myself down, I lost my precarious footing and barely averted taking a swim myself.

Not far below the rapid, I came to the Ledges of Guerrero, a series of three river-wide ledges that are barely submerged. These slabs of limestone extend from shore to shore, and I knew the water running over them would be extremely shallow because as I approached the first I saw a Mexican fisherman standing on the ledge about a hundred feet from shore. From a distance, he appeared to be walking on water. I navigated the first by scraping over the ledge near the fisherman, but at the next one I had to scramble along the ledge as the river tried to sweep me sideways over it, looking for an indentation in the rock deep enough to allow the passage of my canoe. A number of people fished the Mexican side in this area, though none appeared to have any interest in the unusual sight of a gringo in a canoe fighting his way over the rocks.

The third ledge is part ledge, part steep and long rapid, and once I came upon it, I wished I had lined it. The current pours over the river-wide ledge and then falls through a two-hundred-yard rapids, which consists of submerged rock ledges running in every possible direction. The result is that the current fights through a thousand competing channels, none of them deep, none of them much wider than the width of a canoe. Through a combination of lining, pushing, and dragging, I steered the canoe down the slippery descent, at times in the current up to my waist, at other times not having enough water beneath the boat to move it even an inch. At one point, I eased the boat through a turbulent yet shallow section and saw that three competing currents pounded at the bottom of the canoe within its fifteen-foot length. Finally I reached the bottom and, now thoroughly chilled, paddled to the Mexican bank to harvest firewood.

After loading a monster supply of gangly mesquite trunks, I had to navigate more rapids in declining light. The rain fell, and the wind whipped it in sheets across the river. I tried desperately to keep the canoe upright but saw right away that my load was imbalanced. For the first time since I had left Acuña, I settled for a camp on shore, a mucky isthmus, extending out from the Mexican bank a mile below the last of the Guerrero ledges. The rain increased as I unloaded the canoe, and I spent a long time next to the campfire before I felt warm enough to bother with the rest of the chores of setting up camp. When I finally turned in for the night, a dank sleeping bag and a saturated tent awaited me.

-•◆•-

My recipe for protection from hypothermia is simple: I add up all the wet clothes I'm wearing and measure them against the clothes stored in my dry bag. If the wet clothes exceed the dry clothes, I spend whatever time it takes drying them beside the fire. If my dry clothes exceed my wet clothes, I can push on downriver. In the event of a capsize, I know I have enough dry gear to avert hypothermia.

Now, however, I faced a new problem. Night after night of rain had left me unable to dry any clothes, and, unwilling to dress each morning in soaked attire, I had used up every dry thing I had except one change of clothes and one pair of hand-knitted wool socks Eric Clem had given me specifically for this trip. His mother, Shirley, had knitted them, and Eric assured me these socks were as warm as any I could buy in a high-end sporting goods store. As I endured day after day with numb feet, I dreamed of the moment when I could finally wear the wool socks, but I stubbornly persisted with cold feet, wading through the ledges, sloshing through the saturated ground at camps, guiding the boat in and out of the shallows every time I stopped. Unless I hunched over a roaring campfire, I felt cold all the time.

Just as I began to struggle with the cold and interminable rain, I started seeing, for the first time, steady traffic of people crossing the river—and, with the exception of the crowd of guys I had seen before Los Cortines Dam, none of them crossed in boats. While I shivered, though dressed in multiple layers, in the canoe, I would round a bend and see as many as fifteen people wading across the river, some stripped to their underwear. The temperature hovered around 45°F for days, and the water temperature was about 55°F, and still these Mexicans who sought an opportunity to work in the U.S. waded or swam across the wide river wearing next to nothing. Above their heads, they carried black trash sacks stocked with a change of clothes, and when they reached the opposite bank, they seemed in no hurry to don them. I marveled at their hardiness. They never paused to build a fire on the American side, and once they had dressed, they set out quickly across the countryside in single file. My unexpected appearance in the canoe seldom rattled them. Most greeted me with tentative waves, if they noticed me at all.

I found it easy to monitor popular crossing routes. Nearly all the people left trash sacks, wet clothes, and plastic water jugs on the Texas-side bank. On the Mexican side, I spotted countless trails leading to the river—some used by ranchers or fishermen, but most used by undocumented workers. I found it easy to discern the difference: the ranchers and fishermen littered beer cans, while the undocumented workers left empty tin cans, evidence of their final meal in Mexico.

Exactly one year earlier, Celestino López, age thirty-six, had crossed the river illegally in this same area. Not far from the river, he passed near three hunters, who had set up camp. While his two hunting partners cooked supper, Jaime González of Eagle Pass thought he heard javelinas in the nearby brush. Unable to see through the darkness with his binoculars, Jaime took his rifle and pursued the noises on foot. Moments later, seeing movement in the brush, Jaime fired from a distance of 129 yards, dropping Celestino López with a bullet, which tore through the victim's abdomen and the plastic trash sack in which he carried a change of clothes. López died en route to the hospital. No criminal charges were filed against González, but the victim's family filed a wrongful death suit, asking for $8 million in damages.

I thought about Celestino López as I paddled downriver on the one-year anniversary of his death, fighting a lingering chill, refusing to don my pair of wool socks and my long underwear. I rationalized that if guys like Celestino could swim this river naked and then hike for distances sometimes surpassing a hundred miles, I could endure chilly feet. Hour after hour, I paddled steadily, stopping only to eat. I discovered the warmest place was in the canoe; onshore I could not get warm without a robust campfire. At lunch stops, I tried jogging back and forth, but even that produced little warmth in my feet.

For fifty-five miles between Guerrero and Hidalgo, a Mexican village visible from the river, there are no towns on either side. At times I would hear a pickup truck or a tractor driving above the Mexican shore, but I saw no one except those crossing the river. After struggling all day with rain, cold, and wind, I pulled in to scout a forest on the Mexican side for camp, and just as I turned toward shore, a group of a dozen young men marched naked into the current a hundred yards downriver, going single file in water reaching their armpits. For a second straight night, I spent so long warming myself by the fire that I set up my tent in darkness. For a third straight night, rain fell all evening and I could dry nothing by the fire. Human trails crisscrossed the dense forest, and I could hear the drone of a pickup moving slowly along a nearby ranch road. I felt paranoid, haunted by the prospect of a *coyote* leading a group of river crossers directly into my camp. What if the *coyote* who appeared was the same one who had led Celestino López across the river one year before?

Instead I suffered alone, the rain relentless, the cold piercing. Even the fire seemed overwhelmed by the incessant showers.

The Second Half of a Long Winter

Feb. 1–3

By two o'clock the next afternoon, after three days of nearly ceaseless rain and freezing temperatures, I pulled into shore; my toes were so chilled that they burned, making it hard for me to sit still in the canoe. A raw wind penetrated every layer of sodden clothing. I stood shivering in a swampy thicket of willow saplings, and thought, "Enough is enough. I have to change into dry gear."

I withdrew my long johns, my one pair of dry jeans, my Shirley Clem wool socks, and a turtleneck shirt from the dry bag, and then, while hopping on the boggy river shore, completed the fastest change of clothing I have ever executed. Instantly, I felt human again, and those socks eased the stinging cold in my toes.

Feeling armored against the cold, I assaulted the cooler and drained three Tecates as though it were a steamy afternoon.

Back in the canoe, I rounded the next bend in the river and saw a village sprawled on the Mexican hillside above the river. From one of the row of ramshackle homes, a man emerged, and I waved to him. He returned the greeting, and I cut the canoe hard for shore, intending to ask him the name of the village. When he saw me start for shore, he began a quick descent of the muddy trail to the river to meet me.

"What's the name of this village?" I called as he neared my canoe.

"Hidalgo."

I was so happy that I'd arrived, I wanted to hug him. But we chatted for only a minute because I had to pee, thanks to the beers. The man directed me downriver to *la bajada,* or the river landing, and I paddled along the trashy banks to a cobblestone road that reached the river. In a light rain, I walked the slick stones up the hillside into the heart of Hidalgo, a village large enough to have a central plaza. Outside a municipal building, I found two men conversing, and I asked for directions to the village store.

"Which one? There are four. What do you want to buy?"

I followed their directions to a market three blocks away, where I found the women in the store no more curious about my appearance than the two men had been. You would have thought gringos emerged from the river on a daily basis. A *telenovela,* or soap opera, ran on the television in the market, and I committed the faux pas of asking a question while the main action of the drama unfolded—a tense lovers' quarrel between a dignified man in his late forties and his Barbie look-alike concubine, a pouting girl, maybe twenty-five, with high cheekbones, coffee-colored eyes, and dyed blond hair. The women were riveted to the screen, but a minute later, when the show broke for a commercial, the woman behind the cash register directed me to the tortillas, which sat in a cooler below the TV.

Triumphantly, I lugged two sacks of groceries through the muddy streets, waving at the curious passersby who eyed me. A police cruiser pulled alongside, and I expected a terse interrogation, but when I waved and smiled, the young officer returned the greeting. Doubling back to the plaza, I passed the same men I had asked for directions to the store, and they smiled when they saw I had shopped.

A mile below Hidalgo, I found a large gravel island dividing the river into two swift channels, and right there sat an uprooted mesquite tree awaiting my saw and lighter. Just as I pulled the canoe to shore, the rain finally quit. I started a bonfire that I fully expected would lure the citizens of Hidalgo to the river's edge to investigate. Had they come, they would have seen flames leaping six or seven feet into the air, and the entire camp strewn with damp and muddy clothing drying in the heat of the blaze.

◆◆◆

The sun rose brilliantly the following morning, a deceptive harbinger of the afternoon's weather, and when I put the boat in the water, I found myself heading directly into blinding glare. After so many days of reduced light, the sun's intensity overwhelmed me, and even my sunglasses offered little relief. But I didn't have to squint for long. An hour out of camp, clouds hurried in from the north and shrouded the sun—for what would turn out to be the next nine days. By noon, rain fell yet again. With my feet nestled in thick wool socks and my legs warmed by long johns, I welcomed the bad turn in the weather; I saw it as an inspiration to paddle hard for Laredo, where I planned to rest at home for a week before doing the final stretch to the Gulf.

Leaving Hidalgo, the river winds playfully through numerous turns and around a number of thickly wooded islands. Despite this stretch's proximity to the two Laredos (the lights of the twin cities are visible at night from camp), I saw remarkably little evidence of people between Hidalgo and the Columbia Solidarity Bridge, the first of Laredo's four international bridges. This unlikely structure connects a U.S. Customs complex with a Mexican Customs complex, both of which seemed ludicrously misplaced in the middle of arid country thirty-three river miles from the center of the two Laredos. In a subversion of economic and demographic logic, the state of Nuevo León convinced the federal governments of both the U.S. and Mexico to issue the permit to construct the bridge at this out-of-the-way location by promising to make infrastructure improvements here on the Mexican side and to build a new highway linking the bridge with the

Pan-American Highway twenty miles to the southeast. Although the bridge was completed in 1991, little on either side of it has changed. It remains a lightly used bridge linking nowhere with nowhere; the nearest convenience store, gas station, or restaurant on the U.S. side is a dozen miles away. On the Mexican side, a small combination gas station/convenience store/restaurant sits two miles from the bridge, the only service for more than a dozen miles.

Thanks to the failure of the Columbia Solidarity Bridge to attract the traffic and business development the Nuevo León government envisioned, the stretch of river between Hidalgo and the outskirts of Laredo offers a weird river experience. Bridge traffic noise impinges for miles on the tranquillity of the river as trucks cross the half mile between customs stations; the Border Patrol's surveillance towers rise from the Texas riverbank; and for a mile above the bridge and extending far past the two Laredos, the banks are littered with the trash of people crossing the river illegally. Thousands of inner tubes, inflated plastic trash sacks, water jugs, and clothes lie at the water's edge or float lazily in the current.

A couple of turns below Columbia Bridge, I rounded a tight bend below one of the few Texas-side homes in the area and found four young Mexican guys wading across the shallows, stripped to their underwear and holding their bundled clothes above their heads. As soon as I came into view, they retreated to the Mexican shore and walked briskly to a tree some forty yards inland. After struggling for days to stay warm in multiple layers of clothing, I marveled at their fortitude. Raw winds whipped out of the north, and the temperature hovered in the mid-forties. I turned the canoe into the shore near the group of guys, and couldn't resist having a little fun at their expense.

"What the hell are you doing?" I called out in Spanish, sounding like a high school principal. "Didn't anyone tell you it's freezing? Who do you think you are? Canadians?"

One brave young lad responded in a trembling voice, "It's not cold."

Even at forty yards, I could see that his lips had turned bluish, and one of the youths shivered as he wrapped his wet arms around his chest, hopping on the balls of his feet as if dancing on hot coals.

"Listen," I said, trying not to giggle. "If you're tough enough to wade across this freezing river in your damned underwear, you obviously have the balls to make it in the U.S. But I wonder about your mental toughness. I mean, I'm one guy in a canoe and the minute you see me, you go running back to Mexico. What the hell is that? If you're going to do, then do it. Don't let anything stop you."

The youths stared at me, their faces betraying a mix of relief and disbelief at the scolding. Feeling some guilt at prolonging their exposure to the sharp cold, I turned the canoe back toward the current and barked a final order: "Now get your freezing butts back across that river and go to work!"

A hundred yards downriver, I looked over my shoulder to see them dutifully marching across the shallows toward the Texas shore.

-◆◆▶-

By late afternoon, the day had grown colder than any I had experienced in the canoeing part of the trip. Then rain began to fall, making a dismal combination of steady precipitation, fierce winds, and sharp cold. I pulled onto a large grassy island immediately below a Border Patrol surveillance tower and, resisting an impulse to wave for the cameras, set about the long business of amassing a supply of firewood equal to the conditions. I staggered with fatigue along the raccoon trails that crisscrossed the island. An owl in the river cane on the Texas shore hooted. Wild turkeys on the Mexican embankment watched me, their heads bobbing.

Physically, I was a basket case, and I struggled to do even the smallest of camp chores. My hands had so long gripped the canoe paddle or the bow saw that I could scarcely open them, and they looked more like talons than the hands of a man who taught school for a living. When I tried to do fine work—simple tasks like opening a plastic package or turning the page in my notebook—my fingers betrayed me and I resorted to alternative methods such as using my tongue to turn pages or ripping plastic with my teeth. I no longer had enough thumb dexterity to flick the lighter to start a fire, and I improvised by thrusting the striker roller along my jeans. Two sensations dominated my waking hours: soreness and cold.

One minute my cheeks would be so painfully cold that I'd wrap a towel across my face. A minute later, my cheeks feeling better, my butt would ache from hours of sitting on the wooden frame of my canoe seat, so I would adjust an inflated pad to relieve the pressure. Then my fingers would grow numb from exposure while adjusting the pad, so I would retrieve my extra set of gloves. With my fingers warming, I would address my aching knee, aggravated from the daily grind of hauling heavy firewood in the evening and loading and unloading the canoe. Stretching the knee for relief, I would then notice cold creeping up my back. This series of endless adjustments consumed my life, and even while eating or writing in my journal, I moved incessantly to fight off aches or chills.

When my stoicism was challenged, I always resorted to the same elixir: beer. Through the whole trip, I had managed to keep the cooler stocked, and when my frustration with the ceaseless cold, rain, or physical pain threatened to plunge me into depression, I took the river runner's version of a kindergartner's time-out and opened a beer. Unfailingly, it always soothed my discomfort, be it physical or psychological. In a relationship only a beer drinker could comprehend, beer became my companion. If I felt like having company, I opened a beer. If I ached, I opened a beer. If I was miserably cold, I opened a beer. Yet beer drinking never became my principal activity. I opened a beer, then busied myself with a chore—maybe setting up the camp, collecting the firewood, or cooking supper. Beer became the link among an unending series of chores that began the moment I reached camp and ended when I collapsed wearily in the tent late each night.

Now only fifteen miles from Laredo and anticipating the next day's temporary return to life off the river, I heated water and shaved, using my rough fingers in place of a mirror, feeling my way in the darkness over the smooth patches of skin I had already shaved, hunting for the stubble I had missed. Then I cleaned the pot in the river, reheated more water, and, doling out the steaming water with my coffee mug, shampooed my hair. With the frosty air stinging my freshly shaven face and wet pate, I walked to the cooler and opened yet another beer.

⚫⚫⚫

About eight river miles before Laredo, the river bends at the base of a low cliff topped by an impressive estate, and the World Trade Bridge, the newest of Laredo's four bridges, comes into view, looking almost identical to its sister bridge twenty-five miles upriver. Known locally simply as "Bridge Four," the World Trade Bridge opened in 2000 to relieve the congestion of truck traffic in downtown Laredo, which had grown so extreme that it paralyzed Laredo's interstate and its downtown streets. Bridge Four was designated for truck traffic only, and the thousands of semis that cross it every day can bypass the interior of Laredo completely.

Laredo is the United States' largest inland port, and more trade passes through it than any other inland port in the nation, including Detroit. The World Trade Bridge alone carries more than twice as many trucks as pass between San Diego and Tijuana or between Juárez and El Paso. Almost two million loaded trucks use Bridge Four each year, and this makes an incongruous sight from the river. Six lanes of semitrailers, stalled between the two international customs stations, jockey for position on a wide cement swath some one hundred feet above the river. Afloat, one wonders where they all came from and where they're all going; Laredo and Nuevo Laredo are nowhere in sight.

Beneath the bridge on the Texas side, Border Patrol agents cruise rutted paths in all-terrain vehicles, and judging by the glee on their faces and the enthusiasm in their patrolling, I would guess that this beat is the most coveted patrol in the entire Laredo sector. When I passed by on yet another cold and rainy morning, the agents were huddled next to a fire out of the rain, laughing at each other's jokes, and their ATVs sat parked. I crept most of the way past before any of them noticed me. Although they seemed surprised by my appearance, none came to the river for a closer look or an interrogation.

Once past the bridge, I had arrived within Laredo's city limits, though little about the riparian environment suggested that I was now inside a city of somewhere between a half and three quarters of a million people. On the U.S. side, river cane lines the banks and the ubiquitous Border Patrol surveillance towers are the only evidence of man. On the Mexican side, the occasional dusty ranch shacks above the river look as though they are a hundred miles from the nearest city and a hundred years from the twenty-first century.

Despite the cold, Mexicans fished the shallows below the bridge, and I pulled in to talk to them, more because I needed to stretch my legs than because I wanted to talk fishing. They regarded me suspiciously as I jumped out of the boat, and I could see several more men standing on the bluff above eyeing me warily.

"How's the fishing?" I asked a young wiry guy with long, wavy hair and a goatee overgrown into the corners of his mouth.

He stared at the small mountain of gear crammed into my boat, dismissed the question with a shrug, and said, "You must have a lot of fish in those boxes."

As he stared at the small mountain of gear, I realized how it must look to Mexicans who reflected on how I had crammed two seven-gallon water jugs, a fifty-two-quart cooler, a large plastic box for food and first aid supplies, a watertight plastic barrel three feet tall, two dry bags, a tent, a thirty-inch bow saw, three paddles, a bailer, a fire grill, and several sections of coiled spare rope into my canoe. It's possible that I'd packed more gear than these fishermen owned in their homes.

"No, I haven't been fishing this week."

"Excuse me for asking, but why do you have so many things in there?"

I explained the extent of my trip and the need to outfit such a long excursion, but I sensed he had no grasp of the distances involved. Many people from the interior of the U.S. and Mexico assume mistakenly that border people have lateral interests—that is, that we care about and are aware of our neighbors up and down the river. While that may be true in the limited area of the Rio Grande Valley, it is not true for Laredo and cities upriver. It's probably safe to assume that most Laredoans have never visited Del Rio, let alone El Paso. Similarly, most Nuevo Laredoans have little knowledge of Acuña or Juárez. When I explained to the fisherman that I had been on the river for forty-six days already, he shot me a look that seemed to say, "But that still doesn't explain why you have so much gear!"

I felt uncomfortable suddenly, as if the nearer I drew to my home—now only six miles downriver—the more of an alien I became. I had the feeling that these fishermen believed I was some sort of undercover agent patrolling the river, meddling in their business, setting foot on their shore as if the border didn't exist. An awkward silence fell, and I shoved the boat off from shore.

Three miles later, now close to the Laredo Community College campus where I work, I saw a cheap rubber raft tied off to some river cane overhanging the Texas shore. Another hundred yards below it, two men swam the river by clinging to inner tubes, so I knew the raft didn't belong to them. I angled for shore, thinking I might collect the raft for myself. Just as I drew close enough to touch it, I was startled by the sight of a teenaged boy huddled in a tight opening in the cane. Clearly, the raft belonged to him, or at least he was using it to ferry people or contraband across the current. Just as I was about to speak, he raised a finger to his lips, signaling me to remain quiet; taking his cue, I angled my canoe back into the main flow of the current, from where I saw a Border Patrol agent thrashing through the growth of *palo verde* and *huisache* saplings above the river cane. I glided past, and the agent never noticed me.

When I reached the steep access at the fringe of the college campus and tied off to an ash tree at the base of the trail, I realized almost at once that the incessant rains of the previous week had rendered the banks so slick that I wouldn't be able to get out of the canoe without some engineering work. I had to secure the canoe with three separate tie lines before I could even begin to dig steps into the bank. After ten minutes of digging, I'd gouged three footholds into the slippery clay. Gingerly, I worked my way out of the boat, inching up the bank by clawing the ground and saturating my jeans as I moved. When I gained flatter ground eight feet above, I realized I would be unable to unload the boat, so I set off across campus looking for help.

If you ever want to get a sense of how porous our national border with Mexico is, all you have to do is land on the Texas side of the river and walk inland. The likelihood of encountering a Border Patrol agent, even in the heavily patrolled sector of Laredo, is not high. I wandered up the B. P. access road to the fringes of campus and angled for the Environmental Science Center, where Tom Miller, the only guy I know who has canoed the Rio Grande from Hidalgo to Laredo, works as the center's director. He was out having lunch, so I continued to the college baseball field, where the coach sent two of his players to help me haul the canoe out of the water.

These two young players had an interesting reaction when they learned on our way to the river just what their role would be. One asked for assurance that we wouldn't be shot when we went to retrieve the canoe, and as we descended looked as if he expected me to take the first bullet; the other one asked, "Are you sure it's safe to go down there?" and looked with great trepidation at the water below.

──◆◆◆──

Thirty minutes later Tom Miller tossed my gear into the back of his pickup truck with the ease of a man who had far more left in his tank than I had. Tom oversees a living museum of the region's wildlife. Inside the Environmental Science Center live dozens of rattlesnakes and rodents in terrariums; outside in ponds and cages reside alligators, fish, and bobcats. Walking through the center with Tom is like accompanying a happy child seeing the zoo for the first time. Of all the Laredoans I know who were aware of my trip, none was more excited or supportive than Tom. He regarded it in much the way I did—as something "really fun."

While he drove me down the narrow streets of my neighborhood, El Cuatro—the old residential section of downtown Laredo sandwiched between the business district and the railroad—he talked about the Rio Grande mussels that he collects for study. Tom is the first scientist to have located a living mussel here, and he frequently takes river trips to study their habitat. Now he voiced a new concern about the mussels. He'd just learned that the Japanese were willing to pay eight dollars a pound for the shells. "Some yahoos from Tennessee are going to catch wind of that and come down here and raid the mussel beds, so don't tell anyone where you've been finding them. Keith, we'd have a real problem if word got out around here that you can make money from them."

Standing on the sidewalk in front of my house, I suddenly felt homesick off the river.

Los Dos Laredos

Feb. 3–12

A year or two ago many civic-minded Laredoans were incensed to learn that in a national ranking of over three hundred thirty American cities—based on their health, entertainment, arts, climate, education, and business—Laredo ranked dead last, thus earning it the dubious distinction of being America's least livable city. Apologists quickly rallied to its defense, pointing out a number of positives that the ranking had overlooked—things such our bilingual culture, our easy access to the interior of Mexico, and our mild winters. Resident critics counterargued that those positives were actually negatives: our bilingual culture produces generation after generation of students who aren't completely versed in either language; our easy access to Mexico leads to ever-escalating levels of drug crime and drug-related violence; our mild winters last only three brief months, and the rest of the year we are stifled by excruciating heat.

In an ironic twist, another study, released in *Men's Health* magazine in March 2005, ranked Laredo as "the happiest city in the United States," based on such criteria as quantity of antidepressant drugs consumed, stress levels of the citizenry, mental health surveys, and interviews with locals. Not surprisingly, El Paso ranked number two, and Brownsville, another border city, ranked number four. Both of those cities had also fared poorly in the "livability" survey.

My take on the apparent contradiction that Laredoans, despite living in "America's worst city," are a relatively happy population is this: our sales of antidepressant drugs are low because most Laredoans buy their medicines across the river in Mexico, where prescription drugs are cheaper; and we are happier than Americans to the north because we expect less and therefore are less likely to be disappointed. On the other hand, if we *are* unhappy, we're not likely to confess it to outsiders doing happiness studies.

—◆◆◆—

A few days after I canoed into Laredo, I had to take the bus back upriver to Langtry to retrieve my car, which I'd parked at Pete's house. I elected to take the bus on the Mexican side of the river.

In the fifty days I had been away from Laredo, violence between rival drug cartels in Nuevo Laredo had escalated alarmingly—not that the level before my departure was low. The Gulf cartel, which had controlled narco-trafficking in Laredo for years, was being challenged by the Sinaloa cartel for control of the lucrative Nuevo Laredo smuggling corridor, and the resulting violence targeted law enforcement officials, members of the media, and cartel members. In addition to frequent shoot-outs in the city streets, a rash of kidnappings swept the city, with the kidnappers demanding exorbitant ransoms for their hostages; in many cases, the victims simply disappeared. That very morning, when I walked across International Bridge Number One to catch the bus to Acuña, a shoot-out in Nuevo Laredo had culminated in a high-speed police chase. Two gunmen were shot dead in the Mexican Customs complex, and a volley of bullets pierced the tollbooths where crossers to Laredo pay their bridge fee.

I found Nuevo Laredo a changed city. The gun violence had discouraged most Laredoans from crossing to shop for things like medicine, fresh fruit, and herbs, and the absence of gringo shoppers from cities like Houston and San Antonio was notable; normally the sidewalks of Guerrero Street would have been clogged with them. The city's main bus terminal was nearly empty—there appeared to be more ticket agents than passengers—and while waiting for my bus to Acuña to leave, I saw five buses depart, each with fewer than half a dozen passengers.

Patrols of Mexican government soldiers now rode through the streets of Nuevo Laredo in jeeps and trucks painted with camouflage. On the highway leading along the river, my bus stopped at four Army checkpoints in the first thirty miles, where soldiers boarded the bus, asking passengers for identification or checking through their carry-on bags. When we arrived at Hidalgo, which sits a mile off the narrow highway, we were stopped at yet another checkpoint, where we were told to disembark, claim our luggage, and set it on a makeshift table for the soldiers' inspection. Once they were satisfied, the bus proceeded into town, took on two passengers, and was stopped on the way out, where we were forced to repeat the process we had undergone only ten minutes before.

As the bus traveled beside the river, I studied the lay of the river valley. The bus trip to Acuña took less than five hours, but the same trip in the canoe had taken me ten hard days. From high above the river, I recognized little, but in Guerrero, at yet another military checkpoint, I saw a pickup filled with fishermen heading for the river, and I resisted a temptation to wave to them, thinking for one mistaken moment they might remember having seen me battle over the Guerrero ledges a week before.

-◆◆◆-

Back in Laredo the following day, I had a visit from Jesse Bogan, the *San Antonio Express-News* border correspondent. He wanted to accompany me on part of the remaining three hundred sixty miles to the Gulf of Mexico. He saw a story opportunity in my journey, but before pitching the idea to his editor, he asked me, "Are you sure you're the first one ever to make this trip?"

Apparently, a canoe trip the length of the Texas-Mexico border can be news only once. Since I couldn't assure Jesse I was the first, nor did I care, we decided he would accompany me for the first couple of hours out of Laredo, and then, if that went well, he would try to convince his editor to allow him to do a longer stretch later, closer to the Gulf.

At six feet four inches tall, Jesse is a long man by any measure and, despite his trim build, presented a logistical problem. In order to make space for him, I drove some of my gear down to San Ygnacio, about forty miles below Laredo, and left a food box, a water jug, and some beer at the riverside home of my good friend and colleague Sue Rickels. If Jesse and I left Laredo on a Saturday morning, I planned to arrive at Sue's on Sunday, when I'd reload the canoe and paddle on.

Jesse and I met at the river in a cool drizzle about midmorning. Since he didn't have a ride home from where I planned to drop him on the edge of Laredo, he asked if we could squeeze his bicycle into the canoe. I agreed to try.

Jesse's size makes him an imposing presence in nearly any setting. His trim build and bouncy step give evidence of an active lifestyle, and his farmer's tan shows that he spends a lot of time outdoors. Jesse's a good reporter, but he strives for something beyond good reporting; he wants to take part in the action of the news he reports, which is the quality I most admire about him. While other journalists would have been satisfied to cover my trip merely by interviewing me, Jesse believed it was important to be a part of the trip so that he would know for himself what canoeing the Rio Grande entailed. He calls this type of reporting "immersion journalism," and I cracked that he'd better not take the "immersion" aspect too far when we were together on the water.

I had no reservations about taking him along. Thanks to spending two years living in Torreón, Coahuila, he's bilingual, and his love for the Mexican people and their culture rivals my own. Also, he is an accomplished canoeist, a veteran of dozens of river trips in his native

Missouri, including a three-hundred-mile trip on the Missouri River and shorter trips on many of the Ozarks' finest rivers.

As we shoved off, a pair of guys clinging to inner tubes set out from the Mexican shore just below us. Jesse tried to interview them as we passed; not surprisingly, neither showed any interest in conversing with us. A couple of hundred yards later we found a flat landing on the Mexican side, and I pulled in to reorganize the gear; the boat was feeling incredibly unstable, and I feared a capsize.

Even with the gear better distributed, I did not feel at ease with Jesse in the bow. Since he was working on a story as we moved downriver, he swung his lanky frame often to retrieve his notebook, or grab his camera, or readjust the gear at his feet. He moved more in five minutes than I did in an entire day of paddling, and with each of his movements, the gunwale of my overloaded craft dipped perilously close to the waterline.

A mile below our put-in, the river makes a ninety-degree bend at a neighborhood Laredoans call *el rincón del diablo* ("the devil's corner"); the direction of the river shifts from due south to due east as it courses through downtown Laredo and passes under the railroad bridge that connects the two nations, and then under the last two of Laredo's four international bridges. As we approached this bend, we saw three men fishing on the Mexican side, and Jesse directed me to angle the boat closer to them so he could interview them. I had moved us about halfway from mid-river to shore when a group of adolescents standing outside a sordid row of shanties on a cliff above the fishermen suddenly showered rocks into the river all around us. One golf ball-sized stone pelted the stern of the canoe six inches from my hip. Several more splashed within a paddle length of the canoe.

We paddled hard back to the middle of the river, and the next volley of rocks came up well short of us. At the apex of the bend, the river drops quickly through a small rapid, and the channel squeezes close to the Texas bank. As we dropped through this, Jesse turned to me and said, "I think it's probably a normal reaction for a kid to see a canoe and throw a rock at it."

—◆◆◆—

Founded in 1755 and named after a town on the Atlantic coast of Spain, Laredo differs from the other Texas-Mexico border cities in several ways. It is isolated geographically from both the Rio Grande Valley and the cities upriver; unlike them, it has neither agriculture nor neighboring communities with which to trade. It wasn't until the end of the Mexican-American War in 1848 that it even had a "twin" on the other side of the river, now called Nuevo Laredo. And Laredo, alone among the border communities, supported Spain when Mexicans sought their independence beginning in 1810. Then, in 1836, Laredo supported Mexico when Texas declared its independence from Mexico. Ten years later, during the Mexican-American War, Laredo again threw its hand in with the losing side, supporting Mexico. Finally, during the American Civil War, Laredoans aligned themselves with the Confederacy. In between Texas's declaration of independence from Mexico and the Mexican-American War, Laredo leaders declared their own short-lived republic, the ill-fated Republic of the Rio Grande, which lasted a mere nine months, during which Laredo served as the capital. While other Texas cities boast of having lived under six flags, Laredo is the only one to have lived under seven, and the only city on the border to have once been a national capital.

Laredo's history is distinctive, too, in the absence of a sizeable class of landowning Anglos. The tiny minority of Anglos who did settle in the area quickly became assimilated into Hispanic culture, and neither American nor English values had much influence on the city. Even more than a hundred and fifty years after the Treaty of Guadalupe Hidalgo specified the Rio Grande as the Texas-Mexico border, Laredo reflects Mexican culture far more than that of the United States. Over ninety percent of its households use Spanish as their principal language; more families celebrate the Mexican Mother's Day than the American one; Laredoans are far more likely to know about *el grito* ("the cry")—the famous call, issued from the pulpit by Father Miguel Hidalgo on September 16, 1810, that began the struggle for Mexico's independence from Spain—than about the

American colonies' war of independence from Britain.

Still, Laredoans, for the most part, are ambivalent about their feelings toward Mexico. They complain that Mexico is "dirty, corrupt, and unsafe" in the same conversation in which they boast of their Mexican heritage. Racial and class divisions here follow the Latin American pattern in which people of European blood control those of predominantly indigenous heritage. The execution of criminal and civic law depends more on whom you know than on the statutes themselves. Outsiders, whether they be from Mexico or the U.S., are, in general, ostracized. Many of the brightest sons and daughters leave the city to make their fortunes elsewhere rather than be stifled by a border culture that clings to small-town attitudes even as the population mushrooms into the hundreds of thousands.

—◆◆◆—

As Jesse and I passed under the railroad bridge, the skyline of Laredo opened up briefly in front of us. At best it was a modest sight, but seeing it for the first time from the river made it seem exotic. The Spanish tiled roof of the hotel La Posada sat in the foreground under the bell tower of the venerable San Agustín church, Laredo's oldest landmark. An enormous American flag fluttered in the light breeze. The Customs complexes of Bridge Two dominated the bluff above the river, looking more like a sprawling hacienda than a seat of American bureaucracy.

A hundred yards ahead, a raft carrying a number of uniformed men was tied to shore. As we approached we could see a diver bobbing on the dark surface of the river close to the bank, and the attention the boatmen paid to him prevented their noticing our presence until we were nearby. Suddenly, they shouted at us, but with the rushing current, I couldn't make out their words. One waved his arms wildly, seeming to direct us away from the boat. Jesse stared dumbly at him as I steered the boat through the fast water.

Just as we cleared them, Jesse twisted for a better look. "My God, I think they have a dead body in there. I'm pretty sure they had a body bag in the raft. We should pull over so I can interview them."

Then he added, in a mix of bewilderment and sarcasm, "This is a pretty eventful first hour on the river. First, kids throw rocks at us. Then we have Search and Rescue dredging for a corpse."

I guided the canoe to a landing a hundred yards downriver, and Jesse disappeared up the bank. I waited for him onshore. I couldn't see beginning my long push to the Gulf by eyeing a body bag at close range.

Jesse returned ten minutes later, sounding disappointed. "It wasn't a dead body. Just some National Guard guys trying to pull those underwater posts out of the river. That's not much of a story."

—◆◆◆—

Passing below the two bridges made me nervous; I kept expecting a kid to drop a rock or another heavy object toward the canoe. Workers from the Mexican side were constructing an archway above the sidewalk on the Mexican half of the bridge to provide shade for pedestrians, and one painter nodded as we passed directly beneath him, but he didn't even break his brush-stroking as we called up *"Buenos días."* A Border Patrol officer, sitting in a vehicle parked just below the bridge, didn't look up from his newspaper as the river pushed us silently past.

A mile below the bridges we found several groups of Mexican guys in their twenties huddled under lean-tos on the grassy *vega* near shore. It looked to be a semipermanent camp and reminded me of the hobo jungles I had stayed in during my youth. Jesse wanted to pull over to conduct interviews, and then he didn't want to, and then he did; meanwhile, the strong current swept us far enough downriver that the distance ended his indecision. I eyed every person suspiciously, half expecting to see a volley of rocks or hear the piercing report of a gun fired in our direction. Jesse wanted to photograph the inner tubes and trash abandoned by people crossing from Mexico illegally. As I started moving us nearer, three teenagers appeared onshore, promptly stripped down to their underwear, and entered the river, trailing not far behind us.

We proceeded like that, tacking from one bank to the other so Jesse could photograph or interview, until the winds abruptly shifted and our tail wind became a head wind. Finally, Jesse abandoned his work and helped me paddle downriver. In a few miles we found a stopping place with access to a road. I unloaded the canoe on shore while Jesse put together his bicycle for his shuttle back home. (Because you canoe from a different end of the boat when you're paddling solo, I had to reposition all the gear.) Two Border Patrol officers arrived to check us out. They took one glance at the canoe and the two of us and disappeared. Jesse followed them out to the road, and I was left on my own to face the crowded river below.

Laredo to Falcon Dam

Feb. 12–16

About five miles south of Laredo's city limit sits the riverside *colonia* of El Cenizo, Texas. El Cenizo gained national attention in 1999, when its city council voted to conduct town meetings only in Spanish, and also approved a measure making it illegal for any town official to report an illegal immigrant to the Border Patrol. Predictably, patriots and supporters of legislation for an "English only" U.S. rallied against the "un-American" statute. Call-in radio talk shows nationwide bristled with the indignant protests of Americans who believed El Cenizo's actions were tantamount to treason. Op-ed columns in even the most liberal of media railed against the perceived arrogance of this small, impoverished, and under-serviced community.

Many of El Cenizo's 8,000 residents are in the U.S. illegally, but they were dumbfounded by the intensity of the protests. Illegal immigration was so much a part of the fabric of the town that anti–Border Patrol sentiment was keen. People complained that B. P. agents routinely stopped pedestrians in the dusty streets and demanded identification. Since nearly all of the town's residents were first-language Spanish and many did not speak or understand English, the council concluded it was in the best interest of the townspeople to conduct official business in the language that its citizens understood. And since many residents experienced what they perceived as undue harassment from the B. P., the council decided to give them the limited protection it could by prohibiting town officials from reporting illegal residents.

The uproar over the city council's actions was short-lived, and after El Cenizo's fifteen minutes of fame, life in the riverside community settled back into its impoverishment, ignored by all levels of government except the Border Patrol.

As I approached this disadvantaged town on the river, an hour or two after parting from Jesse, I noticed a sudden increase in the number of people crossing the river on inner tubes, or on what I came to think of as "bowtie tubes"—the destitute man's version of the comparatively upscale inner tube. People would fill two plastic trash sacks with air, knot their ends shut to trap the air, then twist the two tied ends together, forming a primitive flotation device that served to get them across the swift currents of the Rio Grande. I saw these bowtie tubes everywhere—some abandoned on shore, others left to float in the river, still others carrying Mexican people not far from the bow of my canoe.

Between the city limits of Laredo and Rio Bravo, which lies a couple of miles downriver from El Cenizo, I saw more people crossing illegally than in the whole rest of my trip. Group after group happily dogpaddled across the river, clinging to their bowtie tubes. One group of twenty-five landed immediately below El Cenizo, and as the four who were *coyotes* collected the tubes, the other twenty-one dashed up the bank toward town, most of them dressed only in underwear. I got the idea that the standoff between the Border Patrol and El Cenizo as a result of the 1999 ordinance had ended and that El Cenizo had won. Yet, given the sheer number of people crossing, I wondered how sweet a victory it could have been. Surely, the already overstretched network of city services couldn't easily accommodate such an influx of immigrants.

Once I passed Rio Bravo, the traffic abruptly ended, and for the next three weeks, as I canoed nearly three hundred fifty miles, I saw exactly fourteen more people crossing the river. If you were evaluating the Border Patrol's effectiveness along the length of the Texas-Mexico border, you might conclude that the Laredo sector is either grossly understaffed or woefully inattentive to the river traffic.

—◆◆◆—

By midafternoon the sun broke through for the first time in weeks, and immediately the river smelled of spring. The cold dissipated, and thousands of birds emerged from their shelters. Scavengers like grackles and ravens squawked noisily as I paddled beneath them. Blue herons hunched on the shoreline. Bees buzzed drunkenly around the canoe. Bathed in sunshine, the river offered a different world from the one I had become accustomed to. Amid all this renewed life, I felt lazy.

The following day offered a solar blast from the minute the sun rose, and Mexicans flocked to the river to fish, drink beer, swim, and do their laundry. I passed one beach where seemingly an entire village lazed on the riverbanks, while below them, a half dozen shirtless men fished the rapids with nets. After another bend in the river, I saw dark-skinned young men lounging in the shade on the Texas side, and I called to them in English, "Can you tell me how far to San Ygnacio?"

One of them leaped to his feet and, pointing downriver, answered in Spanish, "San Ygnacio isn't far, maybe a mile more. It's just over there." I found his estimation off by a factor of ten.

The river dropped through numerous ledge rapids, none of them difficult for the canoe to navigate, and each followed the same pattern: a ledge of submerged rock would extend most of the way out from one bank or the other, forcing the river to drop through a narrow opening, below which the current erupted into large standing waves, some three feet high, that I found easy to elude. Although there were few visible dwellings or villages, I saw people often, and the traffic on Highway 83, which runs parallel to the river, further served to remind me how different the river environment below Laredo is from that above it.

Late in the afternoon, I reached San Ygnacio. My plan was to walk directly up to Sue's impressive house high up the bank, but as I started up the narrow path, I met a man leading a small group of birders. I later learned they were paying him five dollars a head to walk the very path I was climbing.

"I came in by canoe. Is it okay if I camp down at the river?" I asked him.

"That will be ten dollars." He directed me to a landing a hundred yards further downriver, where I found a group of two dozen birders huddled near a primitive birding platform that the guide had been in the process of constructing. As I unloaded my canoe, the guide said, "All these people are here to see a roadside hawk that comes every evening at 6:30. Where are you coming from?"

"El Paso."

"El Paso, Texas?"

"Yes sir."

"That's a long way. Anything happen yet?"

"Not much. But I can tell you one thing. You're the first person to charge me for sleeping on the ground next to the river."

"Well, you'll get to see the hawk."

The birders scarcely noted my presence, and when their guide, who seemed more eager to sell the presence of the hawk than see it, informed them I had canoed all the way from El Paso, they smiled politely but turned their attention back where the hawk was supposed to appear. I was grateful to be upstaged by an absent raptor.

◆◆◆

It was wonderful to see Sue, my close friend and colleague at school, and she had prepared a fine supper for us. When I told her I had decided to camp at the river's edge rather than carrying the canoe and all my gear up the long path, and that I had already paid the birding guide, she said, "I was hoping you would have told that Joel Ruiz to go fuck himself."

-◆-◆-

Ever since Hayesy and I had battled the winds of Amistad Lake, I had been apprehensive about canoeing Falcon Lake, the second of the two large lakes created by dams on the Rio Grande and about twelve percent smaller than Amistad, assuming both lakes were filled to conservation level. The ten-year drought that plagued the Southwest before 2004 had hit Falcon particularly hard, and growths of willow, ash, and elm had crowded in on its receding shores, but by now Falcon was closer to conservation level than it had been in nearly ten years.

The lake begins at San Ygnacio, where the current in the Rio Grande backs up, offering, on windless days, a glassy surface of water interrupted only by the traffic of powerboats. For the fifteen miles between San Ygnacio and Zapata, the lake is contained in a riverlike channel about sixty yards wide, but as I discovered a few miles below San Ygnacio, this channel is deceptive. Much of it consists of tightly spaced willow trunks and limbs that are now partially underwater. If you want to land your boat, you have to navigate through this bayou-like thicket, sometimes for distances approaching a mile. As I neared Zapata and had to deal with the wakes of powerboats, I realized that capsizing in the wide lane defined on either side by this drought-born tree growth would almost certainly mean losing the canoe and most of my gear.

The tree thicket bordering the channel presented two more pressing problems. First, I couldn't get to shore to pee, and attending to that necessity involved some creative improvisation. I would paddle under an overhanging tree limb at the border, wedge the canoe in a fork in the branches, and go about my business. As long as a power-boat didn't come along, this worked fine. Second, I couldn't get out of the canoe to stretch my legs or eat, so I was in effect imprisoned in the boat for hours until the lake opened up below Zapata. At one stretch, I paddled five hours straight without sighting a landing place;

at times I couldn't even see land through the dense growth of willow. When I passed Zapata, I finally located a rocky beach at the end of a rough ranch road, where I hoped to make camp.

But before I could reach this beach and my first access to shore in fifteen miles, I found myself in a terrifying position, thanks to two hard-charging powerboats. Some Mexican fishermen use an outboard engine far too heavy for their boat, so their stern sits dangerously low while the bow rises high out of the water, tilting the craft at about a ten-degree angle. With the bow riding so high, the pilot cannot see immediately ahead of him, and so a couple of times I came close to being run over, until I learned to stay out of the pilot's blind spot. My long moment of terror now occurred because as one powerboat headed straight for me, a second powerboat came equally fast from behind, cutting off my escape from the oncoming boat. My escape was further blocked by the barrier of willow and ash on the Mexican side of the main channel. If I paddled in there, the dual wakes of the passing boats would surely capsize me and then pound my overturned canoe against the tree trunks.

The boat from behind now passed hard, forcing me to spin the canoe into a rollicking wake and leaving me open for a broadside collision with the boat charging from ahead, which closed rapidly, now fifty yards and approaching. At the last possible second, the driver of the other boat signaled to the man about to broadside me to stop, and with less than thirty yards to spare, the hard-charging boat killed its engine. I was spared.

◆◆◆

From my camp, I had seen how the lake now widened appreciably, and in the main channel I could see buoys that marked the deepest water. Only the first three buoys were visible; the others were too far away. On Amistad the distances between coves had always been relatively short, usually less than a mile, but on Falcon Lake the coves were immense, lakes within a lake. I was soon to learn that I would have to commit myself to between thirty minutes and two hours of hard paddling from point to point—distances that would force me to plan each crossing carefully and would test me in ways in which I'd rather not have been tested.

When I broke camp the next morning, I found the lake dangerously choppy, but I committed to a three-mile crossing, only because I worried that the winds would strengthen later in the day. The wider the lake grew, the worse the waves became, and they were at their worst furthest from shore. The swells heaved my canoe so intensely that I felt borderline queasy. It was little solace that the lake water was rough enough to keep the powerboats docked. When I finally gained the next point, after a harrowing hour, I hurried toward the shore, but had to hop from the canoe in knee-deep water to keep the waves from crashing my boat onto the rocky coastline. I paced along the rock-strewn shore, trying to calm my wildly beating heart, and decided to end my canoeing day after a mere three miles of forward progress.

I found a number of curious sights along the shoreline. Most noticeable were shells that appeared to be from hundreds of lobsters. After long study of these coral-colored remains, I realized that the crustaceans were crawfish. A moment later, I saw an enormous live crawfish studying me from the shallow bottom five feet away. For the next half hour, I searched along the shore for crawfish and found half a dozen, each the size of a small lobster, and all quick to take cover under a rock when I leaned over to photograph them.

I also found a weathered wood carving, apparently from Mexico, lodged between rocks a few feet from shore. It featured what appeared to be an Indian man, clothed only in a skirtlike garment, seated in the lotus position and staring stoically ahead. On his head were two Indian children, one on top of the other, identical twins. I stashed it in the canoe.

After more than an hour of beachcombing, I scouted from the end of the point. There I found that the crossing to the next spit of land looked short—maybe fifteen minutes in the boat. Despite the rolling waves, I launched the canoe. Gaining that point, I gambled and stayed in the boat to cross another narrow cove, then another after it, before the anxiety generated by the waves got the better of me, and I again landed on a rocky shore. From this vantage point I could see that I now had to cross my widest inlet yet, some four to five miles, and the swells were simply too large even to consider such an attempt.

And then, miraculously, the winds died.

-◆◆◆-

Three quarters of the way across one large cove, I neared a powerboat manned by four beer-drinking Mexican-Americans. The pilot of the boat killed the outboard the instant he spotted me, and trawled the boat until we were side by side. Even before they asked for my story, one inebriated man offered me cold water, cold beer, and potato chips. I accepted the water. With the absence of wind, the day had grown hot, and due to the logistical nightmare of trying to pee while crossing wide stretches of lake, I had eased off drinking fluids I knew I needed.

After the men heard an abridged version of my story, the most outgoing and generous of the four treated me like a hero; the other three looked only faintly amused by my story. One grabbed a high-tech bow and arrow and began firing the tethered arrow at fish. I recalled the movie *Deliverance* as his first shot missed its intended target.

These four fishermen hailed from Zapata, Texas, and we soon established that we had friends in common. One man warned me, "The lake is going to get really rough when you get around the next point. It gets really wide there, and it's way too rough for your canoe. Be careful."

Seizing on this moment of concern for my welfare, I asked if they could spare some ice, and they gladly obliged me with enough to chill the beverages in the bottom of my cooler.

Generally, though, powerboaters ignored me, and it was rare to get even a distant wave from them. I didn't care. The further away they stayed from me, the more time I had to react to the wakes of their speeding boats. And I had plenty to worry about navigating from point to point without engaging in conversation. Just reaching each spit of land safely made me a feel that the world was very nearly perfect.

—◆◆◆—

As the fishermen had said, the lake did grow wide here, and when it grew so wide that I could make out little on either shore, I set up camp on a peninsula. A tremendous stretch of water separated me from the next point of land, barely visible across the glassy horizon of the now-placid blue water. I had no map for it, but I expected this crossing would be the longest I'd face, and therefore potentially the most dangerous. Even a hint of wind could send swells rolling across this inlet. Although the lake surface looked impossibly calm, I decided to camp rather than attempt the crossing late in the afternoon. Because I was only marginally hydrated, I figured I'd had enough sun for one day.

But next morning I regretted my decision. Winds blew strong from the southwest, pushing swells into the cove. Right away I saw that I had little chance of making a direct crossing to the next point. Instead, I would have to ride the swells deeper into the cove and then tack out against them, adding miles to my crossing. At first, I thought it wise to stay in camp for an hour or two to see what the wind would do, but then I fell back on a logic that often drove me to risk peril: "It may get a lot worse, so you'd better get moving before it does."

—◆◆◆—

I spent two hours crossing the wide section. Most of the time I was sick with fear. My canoe felt tiny in a sea of water that rolled like an ocean. Land was so distant that I seemed to make no forward progress. I paddled steadily but cautiously, afraid that a more vigorous effort might capsize the boat in the swells.

By midday, I reached the distant point, and once I had rounded it the lake current pushed me in the direction of Falcon Dam. The distance between points narrowed—less than a mile now between each pair—and riding the waves' momentum, I eagerly paddled on. The dam came into view, a brick-sized silhouette at first, growing slowly larger as I passed each point. Meanwhile, the swells increased, and now I was riding the biggest water I had yet encountered on either Amistad or Falcon Lake. Although waves broke over the stern of my canoe, soaking my back, I couldn't resist riding them, since they pushed in the direction I needed to go.

My destination, if I could stay in the canoe long enough, was Falcon State Park, less than a mile before the dam. During my eight-day rest in Laredo, I had driven down there to inquire about getting a ride around the dam because, as at Amistad, the land was fenced off below the dam, and I couldn't carry around it. I had met a kind woman at the park office who'd agreed to drive me to a river access not far below the dam, and she had even led me around the park to familiarize me with it for my subsequent approach in the canoe. I hadn't thought I would have any difficulty locating it from the water.

But now I was quickly running out of lake, and I appeared to be heading on a collision course with the monstrous causeway at the base of the dam. I didn't want to get swept in there, so I angled slightly in toward shore, heading for the last piece of land at the edge of the causeway. Above it, I could see an American flag whipping in the stiff wind. Feeling that my boat and I couldn't withstand any bigger water, I paddled frantically toward shore.

Once safely off the water, I found I had a new problem. A hundred yards up the concrete road leading away from the water was a locked gate and an ominous sign: NO TRESPASSING—UNITED STATES GOVERNMENT PROPERTY. On the other side of the locked gate, the blacktop led past nondescript buildings that reminded me of officers' housing on a military base. From this higher vantage point, I looked toward the lake, hoping to see some alternative possibility, but the wild waters offered me little chance of escape.

Just then a man emerged from the building directly below the flag, and I waved. He looked at me quizzically for a moment, then walked to an SUV and drove it down to meet me at the gate. "What happened?" he said.

This middle-aged Hispanic man, dressed in jeans and a western shirt, seemed so dour that I half-expected him to tell me to turn around and deal with the lake.

"The lake was so rough that I missed the boat ramp for the campground."

"Well, we'll just have to get you out of here. I'm surprised you made it down this far."

Talk about surprised. His helpfulness floored me. He said he'd take me to the park and help me find someone who'd follow us back to get my canoe. He said, "I saw you a couple of days ago up near Zapata. I was out fishing when I saw you, and I wondered what the hell you were doing then. If I had known you planned on coming this far, I would have talked you out of it."

◆◆◆

Fran Bartle, the park employee who'd helped me earlier, had also introduced me to a retired couple who spent the winter season as park volunteer guest hosts. Now I asked to be driven to Ed and Rosalie's.

The man who drove me to the campground worked for the International Boundary and Water Commission. He approached the task of helping me with the cool efficiency of a guy who knew he was bending government regulations in doing so, but also knew that the best way to make trouble disappear was to attend to it himself. I introduced him to Ed; then Ed and I followed him back to the IBWC headquarters, where he unlocked the gate above my canoe so that we could drive down to the lakeshore.

The IBWC guy looked relieved when he saw how speedily I worked to load my gear and canoe into the back of Ed's truck. He smiled for the first time when we were about to drive away, as if to say, "Man, am I glad you didn't turn this into the bureaucratic nightmare I thought you might."

Back at the state park, I was assigned a campsite in the primitive camping area near the lakeshore. The sites on either side were occupied, and at once I felt uncomfortable, as if I were intruding on the other campers' privacy. I walked to the shower building to shower and shave, and I lingered a long time for no other reason than that I dreaded returning to my own campsite. To get away from my neighbors, I loaded some food in the cooler, grabbed my journal, some beer, and flashlights, and went to a dense thicket of *huisache* separating the lakeshore from the campground. If I'd thought I could have gotten away with it, I would have taken the tent down there as well and set it up in the thick undercover of the thorny branches. I spent the remainder of the evening and half of the night sitting out of view on my cooler, writing a river report to send to Louis. I don't think I've ever felt so out of place as I did in that campground.

Paranoia

Feb. 17–19

When I returned to my campsite late that night, I found a handwritten note taped to my tent. In beautiful, flowing cursive, Fran Bartle welcomed me to the state park, congratulated me on having made it across the forty miles of lake, and said she looked forward to ferrying me to the bottom of the dam the following morning.

The next morning at eight o'clock I found Fran in her travel trailer, eating breakfast. She invited me inside to talk about our schedule and told me a little about herself. A retired schoolteacher and an accomplished birder, she had set up the birding program at Falcon State Park a couple of years earlier and now winters there. Like Ed and Rosalie, she's served as a guest host, leading birding tours in the park as well as coordinating a birding program in Bentsen Rio Grande State Park halfway between Falcon Dam and the Gulf. Fran spoke with the twang of her native East Texas, and described herself as "a gypsy" whose great passions are birding and traveling. I found her pretty, charming, and charismatic.

We agreed to rendezvous at ten o'clock for our drive to the river access below the dam. I made a long circling walk of the park and then walked back to my campsite. Moments later the couple from the next campsite walked over to chat; Fran had told them about my trip when she came by to leave me the note the night before. They were Swiss and curious to hear of my adventures. As we talked, another woman appeared, and she too was European. I was struck by how much more curious these three Europeans were about my experiences than were even some of my best friends. We talked for an hour, until Fran arrived—along with the rain. Fran offered to return once the rain quit, if I preferred.

"If I let the rain stop me, I'd still be camped in Eagle Pass."

In the tiny hamlet of Falcon Heights near the dam, we stopped at the post office so I could mail my river report. Inside we found the sharp-talking postmistress, a woman about age sixty, who regaled me with one horror story after another about murder along the section of river I was about to travel. She seemed to find humor in most of her tales, as if the only way to cope with the fearful events along the border was to laugh at them.

I asked if I should drop my letter into the mail slot, and she said, "Oh no, honey, if you do that I'll have to bend over and pick it up, and although the view you're seeing of me right now may not be all that pretty, you surely don't want to see that side of me."

Fran seemed embarrassed.

Back in Fran's Ford 350 diesel, we turned off on a narrow, winding road that descended toward the river. She told me about friends who live along the river a couple of miles below the access and whose home was in the middle of a gun battle between shooters on both sides of the river. Bullets pierced their kitchen walls. When they called the sheriff, he refused to come to investigate. The next morning they found a trail of dried blood leading to the water. One of the victims had apparently been dragged there and dumped in the current, where, presumably, he did what I was about to do—float in the direction of

Roma, Texas, and its sister city, Miguel Alemán, in the state of Tamaulipas. I sensed Fran's anxiety about my safety on the river.

After unloading my canoe and gear, I offered to pay Fran for her trouble, but she said she couldn't take any money; she would, however, accept a donation to the park birding program, since the state didn't provide funds for bird food. Fran lingered as I loaded the boat. With a light rain falling, I wasn't nearly as eager to be on the river as I had expected to be. Plus, Fran was delightful company.

"How far do you think you'll go today?" she asked.

"I'll find an island camp somewhere before Roma."

"It feels strange to just leave you here, almost like I'm abandoning you."

"Oh, I'll be fine. It will be fun."

"There have been so many bad things happening on the river lately that it's hard to think of what you're doing as fun. I'm going to be worrying about you."

"The nice people like you far outnumber the bad ones. Trust me, Fran."

I saw sadness in her eyes, and I sensed again, more strongly, that she didn't feel hopeful about my chances on the river.

——◆◆◆——

Starr County, Texas, is often reported to be the poorest county in Texas, the poorest along the entire border, and the poorest in the United States. It's also notorious for drug smuggling and a corrupt enforcement and judicial system. A number of high-profile cases involving Starr County officials have made national headlines in recent years. Jesse Katz, in a brilliantly written exposé of Starr County for the *Los Angeles Times* in 1999, wrote: "It has been portrayed, most often, as alien and irredeemable: the narco-capital of the U.S.-Mexico border, Texas's Little Colombia, a danger zone that only Rambo would love."

Starr County's poverty statistics don't tell the whole story. Certainly wages are depressed and unemployment is high, but as with so many communities along the border, there's a thriving underground economy based on smuggling—primarily drugs, but also people. And its principal towns, Roma and Rio Grande City, appear to be at least as well off as most small cities on the border, and better than many. There's money there; it's not money generated from industry or tourism. In fact, the biggest employer in Starr County, as Katz noted in his article, is the county itself.

Well aware of Starr County's reputation as a violent drug-smuggling corridor, I felt intimidated to be passing through the city of Miguel Alemán, redoubt of the Zetas—gangs of deserters from the Mexican Army who made their livings by kidnapping, murder for hire, torture, and drug smuggling. Their reputation for barbarism had far surpassed the gruesome standards to which border residents had long since grown inured, and no one felt safe treading in their territory. The postmistress in Falcon Heights had said, "You don't even go there to fill a prescription or eat lunch in broad daylight."

The Zetas, everyone warned, represented a new breed of evil that honored none of the codes of old-time *narco-traficantes.*

For days I had nightmares about people being fed to lions.

—◆◆◆—

Fran stayed on shore, waving good-bye until I had passed out of sight. For a half mile or so, I struggled to adapt to the new river, now a much smaller one than I had left on the other side of the lake. As in the area below Amistad Dam, the water ran clear, and I could see the sandy bottom and the darting fish—mostly carp and bass, and an occasional gar. For a short distance, bald cypress trees lined the shores, their drooping branches and pinnate leaves forming a feathery canopy. The river ran narrow, and the banks were steep. Above the cypress, Rio Grande ash, willows, sugar hackberry, and elm concealed the fact that I was boating through an arid stretch of countryside called the Wild Horse Desert.

I had a claustrophobic, uneasy feeling as I navigated through the small canyon. I was easily startled by birds, and later by a raccoon. I passed a few homes, but I saw no people on the Texas side. On the Mexican side, I passed an empty pickup truck parked in a clearing just above the river, and a few hundred yards later, I saw two men armed with machetes walking near shore. Fighting my nerves, I angled the canoe towards them. One of them approached the bank.

"Good afternoon," the bearded man said warmly in Spanish. "Welcome to my ranch. Where are you going today?"

"I'm on a long trip. I started in Juárez, Chihuahua, and I'm going all the way to the Gulf."

"Tell me," he said, "How have we Mexicans been treating you so far?"

"Exceptionally well. Your people have been very helpful, very kind."

"Good. That makes me proud of my country. But tell me, my friend, if I made the same long trip you are making, how do you think your people would treat me?"

"Probably like a bunch of *chilangos.*"

"That bad? Well, I would say you're lucky to have us good Mexicans living near the river."

- - -

Before Roma, El Álamo River enters from the Mexican side, and at its confluence with the Rio Grande, the latter drops swiftly around three islands. Although I had hours of daylight remaining, I set up camp on the largest of these, a sandy slice of land only six feet high, thirty feet wide, and eighty feet long. Completely barren of trees, the island offered no cover. I had to canoe downriver a hundred yards to saw firewood from a fallen mesquite tree lying on the steep Texas-side bank.

I had a long talk with myself as rain pelted the hood of my rain jacket and the wind bent my tent. I decided I needed to check my festering paranoia not only about the Zetas but about the entire river from here to the Gulf before it turned the final weeks of my trip into a sustained nightmare. I called up each of the worst-case scenarios and, one by one, dismissed them as being highly unlikely to occur. If I encountered drug smugglers, I would simply talk to them amicably. If a gang of toughs wanted to rough me up, I would joke to them that beating up a forty-eight-year-old man wouldn't offer much sport. If a suspicious Texas landowner thrust a rifle in my face, I would simply assure him I intended no harm. It would be easy, I thought to myself. I would just canoe right to the end, drinking my beer, eating my meals, building my fires, and piloting my canoe. Any Boy Scout could do it.

━━●●●━

The coyotes were raucous all night, and they woke me often. I lay in the tent, listening to the rain beat against the roof, ears pricked up. At times the noise of the current played tricks on me, and I imagined hearing raccoons or smugglers swimming across the narrow channel to raid my camp. Once I awoke with a start, wildly paranoid: all the rain would flood the river, sweep my canoe away, and strand me on a quickly disappearing island. I peered outside, saw the river hadn't risen an inch, threw another log on the dwindling campfire, and fell back asleep.

In the morning, a shroud of fog clung to the surface of El Álamo River, the rain now a fine mist. I wanted to get an early start so I could get well past Miguel Alemán in time to scout my next camp well before dark. As I folded my tent, a voice not ten feet away startled me.

In the narrow channel between my island and the Texas side, a large man in a flatboat stared at me. On his head, he had wrapped a woman's clear plastic shower cap, beneath which I glimpsed his tightly curled salt-and-pepper hair. A freshly lit cigarette hung from the corner of his mouth. He paddled his boat with an undersized oar.

"You're camping?" he asked in Spanish.

"And you?" I said, as the swift current carried him below me.

"I'm fishing. I have some lines in the water right here." A moment later, his dog came swimming after the boat.

The man kept turning back, watching me. He checked two lines tied to overhanging branches on the Texas bank and then crossed the river to check two more on the Mexican bank. None yielded any fish. Then he tried to move his boat upriver along the Mexican shore, but he wasn't proficient enough with the paddle to make any progress.

Tentatively, he lowered one leg into the water, while his dog swam to shore and shook itself dry, waiting for its master to line the boat along the bank. This big man seemed intimidated by the river, and I sensed he was new to this routine. I could also tell that my presence unnerved him. Hoping to reassure him, I asked, "Did you catch anything?"

"Not yet, but I have more lines up El Álamo. And you? Are you fishing?"

"Not this morning. I don't want to take your fish."

"Oh, there's plenty of fish for both of us," he said. "Where are you from?"

"Laredo, Texas—rather, that's where I live. I've come all the way from Juárez, Chihuahua. Fifty-something days already since I left there."

"I'm from Mier, and I'm fishing, nothing more," he said, sounding paranoid.

I had the sinking feeling he neither trusted me nor believed a word I said. He pulled his boat to calm water, climbed back in it, and paddled up the mouth of the other river, turning every few paddle strokes, looking as if he wished I would leave.

—◆◆◆—

An hour below that island camp, I passed the village of La Guerra, perched above the river on the Mexican side. I saw three men working to grade the slope to the water. One man drove a bulldozer, while the others conferred over a set of blueprints. I waved to the bulldozer operator, but he merely nodded his head. The steep cliff was littered with trash, and ravens and pigs picked through the rubble. At the last house of maybe a dozen visible from the river, a young man noticed me paddling far below, and when I waved up to him, he sprinted to the edge of the cliff and shouted in Spanish, "Go for it!"

The weather turned cold and raw just as I neared the bridge at Roma. Here the river divides around a high, wooded island. I took the narrow Texas-side channel, an eerie route under a canopy of overhanging ash branches. At the end of it, a sign warned boaters to steer clear of the intake pipes for the Roma Water Plant, but because the channel was so narrow I had to canoe right over them.

Miguel Alemán sits on the river's edge, directly across from Roma, offering the best access of any Mexican town on the entire river. I could see a small store only a hundred yards from the river. I needed supplies, but my paranoia got the better of me. I imagined thieves carting away my gear as I piled tortillas onto the shop counter. As soon as I had moved onward, I regretted my decision, and spent much of the next hour trying to find a place on the American side from which I could walk into Roma.

Despite its small size, Roma has more access to the river than Laredo, Eagle Pass, and Del Rio combined, and I landed briefly at several places, hoping to scout a way into town. At one landing, I found a camp equipped with two barbecue pits, tables, and folding chairs. This looked encouraging until I saw and heard dogs barking up ahead, and I retreated. Another river bend later, I docked again and pursued a ranch road for almost half a mile before turning back. A hundred yards later, I docked a third time at yet another rutted road reaching the river, only to realize when I topped the embankment that it connected with the same road I had just abandoned upstream.

I found a young Mexican man fishing in the rain below this third stop, and he directed me to a store downriver at Rancho Los Angeles. After a couple of stops on the Mexican side, I thought I'd located this tiny village, but again I weighed the possibility of a theft against the payoff of getting food, and I opted to continue downriver. What had become of my resolution to check my fear? I wondered.

Rain fell, and by late afternoon I was saturated and dangerously cold, but I couldn't find an island on which to camp. Every turn opened into yet another long straightaway thickly lined on both banks. At the end of one long straightaway, when the river abruptly squeezed into a swift drop, I heard the telltale roar of a rapid just ahead.

The river narrowed from seventy yards to twenty as the current shot through a nasty drop with undercut ledges, creating a mess of crosscurrents. I braced my paddle, trying to keep the boat upright as the competing waves surged under me. At the bottom of the drop, a string of standing whitecaps defined the tight channel, and I struggled toward the edge of the restricted course. My canoe leaped into the air and then smashed hard into the first of the waves, teetering for an interminable moment on the verge of capsizing. A surge of water righted me, and I sliced into another wave. Ahead I heard a second roar, signaling the next of the rapids. At the end of the wave train, I cut hard for the Mexican shore and beached the boat under an awning of Rio Grande elm. The bank rose steeply behind it, and my beach was scarcely above the water line, but I felt so chilled that I couldn't face the prospect of more rapids, so I set up camp, while across the constricted channel that separated me from Texas, a raccoon family eyed me hopefully. Above them, beside a ramshackle cinder-block dwelling on the precipice, lay many months' worth of trash half-burying two '50s-model Ford cars.

—◆◆◆—

While the raccoons puzzled over me, I scaled the embankment above my camp and extricated a half dozen thin trunks of elm from a webbing of vines that apparently had choked them to death the summer before. A deliberate process of feeding wet twigs to a limp flame rewarded me with a small fire base that I then fed with larger kindling for another fifteen minutes, encouraging the fire with hopeful words and extravagant compliments until I'd nursed it to a steady burn capable of digesting the larger elm boles. Meanwhile, the raccoons poked through the high grass on the opposite bank, unmoved by the threats I shouted at them.

Once when Hayesy and I had camped in the Lower Canyons, we played tag with a persistent raccoon drawn by the aroma of our supper cooking in the fire. Every time we tried to run it off, it retreated to its den in the river cane only long enough for us to sit down; then, moments later, it reappeared, eyeing our stewpot hungrily. As I vented aloud about what a nuisance this critter could be while we tried to sleep, Hayesy said, "How about if we get him drunk? Maybe he'll pass out and leave us alone."

We spooned out a bowlful of camp stew, then added three shots of top-shelf tequila. I dug a bowl-sized hole at the edge of camp and snuggled our bait into it. We watched the raccoon devour the meal, hoping it would soon stagger back to its lair, but twenty minutes later it just licked the empty bowl and stared at us. "I think he liked it," Hayesy said.

We repeated the exercise, this time adding only two shots of tequila to the stew, and the raccoon ate as if ravenous. This time it walked off in the direction of the river cane, sated but walking a very straight line. We raccoon-proofed the camp just in case, stacking large stones on top of the food box. Next morning I found the tequila bottle lying on its side and raccoon prints circling it. It was clear from the tracks that the wily critter had spun the bottle numerous times, trying to have a nightcap.

So tonight, when darkness descended and the raccoons became really loud, I imagined them bickering over how best to assail my food supply. Then came the howl of coyotes, and I hoped they'd chase off the raccoons, but no such luck. As the rain fell, I began the long job of raccoon-proofing my camp. I thought that if I'd brought tequila along on this trip, I sure wouldn't be sharing with raccoons.

During the night the rain quit and the raccoons stayed away—perhaps intimidated by the coyotes, which barked and yipped until dawn. I crept outside the tent several times to check the water level; content that I wasn't going to be flooded out of my already saturated camp, I drifted back to sleep until the coyotes woke me again.

I calculated I was about three hours from Rio Grande City, the second of the two significant towns in otherwise sparsely populated Starr County, and I vowed to make a more determined effort to get ashore there to restock provisions. I had exhausted my beer supply and had also run out of tortillas and fruit juice, two staples that formed a significant part of my daily diet.

The next rapid ran much like the first one the day before—an angry push of constricted water careening off barely submerged ledges—but fresh from a night's rest, I had better command of the boat and sailed through easily.

Later in the morning, the sun hinted at pushing through the thick haze, and suddenly the morning became heavy and humid, far warmer than the previous day. As I approached Rio Grande City, I encountered a group of Mexicans swimming the river on inner tubes, and they reached the Texas shore just as I passed them. But one guy, muscular and tattooed, approached me as I neared him. I asked him in Spanish how far to the bridge, and he replied in heavily accented English, "It's two or three blocks, man."

"Two or three blocks" translated to a half mile. As I entered the straightaway leading to Rio Grande City, I saw three men clearing brush high up the embankment. I landed at a public access where a dirt road drops down a steep grade behind the high school football field. Though I was determined to walk into town, I had reservations about leaving my canoe unattended, so I first walked up to where the three men were working. When I approached, one broke from the group and came to greet me, introducing himself as Dan Treviño, a Rio Grande native. He extended his hand and called over his two friends, Tom Patterson, a biology instructor at the local branch of South Texas Community College, and Carlos Lara, an older man, who gazed at me with sad, penetrating eyes. They were clearing brush as a first step toward building a birding platform, but were eager to hear how far I had come on the river. "We don't see many canoes down here," Dan said.

Dan and Tom were river enthusiasts, part of a tiny but vvvgrowing force of intellectuals and environmentalists attempting to draw attention to the plight of the Rio Grande, challenging long-ingrained abuses of the river, studying habitat and monitoring pollution. They were men like Laredo's Tom Miller, who viewed the river not as a sordid dividing line between two disparate worlds but as a living force worth preserving, exploring, and celebrating. When I told them about being pelted with rocks in Laredo the week before, Dan warned, "Watch out when you pass below our bridge. The last time I canoed down there, Mexican kids threw rocks at me from the bridge, and one split my head open. That's a bad way to begin a canoe trip."

Tom agreed to watch my boat while Dan and Carlos dropped me off at the supermarket a half mile away. I then carried six plastic sacks weighted down with a week's worth of provisions back to the river, where I found Tom still hacking away at the thick growth of brush. He talked about his frustrations in the struggle to educate the locals about the importance of preserving the river.

"We're making some progress. Just little things so far. But that's all we can do, go step by step. It's going to take a long time."

"Seems to me that most people on the border don't care much about the river," I said.

"They just don't care about much of anything."

Before I set off I had an exchange with a corpulent teenager fishing for white bass just before the bridge.

"Where are you going with all that stuff?" he asked

"All the way to the Gulf," I said.

He raised his eyebrows, let out a low whistle, and said with a straight face, "You're probably not going to make it there today."

Symbols of Power

Feb. 19–23

Leaving Rio Grande City, the river runs wide and slow, and I had a sinking feeling that I had two hundred thirty-six miles of dead water ahead of me. River cane lined the Texas bank, and numerous beaver chutes led down the slick embankment from dens hidden in the cane. Despite the dead-water feeling, I was relieved to have Rio Grande City behind me, and I appreciated that the next seventy-five miles to Reynosa would offer a tranquil stretch of canoeing. With fresh supplies, including cold beer, and improved weather, I felt no hurry, and the river seemed in no hurry to carry me.

After three miles of calm paddling, I heard the dull roar of a rapid around a bend, but I thought little of it except to feel relief that the river might finally narrow and give me more current. I saw a ledge extending from the Mexican shore and, reasoning that it would open near the Texas shore, I cut hard to the left, just as the current grew swift and pulled me around the blind turn. Now I saw that the river dropped precipitously over a ledge, and awaiting me at the bottom were large cross-checking waves capable of swamping the canoe. After the drop I tried to skirt them, but the force of the river pushed me directly into the maelstrom. I crested the first wave precariously and prepared to be slammed by the second, when I noticed a terrifying sight directly below: not thirty feet away, the river dropped yet again, this time by six feet or more, and a large boulder divided the narrow channel. The waves led directly into the boulder.

I saw that my only escape lay on the right side of the boulder; to the left of it, the river dropped into a powerful eddy that swirled in a tight space between the bottom of the falls and the shoreline. A large snag stood in the river directly below the boulder. To its left was the eddy; to its right, the current escaped downriver along the Texas bank. If I could get to the right of the boulder, I'd avoid both the eddy and the snag. I ruddered hard to go right, but the waves were pushing me toward an ugly collision with the boulder. At the last second, inches away from slamming the boulder, I steered hard left and barely grazed the left side of the rock. The river poured me over the steep vertical drop into the eddy, swamping the canoe as I hit the bottom of the falls.

Now I was caught in the tight swirl, and with my canoe filled with water, I struggled to keep it from capsizing as the eddy fed the boat back to the base of the falls. I was in deep trouble. I had to escape from this powerful eddy with the canoe upright, but how? The snag blocked my route to safer water.

Between the boulder and the snag was a narrow lane that offered my only chance for escape; however, the current dropping around the boulder plowed directly into the snag. I tried to hit this lane, but the surge of water nearly pinned the boat against the snag, and I had to steer back into the eddy to avoid capsizing.

It fed me around its tight circle a second time, but now, as I came to the lane between the boulder and the snag, I paddled with all my power, and the canoe nearly tipped as I dug deep into the current. I ruddered hard against the current, and the canoe barely cleared the snag.

I had escaped.

━◆◆◆━

On the following day, for the first time all trip, it was hot. The ninety-degree heat made me lazy and eager for a bath. All day I looked for an island camp where I could wash my clothes and let them dry in the sun. All day I rounded bends in the river only to find another long stretch of river with no islands in sight. About midafternoon, after passing a group of Mexican boys tubing in the river, I pulled in to saw firewood, certain that I would find my camp around the next bend.

Nothing. As the sun sank lower, I realized I wouldn't be doing laundry this day.

In this stretch, Mexicans fished, picnicked, and drank beer. One proud teenager standing on the bank with two pretty girls, still dressed in their church dresses, said I was passing Valadeces, but I didn't know the town. I asked which town I would arrive at next, and one of the girls answered, "Díaz Ordaz." That town was on Jack Richardson's list, but I couldn't determine how far ahead it might be. I pushed on, now eager to find any camp at all.

From a ranch just above the river, I heard a series of twenty or so gunshots, and I imagined a grisly murder scene with Zetas shooting people at close range. I paddled swiftly as I passed, but not a person was in sight.

A little while later I found a middle-aged man perched about ten feet above the river on the Texas side. I greeted him in English, and asked if he could tell me how far it was to Los Ebanos, a small village on the Texas side, where a hand-drawn ferry still operated. He replied in a mix of languages, "*No está lejos. No te falta mucho, no más* three or four miles."

Not far below him, I saw a U.S. Parks and Wildlife Department sign, affixed atop a pole twenty feet above the Texas shore, and I landed to investigate. The sign marked a National Wildlife Refuge, but except for the name of the government agency, the rest of the sign was written in Spanish. One line caught my attention: "*Se prohibe la entrada sin autorización*" (Unauthorized entry is prohibited). At the base of the sign, I saw several small piles of clothing left by undocumented workers who had swum the river and walked the wildlife refuge.

And wildlife was seemingly everywhere except the refuge. I saw my first armadillo of the trip, three javelinas, a coyote, wild turkeys, and more beavers than I could count.

Finally, with little daylight remaining, I found camp on a sloping Texas-side beach, and I slept that night at an uncomfortable downhill angle.

--◆◆◆--

A second warm, sunny day greeted me in camp the following morning, and I decided to do laundry in the river, shave, and shampoo my hair. I expected to go into the village of Los Ebanos not far away, and that meant having to clear American customs. I was bent over a saucepan of warm water, ladling it out with my coffee mug to rinse the shampoo from my hair, when I heard a gleeful voice call out, "Good morneeeng, sir!"

There in the river, clinging to a high stack of inner tubes, floated a young man with a wide, infectious grin.

"Well, I finally see someone is smart enough to collect those damn things," I said as he floated close and I counted about twelve inner tubes. "I've been on this river for two months wondering why no one was clever enough to scavenge them."

"Man, they're like gold!" he grinned, and then the river swept him out of sight.

Why had no one run scavenging operations on the river? I wondered. Besides thousands of inner tubes, the banks were littered with all manner of clothes–jackets, footwear, underwear, and thousands of T-shirts. Later on I would see dozens of large beer coolers floating in the current, each worth twenty dollars or more.

I didn't break camp until late morning, and Los Ebanos turned out to be a lot further than I expected. I paddled turn after turn, thinking I would find it around the next bend. After about an hour and a half, I was startled by the noise of fast-approaching motors; I looked to the sky, expecting to see crop-dusting planes. But seconds later, two powerboats sped around the bend downriver, approaching me at a terrific speed. About to be blasted with the most threatening double wake I had ever experienced, I waved my paddle wildly to alert them to my presence.

When they cut their engines, I saw that the boats belonged to the Border Patrol, and each was manned by two agents in bulletproof vests, all four of them with automatic rifles positioned for use. I paddled toward the lead boat, but the Hispanic agent on the bow did not encourage me to come any nearer.

"What's going on out here?" he barked.

The other three agents eyed the Mexican embankment as if they expected to be sprayed by gunfire. I tried to stop the canoe's forward momentum.

"Are you carrying any weapons?"

"No, I'm just canoeing."

The other agent on the lead boat, looking like one of those handsome young actors in *telenovelas,* said, "How far up did you start?"

"You mean this morning, sir?"

"You were on the river last night? Are you crazy?"

"Yes to the first question, and it depends who you ask on the second."

Two young Anglo agents in the second boat eyed me grimly, and all four of them kept both hands on their automatic rifles.

"Wait a minute, damn it. Are saying you camped on the river last night?"

"Yes, sir. And the night before that and a lot of nights before that."

"What the hell! You *are* crazy! Where are you going?"

"To the Gulf of Mexico."

"In that thing?" He pointed to my canoe.

"That's the plan."

"We're looking for a dead body that's supposed to be in the river a couple miles up from here," he said.

They all relaxed, and one guy even let a hand drop from the trigger of his weapon.

"You're probably referring to the guy floating down the river collecting inner tubes. If you were far away you might mistake him for a corpse."

I described for them my encounter with the grinning scavenger and assured them that he had to be the source of the report. Inner tubes nearly always go across the river, not down it; it would have been easy to mistake that young man for a dead body.

The agents seemed to trust my logic enough to end their patrol, and we spent a few pleasant minutes talking about my trip. Even as some of my answers to their questions drew smiles and soft laughs, I watched them scan the Mexican embankment while fingering their weapons. Clearly, I wasn't the only one on the river who worried about the Zetas.

<hr />

As the agents had assured me, I found the antiquated Los Ebanos ferry just around the next bend in the river. More of a barge than a ferry, it is a flat platform that holds three cars. A crew of five Mexicans pulls the ferry across a narrow part of the river with a cable—or, as the Border Patrol called it, *un chilán* ("a helper"). Hand over hand, they inch the ferry toward either shore in about five minutes. At the crossing, the river is only about three times wider than the ferry is long, so the course is short.

This unique ferry attracts a large number of tourists in the winter months, when so-called "winter Texans"—"snowbirds" from northern states who winter in the Rio Grande Valley—descend upon the ferry landing to snap photographs. My arrival there coincided with the ferry's arrival, and I found myself the subject of many photographs taken by a throng of geriatrics. The workers lowered the ramp, the three vehicles inched off the ferry, and all five workers came over to ask me numerous questions (in Spanish) about my trip. Simultaneously, the most outgoing of the winter Texans asked some of the same questions in English. For a few brief minutes, I upstaged even the venerable old ferry.

I dragged the canoe out of the water, and began walking up

the road toward Customs just as two Customs agents walked down toward me. When we met halfway, the senior of the two asked for my driver's license and then said dryly, "Let's go have a look at your canoe. Do you have a weapon?"

"No, sir," I said.

The winter Texans ogling the ferry got a bonus that afternoon, as I unloaded the boat and opened my boxes and dry bags, one at a time, as the senior agent ordered me to do. About halfway through, he said he'd seen enough; I was cleared for entry into the United States. When I walked up to Customs, two young agents greeted me warmly there, and the two agents who had searched my belongings became less officious.

"We have one big question for you," the lone female of the four said. "Why on earth are you doing this trip?"

"So I can give you all something to do," I said, and they all laughed. "But seriously, I'm thinking of writing a book. "

"You're not scared of what's going on in Mexico?" she asked. "I mean, they're killing people like crazy along this river. You're not going to write much of a book if you're dead."

<hr />

The store in Los Ebanos turned out to be a souvenir shop with a short bar where the owner sold beer to winter Texans and told them tall tales about life along the river. I was about twenty years younger and a whole lot more fit than the handful of customers who roamed the aisles. The bar, like the ferry, had room for three. I asked the owner the price of beer, and when he said "Two dollars a can," I asked for the six-pack price. "Six times two dollars," he said sarcastically. "If you can't do the math, that's twelve dollars."

"Can you give me a bulk price? I'm on the river canoeing and I can't get to a store."

"If you don't like my price, take the ferry over to Mexico, walk two miles into town, and buy your beer there. Of course, they'll charge you two dollars each way on the ferry, so you're not going to save any money."

"I think I'll do that," I said. "Anything to keep from spending my money in here."

When I passed Customs on my way to the canoe, the agents wondered why I had no shopping bags. When I told them the beer prices, the senior agent said, "Do you want a ride to the store out on the highway? It's four miles, too far to walk."

Unbelievably, the uniformed man was willing to take me out to Sullivan City on Highway 83. As we left to get into his Chevrolet Suburban, the woman agent joked, "This means you're going to have to include all of us in your book."

You can learn a lot about a man in an eight-mile round trip between the river and the convenience store. Alfredo Ruiz Jr., a Laredo native, had worked twenty-four years for the Department of the Interior, first as an Immigration officer, later as a Customs official. He harbored a deep distrust of Mexico: "I never go over there," he said. "I just stay over here and do my business. There's no reason to go there unless you're looking for trouble. That's all you're going to find. And they don't have real laws."

I asked him about the Zetas, and he sighed. "I just know what the newspapers say. They're rival gangs. Just punks. I don't trouble myself with them."

"I hear they feed their enemies to lions."

"Down here, if you have a lion or a tiger, it's a symbol of power. That guy who owns the store where you didn't buy anything, he kept a lion tied out back. It was his symbol of power. They think they're big men if they have one, but it's just an animal. It has nothing to do with what a man is."

At the convenience store, I sprinted in and bought beer, ice, and snacks. Alfredo could see through the plastic bag that I had bought Tecate. "You drink that Mexican beer?" he said with disgust.

We talked about Laredo until we parted at Customs.

"Thanks for the ride. You really made my day."

"It's nothing. I like helping people. One time a group of doctors rented a limo and drove along the Mexican side. The limo broke down over there and the doctors and their wives came running to catch the last ferry, but it had already docked over here. I made the ferry go back and get them, and then I drove them all the way back to Brownsville. It was nothing."

—•••—

Below Los Ebanos, the river slows to a crawl as the waters back up behind Anzalduas Dam, a Mexican diversion dam some thirty miles downriver. About twenty miles before the dam, the current dies altogether, leaving a narrow lake, and the prevailing winds blow upriver. Here the river rolls in waves as if it were headed back to Laredo rather than down toward the Gulf, and for most of the way I had to hug one shore or the other, canoeing under overhanging branches, out of the worst of the waves. Powerboats compound the dangers, and the sound of approaching motors around a blind turn often sent me into a panic. I couldn't venture into the main part of the river because of the waves, which often whitecapped as they hurried upriver, yet taking the wake close to shore meant being rolled backward into the overhanging branches.

The only powerboats displaying any boating etiquette belonged to the Border Patrol, and I saw them twice a day, once on their way upriver on their daily patrol, again late in the afternoon as they returned to Chimney Rock. I looked forward to these encounters; the officers were invariably friendly, inquisitive, and helpful. They stopped to chat each time they passed, always offering encouragement

The only downside of my new friendship with the McAllen sector of the Border Patrol was that I got unwelcome advice from an especially friendly senior agent when I explained my need to portage Anzalduas on the Mexican side. Before beginning my trip, I had scouted the dam to find the best way around it and had noted that a Texas-side portage involved a carry of more than a half mile, while portaging on the Mexican side reduced the carry to less than two hundred yards.

"I can't tell you what to do," this agent said, "but I'm asking you as a personal favor not to break the law by portaging on the Mexican side. Technically, if you land over there and then cross back over here, you must report directly to U.S. Customs. I'm not saying we would arrest you, but you would be—technically, I mean—breaking the law. Plus, you don't want to go over there. Bad things are happening, really bad things, and it's not worth it."

—◆◆◆—

The camping possibilities deteriorated between Los Ebanos and Anzalduas, and for the next two nights, I was forced to stay in abysmal sites. Clusters of mosquitoes attacked me the minute I landed on shore, and no amount of repellent kept them out of my ears and nostrils. Despite the stout winds sending waves upriver, no air penetrated the thick undergrowth where I was forced to camp, and it felt intolerably muggy. Moreover, the forests were rife with critters, principally coyotes, raccoons, skunks, and armadillos. At one camp I spent five minutes using my paddle to slap-shoot coyote droppings into the river before I erected the tent. At the other, I listened to the fractious chatter of raccoons half the night, waking in the morning to find that they had decimated a half-gallon box of mango nectar I had left unprotected. The dense air in the tight forest made the tent particularly claustrophobic, and this feeling was compounded by my inability to find flat ground: each night I'd slip into the lowest end of the tent.

The second of the two nights brought clear skies and a full moon, and the moonlight played tricks on me as it filtered through the tree canopy above me: I swore I saw headlights approaching, and then, minutes later, I thought I saw flashlights coming at me through the woods above camp. The sounds of the wind tossing the treetops fed my paranoia, and the coyotes filled the sound gaps between wind gusts. Just as I wrestled my paranoia into submission, the beavers would suddenly thump the water surface just below me, setting my teeth on edge. An armadillo scampered toward its den five feet from my tent, and owls hooted across the river. I spent the evening peering nervously at the Mexican embankment, watching the moonlight shifting through the trees, lathering myself with insect repellent, feeding the fire. Halfway through the night, roosters on the Mexican side crowed. I mistook the moonlit sky for dawn, so I emerged from the tent, stoked the fire, and spent four interminable hours waiting for the sun to rise.

—◆◆◆—

I reached the neatly landscaped retirement community of Chimney Rock just as the morning winds made the river nearly impassable for a canoe. Rolling waves moved upriver as I moved down a final straightaway and asked a Hispanic maintenance man working along the shore where I could dock. "Wow," he said, pausing to eye my packed canoe, "we don't see too many canoes down here. Where are you coming from?"

"I started way back in El Paso in December."

"Holy shit!"

The boat ramp happened to adjoin the pitch where a group of senior citizens engaged in a spirited game of horseshoes, and the nearby benches were full of spectators. These old men talked in accents that suggested they had grown up at least a thousand miles to the north. My arrival caused several of the spectators to abandon the match and come to greet me. One of them told me there was a store nearby, but said, "You're not going to find very much there."

Across a four-lane road on the south side of Mission, Texas, I found a convenience store, which catered to a Mexican clientele. The shelves were stocked with tins of beans and jalapeños, stacks of tortillas and Mexican sweet breads, and Mexican snacks like dried shrimp and *machacado,* a kind of shredded jerky. The cooler was filled with Jumex fruit juices, soft drinks, Topochico mineral water, and countless six-packs of beer, most of it American. Calling cards offering terrific rates for calls to Mexico and Latin America hung behind the cash register. As I stacked my groceries on the counter, an attractive, full-figured woman with dyed and permed blond hair came from a back room, talking on a cell phone in Spanish as she assumed her place behind the counter.

Eyeing the Mexican groceries and beer I had stacked on the counter, she said to me in Spanish, "Is that all?"

I told her I needed something else, insect repellent, but I didn't know its name in Spanish. She asked me to explain it, and then took a can of exorbitantly priced Off from a shelf behind her. After she totaled the goods and I paid her, I asked her to double-bag everything because I had to carry it all back to Chimney Rock.

"Where are you going?" she asked with a flirtatious smile.

"I'm canoeing on the river, and I'm going all the way to the sea."

"How interesting," she sighed. "I'm stuck in this store every day of my life. You know what? Your eyes look like the sea."

Whoa, sweetheart!

Reynosa

Feb. 23–24

Reynosa, Tamaulipas, a city of a half million residents, begins at Anzalduas Dam and sprawls along the river for the next dozen miles. Reynosa gains frequent media attention for the same reasons that other large border cities do: frequent drug-related violence, police corruption, pollution, and poverty. Two months before I began my trip, the Mexican consulate took the unusual step of issuing a warning to Americans visiting Reynosa, advising them to take extreme caution and avoid going out after dark.

I grew apprehensive every time I thought of having to pass through it. During my many travels in Mexico and other Latin American countries, I have been the victim of crime only once: a pickpocket stole my wallet in a Reynosa pool hall. My only two negative encounters with police also occurred in Reynosa. Once I paid a bribe for a fabricated infraction; the second time I refused to pay the bribe only because the thief had already relieved me of all my money.

In the late 1990s it was reported that the entire police force of the city had been dismissed due to entrenched corruption.

I decided that the best strategy for getting through Reynosa would be to portage Anzalduas Dam, float down the river until I found a secluded camp on the Texas side, then start early the next morning and power-paddle right through the city while the kids were still in school and many of the hoodlums were sleeping off hangovers. I would hug the Texas shore as much as possible.

But first I faced the daunting prospect of the long carry around Anzalduas, which I tackled in stages, moving the gear a hundred yards at a time, from one shady spot to the next. This involved crossing a city park, crossing a levee bridge, and then following the Border Patrol access road nearly a half mile to the steep embankment below the dam. I calculated this would take all afternoon.

An SUV with Montana license plates pulled up alongside one of my resting spots, and a grandmotherly woman in the passenger seat asked if I would like help with my portage. She and her husband had watched me carrying gear, unsure exactly of what I was doing until they drove past my canoe. Then her husband, an accomplished canoeist himself, figured out that I was portaging around the dam.

I accepted the offer with copious thanks, and watched as a grayhaired fellow wearing dress slacks and a pressed shirt extinguished his cigarette, put the vehicle in neutral, and dove into the work of hoisting my canoe into the rear of the SUV, half of it left to protrude out the back. We loaded the front end with my heaviest gear to keep the boat stable, and drove toward the bottom of the dam.

Fred and Sherry Kraeplin had recently moved to Mission, Texas, from Columbus, Montana, and we became fast friends. My familiarity with many of the Montana rivers Fred had floated jumpstarted our conversation, but this handsome couple took such an interest in my trip that had I never been in Montana, it wouldn't have mattered.

"Oh, Fred," Sherry said as her husband carried the heaviest of my gear down a steep grade in his dress shoes. "That's too dangerous for you. You'll fall and then what?"

Fred kept right on huffing the gear down the precipitous trail, and I had to force myself not to stare in awe at his determination. He would hand me a box and then charge back up to the SUV, seemingly more fit than I was. I enjoyed the work and their company so much I had little desire to leave. After we exchanged addresses and phone numbers, I descended the long trail, turning every few steps to look back up at them over my shoulder. I thought, "Oh well, if I die trying to get through Reynosa, at least I was fortunate to spend my last day alive with them."

-◆◆◆-

Below Anzalduas Dam, the river narrows, and the current charges out of the dam and over a scattering of boulders. I put in below the rocks, adjacent to a group of young men fishing the Mexican side of the river, none of whom appeared curious about my presence. A Border Patrol agent descended to the shore as I was gliding the boat into the water and, like all his colleagues in the McAllen sector whom I encountered, greeted me warmly. He estimated the distance to downtown Reynosa at seven or eight miles and said I should find plenty of good places to camp on the U.S. side before there.

"But be careful," he warned in accented English that suggested he'd lived much of his early life in Mexico, "and if you need help, call us."

Two miles below the dam, I turned a bend and saw a group of about ten adolescents brawling in mid-river. As I approached, I could see that the fight was make-believe, just a swimming game. They threw punches and sweeping roundhouse rights. Then the recipient of the non-contact punch would pretend to be driven off his feet, launching himself into the river as if knocked out. Seconds later he would emerge and return the fake blow, and his fighting partner would fly into the air, arms and legs akimbo, and crash into the water. It looked like riotous fun, and I only hoped the group didn't turn into a bunch of punks once they saw me.

When one of the group, a tall kid with dyed blond hair and a voice a full octave lower than those of his smaller playmates, noticed me approaching, the wild horseplay abruptly stopped, and the boys stood motionless in waist-deep water watching me. I called out a greeting in Spanish, and they returned that greeting respectfully, dispelling my fear. I angled the canoe toward them and let the current carry me.

They showered me with questions in Spanish: "Hey *señor,* where do you sleep at night?"

"Do you make your tortillas from scratch?" "Where do you buy Coca-Cola?"

One small boy asked, "Did your wife give you permission to go on the trip?"

I fielded questions for ten minutes or more, and though the kids came right to the edge of the canoe, they never touched it. Finally I asked if I could snap their picture, and they began lining up for a posed shot.

"I want to see you fighting like in a Hollywood movie."

And with that they broke into one of the most impressive staged melees one can imagine. If only Hollywood were that entertaining.

—◆◆◆—

A couple of turns later, the river narrowed and the current sped up, and for the next hour I moved as quickly as I had all trip, winding around bend after tight bend. On top of the Mexican-side embankment, shantytowns filled with people living in wretched poverty sat on bare, dusty earth. In one river cove, three generations of a large family bathed, the mothers and aunts washing the hair of the children by scrubbing their scalps with bars of soap. In another cove, dozens of pigs rummaged in trash littered on the mucky shore. When the sows with piglets saw me approach, they lumbered into the water, forming a barrier between my boat and their young. Roosters and hens pranced above the piglets, pecking at each other, squawking loudly. Women in faded print dresses swept dirt courtyards in front of the ramshackle houses. Children, underfed and barefoot, ran along the top of the embankment, imploring me in shrill Spanish to give them a ride in the canoe. Mules and donkeys stared, worried that my presence might force them to have to move. Had the river suddenly made a wrong turn and led me deep into the underbelly of Latin America? I wondered.

After two miles of squalor, the river bent again, now revealing an entirely different landscape. The shacks were replaced by growths of ash, willow, and Rio Grande elm, and this pristine landscape stretched for three miles. Despite my proximity to Reynosa, I saw no one except a shirtless man pushing a power lawnmower through some high grass at a river landing, and his obese wife and daughters waiting on the bed of their old Ford pickup truck. I pulled into camp on the Texas embankment adjacent to them, and felt as though I were a hundred miles away from the shantytown squalor I had observed less than an hour before.

As darkness fell and the flames of my campfire leaped into the blackness, hundreds of fireflies emerged, twinkling in the fresh spring air like raindrops of starlight.

After I left camp the next morning, my pristine river quickly found the Third World again. Tens of thousands of people flock to the border from the interior of Mexico, many seeking to cross illegally into the U.S., others seeking work in the *maquiladoras*. They arrive destitute and often face a sordid life of scavenging and begging in the streets. With nowhere else to go, they set up makeshift cardboard homes on public land near the river, which serves as their only source of bathing and cooking water. For the most destitute, the river doubles as a bathroom and a kitchen.

For two miles I boated past the abject filth of the *colonias* on the outskirts of Reynosa. Dozens of swine rummaged through a foul-smelling trash dump extending right to the river's edge. Swarms of flies and bees hovered over it. Holding my breath, I attempted to race past the stench.

Another river bend later, I saw tumbledown shacks, with walls made from splintered warehouse pallets, lining the embankment. A man, his wife, and two small children walked along a path at the cliff edge, and I waved to him. He called down in Spanish, "Give me a ride across the river so I can get some work."

"Sorry, but you won't fit in the canoe. I have too much gear."

Although he and his family had been walking in an upriver direction, they turned and hurried along the path, following my canoe.

"Pull over," the heavyset man demanded, "and give me a ride to
the other side. I need to find some work to feed my family."

I paddled harder, but that merely made him walk faster, leaving
his family behind. "I already told you, man," I said, "you won't fit in
the canoe. And I can't take you even if you did fit. The Border Patrol
would throw me in jail."

"No they won't," he said. "You're an American. They only throw
Mexicans in jail. Now pull over and give me a ride." He was beginning to sound angry, and he quickened his pace to a lumbering jog.
I couldn't outpace him. I noticed that women overhearing our dialogue had emerged from their shanties to watch the drama.

I tried to ignore him, but he persisted, and only the steepness of
the bank kept him from charging into the river.

"Hey," he shouted angrily. "Pull your fucking boat over and get
me right now! My kids haven't eaten today. I have to work!"

I was prepared to pull over and defend myself if I had to, but I
still hoped the river would offer an escape. I expected him to throw
rocks. Instead, I saw him slowing to a stop, winded.

"Hey," he called, "fuck your mother, *gabacho!*"

—◆◆◆—

One of the things I had feared most about the trip before I set out was
repeated encounters with the Border Patrol. Down here, we deal with
B. P. checkpoints every time we leave our cities, and few of the agents
are cordial. I'd even heard stories of agents prohibiting people from
launching boats on the Rio Grande, saying it was illegal. I expected
the Rio Grande Valley leg of the trip to be a test of wills: my determination to boat all the way to the Gulf versus the B. P.'s determination
to stop me. I was dead wrong on that call.

And beginning on Day Sixty, with my trip through Reynosa,
I received so much help and favorable attention from B. P. agents
that I almost felt as though I had a personal escort. For starters, the

morning I paddled under the bridge in the center of Reynosa, I found a B. P. boat parked not far downriver. As I approached, the two agents greeted me with big grins, and one said, "We've been expecting you." When I departed after a short conversation with the guys in the boat, the agent pointed at two more B. P. vehicles parked further down on the banks, and said, "Those guys will look after you for the next mile."

With approximately eleven thousand agents nationwide, ninety percent of whom are stationed along the Mexican border, the Border Patrol has a heavy presence in towns, on ranches and farms, and along highways. On the river, however, I had seen surprisingly few agents. From Reynosa to below Brownsville, they are considerably more visible. In addition to river patrols, I saw Border Patrol riding the riverbanks on ATV's, horses, and bicycles. A couple of times I saw them tracking on foot. Their white and green SUV's, Jeeps, and pickup trucks monitored seemingly every outlook above the river for the next hundred miles. There is little doubt the McAllen sector of the B. P. has been effective at reducing the tide of illegal immigration, though critics argue that the B. P.'s heavy presence in the Rio Grande Valley merely forces would-be immigrants to more remote and less patrolled regions of the border. In the Laredo sector, for example, I saw approximately twenty people crossing illegally for every B. P. officer I saw. In the McAllen sector, the ratio was reversed.

As my admiration for the agents in the McAllen sector grew, I found it increasingly difficult to maintain the attitudes I'd had for most of my twenty years on the border. For years I had treated the river as a river, not as an international border. I preferred camping in Mexico not only because private property owners there were more tolerant of trespassers but because I wanted to avoid the B. P. agents who would sometimes burst into my camps on the U.S. side. If I had to portage around an obstacle, I nearly always chose the Mexican side because, in general, Mexicans used the river, and there were paths, whereas on the American side river cane usually blocked my access to shore. In the past I'd been guilty of transporting Mexicans stranded by floodwaters, stuck in remote areas of the river days from towns, to the U.S. side. My rationale had always been that they were going to cross anyway, so why force them to risk their lives swimming dangerous currents when I could ferry them safely across in my boat? Now, in the final weeks of my push toward the Gulf, I began to experience a change of heart about the river as an international border. Although I couldn't share the Border Patrol's view of Mexicans seeking work as criminals, I no longer wished to make the job of its agents more difficult. For the first time in my life, in the cat-and-mouse game between U.S. immigration officials and undocumented workers trying to circumvent them, my support for the Mexicans began to waver, but not through any fault of the Mexicans or any diminishment of my empathy for their plight. Instead, I found myself thinking that the B. P. truly were good guys—no better than the people they sought to stop from crossing, but certainly no worse.

◆◆◆

Both the B. P. agents I met near Anzalduas Dam and those in the boat further downriver had warned me about a "rock crossing" somewhere below the dam, where "it's too dangerous for us to take the boats through. So we patrol only that far." When I asked for more information, they said I'd see what they were talking about when I arrived there. They felt sure I'd be unable to navigate it safely in the canoe.

This "rock crossing"—or *piedras* ("rocks"), as the Mexicans called it—was the first of a dozen manmade rapids between Reynosa and the Gulf. Most of them were sharp drops between boulders and cement slabs that had been dumped in the river in order to dam the current enough so that the pipes of pumping stations would reach the river in times of low water. B. P. agents further downriver used the terms "rock crossing" and "dam" interchangeably. Each time the Mexicans warned of *piedras* ahead, I'd later learn that a dangerous manmade falls waited. A few of these I could run in the canoe. But if Mexicans warned of a *presa* (dam), I knew that a conventional dam lay ahead and that a portage was mandatory. Since I hadn't yet seen a "rock crossing," I had no idea what to expect.

A mile after I passed the B. P. agents, I heard the dull roar of a rapid ahead, and saw a clear landing on the Mexican side, so I angled for shore to scout the rapid. I found a weir dam, after which the river dropped through a rocky chute in a simple Class II rapid. Dead center, the river offered a relatively easy channel to run, and all I needed to do was to avoid some large waves at the base of the drop, a simple maneuver. As I scouted this drop, I saw five Mexican guys fishing the bank below the drop, spaced about thirty yards apart. Only one noticed my presence, and he was the best dressed of any fisherman I had seen the entire trip: designer jeans, Nike tennis shoes, a knitted sweater. This young man looked more like an engineering student at a Monterrey university than a Mexican fisherman. Once I'd picked my route through the rapid, I got back in the boat, and as I angled toward the center of the river, I noticed him eyeing me nervously. I flashed the thumbs-up sign, but he only nodded grimly, as if to say, "I hope you don't expect me to go into the river to rescue you after this rapid destroys your canoe."

The run over the weir and through the ensuing rapid was even easier than it had looked from shore. I glanced over at the fisherman, who now stood quite close to my boat, and again flashed him the thumbs-up sign. This time he flashed it back, smiling broadly. He let out a hard, short whistle to alert the next fisherman downriver, and when I arrived near him, this young guy called out, *"¿En esa la pasaste?"* (You went over that?)

I assured him that I had indeed gone over the drop in the canoe, and he uttered an English word that has crept into Mexican Spanish over the last ten years: *"¡Guau!"* (Wow!)

A couple of miles below the rock crossing, I was suddenly overwhelmed by the stench of raw sewage, and one turn in the river later, I saw why. A reeking canal entered from the Mexican side, emanating a stink so thick that I struggled to breathe. Ironically, the canal entered through a pastoral ravine, thick with overhanging tree limbs, free of trash. If it hadn't been for the smell, this narrow stream would have been the ideal place for a shade break or a picnic lunch, a quiet spot for fishing or napping. Not surprisingly, I saw no fishermen or picnickers, and anyone napping onshore would likely have been dead, killed by the noxious air.

Up till now, the river had been remarkably clean, at least compared with my expectations before leaving on the trip. Except for the smell of effluent entering the river in Nuevo Laredo, I'd had no olfactory indications that sewage, treated or untreated, was entering the water. Certainly, all manner of trash lined the banks, especially on the Mexican side, and in small towns and villages along the way. But the river itself had not seemed to be the riparian basket case that had got itself added to the "Most Endangered Rivers" list in 2000 and 2003. Reynosa put an abrupt end to any illusions I had that the Rio Grande was a waterway returning to health.

For the rest of the afternoon, I paddled through the stench, which rose from the current for more than a dozen miles. After about four hours, thanks in part to stout head winds, I finally could breathe, smelling only a faint hint of sewage. I decided to wait a couple of days before I used the river water again for anything, even washing my hands.

Holding Cell

Feb. 25–26

With Reynosa behind me, I allowed myself for the first time to think about the end of the trip. My confidence in being able to reach the Gulf, now less than a hundred fifty miles away, was growing, and spring was blossoming along the river. As delightful as the season made the riverside scenery—*huisache* flowering with golden yellow puffs that fell in a fine mist of color when the winds kicked up—I worried about the potential for dangers that the warmer weather posed and decided to make a concerted push for the Gulf. Nearly all of the fatal attacks by Africanized honey bees, or killer bees, in Texas have occurred in the Lower Rio Grande Valley, and since I was spending a lot of time thrashing around in their habitat, I didn't want to be the next victim. Snakes too could be a problem, but rattlesnakes rarely wandered into the floodplain, and I rarely wandered above it. I kept a close watch for copperheads, though I saw only large black snakes that I couldn't identify, nor did I meet anyone who could. I took this as a good sign, reasoning that if they were poisonous, people would know.

The days were nearly always pleasant, thanks to strong gulf breezes that played havoc with the canoe but kept the afternoons fresh. Nights, however, were growing increasingly warmer, and often I found my sleeping bag too warm. Any time I could find my way to a store to buy ice, it melted quickly in the cooler. Cold beverages became a luxury. I drank cantaloupe juice at the rate of a half gallon a day when I could keep it cool, but when I couldn't, I drank far less. Beer became an unusual treat rather than a sustenance beverage. About every third day, I found a store that sold it, but I would buy only enough for that evening, knowing that I would be drinking it hot if I had any left the next day.

I began trying to structure my days around finding a store, but it was never easy. If I had been willing to leave my canoe unattended for hours at a time, I could have walked every day to Highway 281, usually about three miles from the river, but I never seriously considered that option. Carrying ten pounds of ice, one six-pack of beer, and three cans of beans even a mile and a half seemed like more work than the reward would be worth.

The day after I passed Reynosa, I arrived at Retamal Dam, an immense suppression dam (a type of dam that blocks the river in times of flood). Its massive concrete frame holds three monolithic steel gates that can be lowered by cable to prevent surging floodwaters from inundating farms downriver. Fortunately, I found the suppression gates raised, so I knew I could float underneath them. I used the opportunity to scale the ten-story-high structure to get a vantage point to scout for a nearby store, but all I saw was a mile-wide expanse of pasture ending at fields of sugar cane.

This stretch of river is remarkably serene. Enormous farms and orchards insulate it from the towns along the highway three miles in on the Texas side, and on the Mexican side are patchworks of tilled fields. I saw few people who weren't driving large tractors, and most of the time I slipped by them without their operators having noticed me. The river passes through the Santa Ana National Wildlife

Refuge, a temporary break in the vast swath of agriculture border-ing the river, but from the water I could not determine where the refuge began and ended. I sensed that tens of thousands of birds and thousands of raccoons, coyotes, and beavers couldn't make the distinction, either.

The two ubiquitous signs of humanity were water pumps and radio towers rising from the land above the river. Most of the water pumps weren't operating; the rainfalls had been generous for weeks, and there was no need for farmers to draw from the river. I suspect that canoeing this section of the river in drier times would be a very noisy experience.

◆◆◆

Late on the afternoon of February 25, I reached the international bridge separating Progreso, Texas, from Nuevo Progreso, Tamauli-pas. I hoped to find a small store on the U.S. side near the bridge or, in the worst case, land on the Mexican side and make a dash to the nearest store in Nuevo Progreso. That town attempts to appeal to the older crowds of winter Texans and retirees who come to the border to purchase prescription drugs and low-cost medical and dental treat-ment at a fraction of the U.S. cost. I counted this international bridge as my last best hope to access a store.

The American side of the international bridge is nearly impen-etrable, walled off by boulders and river cane. I found a drainage culvert at the beginning of a wall of boulders, parked the canoe there, tied it to a *huisache* tree, and scaled the steep grade.

Across the river, where the bridge dips toward Mexican Customs, a crowd of young children, chaperoned by their mothers, begged vo-ciferously from beneath the bridge, shouting "*Dáme* money (Give me money)" in shrill voices, like seagulls hovering over fishing boats. The elderly American tourists walking the bridge showered coins from the pedestrian walkway ten feet above, and the kids scrambled for each peso and quarter. Most would obediently carry their prizes to their mothers, who waited off to one side. As I scaled the embank-ment, three little boys broke away from the pack of beggars to sprint down to the river's edge to look at my canoe, which lay only a quick swim's distance away.

I stood on the edge of the higher ground, studying the boys, trying to assess what their intentions were. Would they steal from me while I walked to the store? As I stood there, a nearby Border Patrolman spotted me and raced his truck over to interrogate me. When I identified myself as an American citizen who was canoeing the river, the young agent warmed to me.

"Canoeing the river? I've never heard of anyone doing that."

When I asked about a store, he said, "You're a week too late. The store over there just closed down last week. There's a gas station up the road and you can get a few things there."

"I'm worried about leaving the canoe. Those kids across the river look pretty interested in it."

"I'd be worried too. Those kids swim that river every day just to get the clothes the wetbacks leave behind. They won't think twice before coming over here. Tell you what. I'll watch the canoe while you're gone. Just show me where it is and I'll park my truck above it. If I get a call over the radio I'm going to have to leave, though. Do you think you'll be long?"

I told him no, and jogged in the direction of the Customs complex and then around it to the road. About a third of a mile away I saw a combination convenience store/gas station. Halfway there, I passed another B. P. vehicle parked beside the road. The agent rolled down his window and called, "Whoa there. Are you coming out of Mexico?"

"No, I'm canoeing on the river. One of your guys is watching my boat so I can buy some food."

After I had loaded up with beer, ice, snacks, canned beans, tortillas, and fruit juice, I realized it would be slow going on my way back to the canoe. Outside the store, I stopped to use the pay phone. Jesse Bogan wanted me to phone him periodically because he'd convinced his editor to allow him to rejoin me for part of the trip, and we needed to coordinate our rendezvous. Just as I hung up and lifted my heavy load of groceries off the pavement, a B. P. truck driven by the young agent who had volunteered to watch my canoe appeared.

Fearing that I had undertaken the four-mile walk to Progreso and back, he had radioed a fellow agent to watch my gear and had taken off to find me.

"I can give you a ride back to your canoe," he said. "The only thing is, you're going to have to ride in the back in the holding cell. I'm not allowed to let you ride inside the cab. Or if you don't want to get back there, I can put your things in back and drive them to the river while you walk."

"Man," I said, "I've dreamed about riding in the back of one of these."

The agent unlocked the door to the paddy wagon to reveal two facing metal benches, each supplied with four sets of seat belts. Then he locked me in and drove back to the river. Despite the three-minute ride, I felt claustrophobic when the truck stopped above my canoe.

The agent introduced himself as Joe Carrion, a native of Browns-ville. He introduced me to the colleague who had watched my canoe in Joe's absence, and this young Hispanic fellow extended his hand and said, "Are you really canoeing all the way to Boca Chica from Laredo?"

"Actually, I started a lot further away than Laredo."

"Wow!" He made me feel that I was doing something very impressive.

"Look, I can drive you into Progreso if you need anything else," Joe offered. "You may not get another chance to buy anything for quite a few days."

"That's okay, Joe," I said. "You may not believe this, but you've already done far more than I would ever have expected. I could stand here for an hour thanking you and I still don't think you'd understand how grateful I am."

Joe and his partner stood at the edge of the embankment as I negotiated the slippery descent, loaded my groceries in the boat, and shoved off.

"You have a good trip," Joe called down. "Be careful."

I paddled back into the current, tingling with childlike excitement. Larger men might respect the solitude I had endured, the rapids I had run, the weather I had suffered, and the dangers I had sidestepped. But, I thought proudly as I passed under the bridge, "You were taken on beer runs by both U.S. Customs and the U.S. Border Patrol in the same week. Wow, nobody's going to believe that one."

—◆◆◆—

I found a camp about three miles below the Progreso bridge, a brushy Texas-side bench opposite Mexican pasture land. The beavers were thick here, their trails and prints everywhere, and the pointed trunks of gnawed willow trees indicated that this was a favorite feeding ground of a large colony. No sooner had I set up the tent and collected firewood than the assault began. Numerous tail-smashings in the water just below camp were attempts to intimidate me into vacating the site. Other, more brazen beavers darted right through the edge of my camp. I had suspected before I began this trip—and now I felt pretty confident it was true—that beaver, my least favorite of the river's denizens, outnumbered any other species of wild animal in the state of Texas. All evening they persisted in trying to evict me from their territory, but nothing short of an armed man or a ravenous bear or mountain lion could have dislodged me from that site.

As it turned out, I would spend more time at that campsite than at any other single site on the entire river, for during the night I was awakened by the hard fall of raindrops on the roof of the tent. The rain persisted for hours, falling in diagonal sheets. I spent the morning scavenging for wood at the base of a sugar cane field, where I found some bulldozed elm trees in the woods that edged the field. There I returned often, sawing large sections of wood and then dragging them back through the mucky floor of my campsite to feed them to the fire. Morning gave way to afternoon, and the rains grew stronger—so strong that at times I could hardly see the other shore of the river, not sixty yards away.

For the first time all trip, I didn't break camp.

Entradas

Feb. 27–Mar. 1

Early the next afternoon I found the rock crossing for the pump house at La Feria, Texas, announced by the roar of the falls and the sudden disappearance of the river as it dropped. Uncharacteristically, the Mexican bank was choked with river cane, and I steered the canoe to the Texas side, tying off to a tree and ascending the manmade bank of the canal. I wanted to have a look at the falls that had been created when large boulders and cement slabs were dumped into the river. After studying the powerful eddy at the base of the drop, I decided to portage. Capsizing in that eddy would mean losing the boat and perhaps my life.

But I faced a problem with the portage: no good place to reenter downriver. I explained my problem to the pump house caretaker, a Spanish speaker returning to his bungalow from the pump house. He listened patiently and then said, "The only thing you can do is load everything into your truck and drive down to the access at the end of the tree line." He pointed across a tilled field bordering the pump house grounds. *"Mira,"* he continued. "Just drive along that road and you'll find a tractor cut and you can get in the water there."

"How am I going to drive?" I asked. Obviously he'd missed the point of my story.

"In your truck, of course."

"But I'm in a canoe. I came all the way from Juárez by the river. I don't have a truck. It wouldn't fit in the canoe."

"Pues," he said, not taking the bait I had hoped would get me a ride, *"hay que caminar"* (Then you must walk).

—◆◆◆—

I stared at the powerful drop in the river for probably fifteen minutes, and then at the grade leading to the river past the dam for another five minutes. I couldn't decide which was more dangerous. I saw that the Mexican side below the falls offered easy access, but getting around the falls there posed its own set of problems: the river cane was thick on the bank, and in order to portage, I would have to cut a path a hundred feet or more from the river's edge. And even if I were willing to cut such a long path, the embankment was so steep that I worried about getting myself and the gear out of the canoe without falling into the river.

Then I saw a chance to shorten the work. The cane at the top of the rapid was not nearly as thick as the cane just twenty feet upriver. If I were to land the canoe at the top of the falls, I could shorten the path I'd have to cut, but the margin for error in landing there was disarmingly narrow: at the precise spot where I had to get to shore, the river began to spill over a vertical drop of twelve feet.

Despite the Border Patrol's wish to keep me off the Mexican side, I opted to land at the brink of the falls, knowing one small mistake could be fatal. The landing required that I position the boat parallel to shore and then creep to the bank, fighting through the overhanging river cane, until the bow of my canoe touched the fast water at the beginning of the drop. When I reached that harrowing position, I would then tie the stern line to the river cane so that the stern couldn't be swept out from shore. Once I had tied that line, I expected to be able to get out of the boat and tie the bow line. With both ends secured, I could begin clearing the trail. There is something ineffably unnerving about taking a canoe to the precipice of a dangerous rapid you don't intend to run. At least when you're going over the drop, the business of steering the boat into the entry channel gives you a focus as well as a release of energy; you're not battling the current so much as using it. But launching into a river when your intent is to keep the river from taking you where it wants you to go is daunting. The river's sole purpose is to push relentlessly over that drop; your sole purpose is to keep it from taking you with it.

I paddled hard across the river and then inched along the bank, the roar of the falls already vibrating under the boat when I was still fifty feet from the drop. Fighting the urge to spin the boat around and head back to the Texas shore to begin a killer portage, I crept forward, talking to myself as I went. "Just a little more," the daring side of my brain urged. "Come on, don't be a baby."

The cautious alter ego shot back, "What? Are you crazy? You're way too close. Get out of the boat and cut the trail from here."

Inch by inch, I moved forward, reaching the precipice, and from the stern of the canoe my bow appeared to be suspended in midair above the drop. With trembling hands, I tied the stern rope to river cane and eased myself onshore.

I've never been so eager to portage as I was at that moment.

--◆◆◆--

A mile below the rock crossing, I heard gunshots, but their cadence suggested a shooter taking target practice. Still, I eased around the bend in the river, peering hard at the shores up ahead. First, I saw a minivan above the Texas bank, and as I completed the turn, I spotted two teens, one shooting a .22 at a target on the Mexican side. For reasons I've never comprehended, it's not uncommon for Texas gunmen to fire across the river into Mexico. When the reverse happens, however, it's cause for national media attention.

Once the pair of Anglo teenagers noticed my approach, they ceased firing and watched as I neared. I asked the older boy if he could tell me more or less where I was.

"Over my left shoulder about one mile is Blue Town, Texas," he said. "There's a convenience store there, but it don't have much."

Following the kid's directions, I beached a quarter mile later at a tractor cut and walked up a dirt road. Once I reached higher ground, I could see the town water tower standing tall. I set out in that direction, following a hard-packed dirt road that appeared to end a mile later at Highway 281, where the kid said I should take a left turn. En route, I passed under a B. P. surveillance tower, the first I'd seen since the Reynosa area, and I noted that it, like nearly all the ones I would see after it, stood far off the river, its camera aimed at the flat fields abutting it. I expected a B. P. vehicle to arrive at any minute, but I made it all the way into town and back and never saw an agent.

The small store stocked little, but I did find tortillas, *queso fresco*, Tecate, canned beans, and ice. The clerk, a wiry Mexican about thirty years old, listened eagerly to my story. As he double-bagged my supplies, he said in accented English, "You don't have far to go now, sir. You'll probably be there tomorrow."

━◆◆◆━

Invariably, finding a store and toting fresh supplies and ice back to the canoe lifted my spirits. For one, I loved having a celebratory beer as I paddled on toward the next camp. Also, the walk invigorated me after so many days of sitting in the canoe. But what most pleased me was the sensation of returning to the slow pace of the lazy river after a brief dose of the fast-paced and deafening world of the automobile. Even in a tiny town like Blue Lake, the traffic noise was earsplitting. When not in their vehicles, people surrounded themselves with racket—noise from televisions, radios, lawnmowers, telephones, their own voices. It seemed as if the one thing people off the river feared was silence. I found it soothing to return to the river and hear nothing but birds and rippling water.

The following morning I arrived at the most intimidating rock crossing of them all, the one that had claimed the lives of the two Border Patrol agents in August of 2004. Before I came to it, I met three Mexican men fishing, who assured me I would find a landing on the Mexican side before the dam. When I asked for a specific description of the landing, one man said, "You can't miss it. There's a building on the bank above it. Stop there. If you don't stop there, it's [and here he switched to English] 'Bye-bye, my friend.'"

Sure enough, I found the building, which held the office of the *Comisión Nacional del Agua, Sector Valle Hermosa*. A steep cement stairway dropped from it to a concrete walkway atop the dam's inflow gate, through which water was diverted to irrigate crops on the Mexican side. I landed here. Ahead the river dropped out of sight so abruptly that I couldn't see the water below the dam until I had scaled half the stairway leading to the water commission office. I judged the drop to be thirty vertical feet. A barely submerged weir extended across the river at the top of the drop. About halfway down, the jagged edges of large boulders divided the cascading torrent. Going over this dam would mean certain death. If the boulders didn't kill you, the furious backflow at the bottom certainly would.

At the water commission office, I startled two men who were listening to the radio when I appeared at their open office door, and they quickly rose to greet me as if I were some sort of authority figure.

After I explained my purpose, the older man offered to accompany me to the edge of the river to show me the best way to portage around the dam. At the top of the falls, he stood on a cement slab beneath a *huisache* tree and, shouting above the roar of the cascade, said, "Get in your canoe and paddle it to here. I'll catch you, and then the three of us will carry your things along this path."

I stared in disbelief at what he expected me to do. The cement slab sat next to the start of the pour-off, and the current there was already beginning to rush toward its long fall. Even if this man were adept enough to catch the front of my boat, the rush of current would sweep the stern of the canoe sideways over the vertical drop.

Seeing my worried face, the man shouted, "Don't worry. I'll catch you."

I worried. Directly below him, the current thundered in a rage of white water colliding with a barricade of sharp rocks. "It's not nearly as easy as it looks," I said. "And if anything goes badly, forget it." I made the sign of a knife slashing my throat.

To the man's disappointment, I portaged by carrying the gear up the stairs to the water commission office and along a dirt road on a bluff above the dam. This carry required a quarter-mile walk in each direction and consumed hours. When I returned to the office to thank the men for allowing me to portage on water commission property, the older man said, "We would have been glad to help, but you did it the wrong way."

❧

An hour later I arrived at the first international bridge below Progreso—Los Indios Bridge—and, knowing I still had three days of paddling before I reached Brownsville, I decided to enter the U.S. there. I needed ice and drinking water. But as I passed under the bridge, I saw no place to get ashore, and the speed of the vehicles passing above indicated that the Customs stations had to be some distance from the river. The river bent northward, paralleling the bridge for a quarter mile, and when it bent back to the east, I landed the canoe, grabbed the empty water jug, and set out through the woods in the direction of the U.S. Customs complex, a half mile away.

Guided by the bridge noise, I angled across two bogs, scaring up a family of armadillos as I did so. After considerable sweat, countless mosquito bites, and several bloody skin tears caused by mesquite thorns, I reached a high chain-link fence separating me from the Customs import lot. The fence encircled the complex for as far as I could see, so I walked along it until I reached the bridge, but there again the fence denied me access to the road. By this time, a Customs agent had noticed me wandering around, and I walked toward him till we met at the fence line. I asked if I could get in to fill my water jug, and he promised to call security to help.

About ten minutes later, two overweight security guys, riding a golf cart, located me. The younger Hispanic man did all the talking. "What's up, bro?" he said through the chain-link fence.

"I'm on the river canoeing, and I'm running short of water. I'd like you to let me in so I can get some drinking water."

"Sorry, bro," he replied. "Can't do it. Only the Border Patrol can get through this gate. If you want me to, I'll call them and have them bring you some water."

"Can't I just throw you the water jug and you go fill it for me?" I pleaded.

"Sorry, bro. Regulations. You know how it is, bro," he said, as if he really did expect me to understand why an American citizen had to step-dance around layers of Homeland Security regulations just to get some tap water.

"Forget it," I said, turning away. "I'd rather boil the river water than deal with this nightmare."

◆◆◆

A couple of river bends later, I heard the telltale roar of a rock crossing. This time, though, I found no landing on either side. I paddled right up to the brink of the drop, fighting the pull of the current, and saw I had no option other than to paddle back upriver a quarter mile to a tractor cut I had passed on the Mexican side. There I carried all the gear and the canoe up to the edge of a farm field rimmed by a rutted tractor road. I followed the road along the river a hundred yards past the rock crossing until I found a steep coyote path leading down to the river. It would have to do.

Across the field, some five hundred yards away, I could see a rough shack with an old pickup parked beside it. For some reason, this made me paranoid, and I worked quickly to move the gear, taking it in stages small enough to prevent my being separated for long from any one item. It was a ridiculous fear, and made me realize I

253

was guilty of the same prejudices as many other Americans: I was hurrying to complete the portage because I was in Mexico, and the sight of the truck prompted me to think someone might drive over and steal my gear. The realization made me ashamed.

When I found camp—a gorgeous sandy beach on the Texas side about a mile below the rock crossing—I was startled by the sound of a pickup truck. Opposite me, on the Mexican-side embankment, sat the same pickup I'd seen at the shack. I waved to the driver and he gave his horn a short toot, as if to say, "Hey, just checking to make sure you found a good camp. Have a great trip."

—◆◆◆—

The next day, I saw a water tower on the Texas side above a tight bend in the river, an unusual sight on that side of the river to that point, and I landed the canoe to investigate. I was shocked to find myself just a couple of hundred yards from Highway 281 and the small town of La Paloma, Texas. I hadn't heard any highway sound from the river, but as soon as I scaled the bank, it seemed as if the highway was rushing right through my ear canals.

From the small store on the north side of the highway, I called Jesse to confirm our plan to meet in Brownsville two days later, and we decided I would look for him near the international bridge that connects downtown Brownsville with Matamoros. Then he would jump into the canoe for the final leg of my trip to the Gulf. Our plans set, I shopped in the convenience store, hauling back to the river my staples of tortillas, beans, fruit juice, and beer.

Back at the river, I felt intense regret that I'd agreed to share my canoe and my camps. I simply didn't want to face the end of the trip, and I knew that the minute Jesse boarded the canoe, my trip would effectively be over. Though most people would have been desperate for company after so many weeks of solo canoeing, I dreaded it. I relished the challenge of doing everything alone, of being responsible for all the decisions and actions, of facing my fears and conquering them. I had long since fallen into a beautiful rhythm, and any needs I had to communicate with people were more than satisfied by the fishermen and Border Patrol agents I met along the way.

Head winds kicked up almost the minute I got back in the boat after my walk into La Paloma. I had to fight big waves coming upriver, and I took this as a sign: the river didn't want me to reach Brownsville and pick up Jesse any more than I did.

I lost my appetite for conversing with people I met along the river. I met a cheerful-looking father and son clearing the riverbank on the Mexican side, and the father hailed me in to shore to talk, but politely I refused. A little while later I passed a fisherman trying his luck at a turn in the river. I merely waved to him as I paddled by.

I had no eagerness to reach the Gulf, no desire to return to Laredo, no longing to end this life of finding a camp every night, bathing in the river, struggling to find small stores to replenish my supplies. I didn't mind portaging the rock crossings or fighting the head winds. I had long since grown accustomed to the endless howling of coyotes cutting through the night air. I had taken comfort in the idea that the trip's ending had been too far away to contemplate; now that the end neared, I felt uneasy, disbelieving, sad.

Then, in camp, while scolding myself for feeling down about the trip having to end, I suddenly stopped. "You haven't finished anything yet," I told myself. "A lot can go wrong in eighty miles."

Sharing the River

Mar. 2–3

For the last two weeks, nearly every Border Patrol agent I had met warned me about passing through Matamoros, the twin city of Brownsville. The Mexican military was camping along the river at several points, and the B. P. seemed to think I should fear the soldiers. I considered their fear laughable at first, but the onslaught of warnings began to achieve its intended effect: I did start to worry about encountering the military. On the other hand, I was curious to see how the soldiers would react to my presence. I hadn't seen another canoe since Big Bend National Park, more than seven hundred miles back upriver, and I felt it a pretty safe bet that I would be the first and last canoeist these soldiers would see during their encampment.

The military had been called to Matamoros for the same reason it had been called to Nuevo Laredo and Reynosa: a rash of drug-related violence between rival drug cartels had resulted in frequent shoot-outs in the city streets. Murders and kidnappings had increased to an alarming level. When I had mentioned to one B. P. agent that I had already passed Nuevo Laredo and Reynosa, both of which had a heavy military presence, and hadn't seen a single soldier, he replied, "There's a big difference. In Matamoros, they're camping right on the riverbank. You'll see them, no doubt about it. And you may wish you hadn't."

Another thing bothered me. I didn't know Matamoros well, and my one visit there had discouraged me from ever returning. In 1998 the college baseball team I coached had played a weekend series against the Brownsville college. After Saturday's doubleheader, I walked with a friend across the bridge to Matamoros to have a few beers.

On our way back, I noticed a fistfight happening on the median between the lanes of the wide boulevard leading to the bridge. I would have been content to pass it by except that, as we drew closer, I saw that a group of five men were soundly beating one small man, each taking his turn administering the thrashing. As we drew nearer, I saw the man drop to his knees and then, seconds later, flop to his stomach. The five men continued battering him, mostly kicking him, though one overly zealous punk did drop down and punch him in the side. The automobile traffic continued streaming past, even as the beaten man collapsed onto the roadway next to the median. Just then, my friend said, "I'm going over to that taco stand on the sidewalk and getting something to eat."

Seeing an opening in the traffic, I sprinted the half block toward the scene, and seconds before I arrived the assailants retreated, leaving their victim bleeding in the street. I cradled his body in my arms and immediately felt his warm blood soaking my shirt. He looked in terrible shape—his eyes rolled back into his head, face badly bruised, blood running from his nostrils. I stood there holding him, feeling his blood saturate my jeans, and thought, "I have to get him off the street before someone runs over him."

Remarkably—and this is why I'd never returned to Matamoros—none of the bridge-bound cars would stop to allow me to carry the man across to the sidewalk. When I spotted a gap between cars, I would step out tentatively, hoping the oncoming driver would yield so that I could cross to the next lane, but driver after driver refused me passage. None of the cars was moving faster than fifteen miles an hour, but still I couldn't dart in and out of traffic as I might have done had I not been carrying this wounded man. I stood there for several minutes, hoping for a break in traffic, my arms growing weary with the weight of this middle-aged dying man.

Suddenly, five men darted through traffic, and I found myself surrounded by the same thugs who had beaten him so mercilessly. One did most of the talking—shouting really—and he was neither polite nor tactful. I stood there, numb. Now the traffic came to a halt, as if nobody could be bothered stopping to allow me to assist the victim, but they were all eager to stop to see me become the next assault casualty.

My friend came running to the rescue, and his intensity appeared to scare off the assailants. Then, with my friend parting the cars, I carried the man to the sidewalk, laying him on a bed of grass next to the taco stand. A woman said an ambulance was already on the way, and she suggested I get across the bridge before the police arrived and tried to pin the assault on me. "After all," she said, "you're covered with blood."

—◆◆◆—

Matamoros was also the scene of the 1989 slaying of Mark Kilgore, a University of Texas pre-med student who disappeared while vacationing at South Padre Island during spring break. He was last seen in Matamoros, and when he failed to return, his friends contacted police, who, at the urging of the Kilgore family and the U.S. consulate, initiated a search and investigation.

Under intense pressure from Americans, Mexican detectives broke the case. Kilgore had been kidnapped by a cult of drug traffickers. His body was discovered with at least a dozen others on a ranch outside Matamoros.

Reportedly, Kilgore had been sodomized, and his skull cracked open. Near his body, detectives found a kettle filled with blood, scorpions, and Kilgore's brain.

I love the border and am a hard guy to intimidate. But I can never think of Matamoros without thinking of that kettle.

—◆◆◆—

The following day I saw a Border Patrol vehicle parked on the embankment above a tight bend in the river. The officer stepped out of the vehicle and walked upriver toward me. We waved at each other, so I took the canoe into shore at the base of the cliff on which he stood about thirty feet above me. I had to shout for him to hear me over the blustery winds I'd been fighting for several days.

Although he appeared to be Anglo, his accent suggested he was Hispanic, since he had none of the South Texas drawl common to gringos. Unlike every other B. P. agent I'd met, he seemed entirely unconcerned that I might be involved in criminal activity. His tone of voice was warm from his first word. When I told him what I was doing, he stared down at me in disbelief.

"You couldn't have done that. Wait, tell me again."

After introducing himself as a native of Rio Grande City who had been stationed in Brownsville for "too long," he reminisced about growing up on the banks of the river.

"Do you know that I used to cup my hands and drink right from the river on a hot summer day? I'm telling you. I used to do that. Hell, you'd probably drop over dead if you tried that now. Yeah, I used to scoop that water right out of the river and let it settle into my palms and then drink it up like nothing.

"In the mid-seventies, big changes occurred along this river," he went on. "First, it was the drugs—just marijuana—but when that cocaine hit, forget it. Even on your own property, it came night, you didn't go near that river anymore. Too dangerous. And that's when the river got real dirty too, real polluted. I don't know how that happened so fast. It didn't seem like no time before the water got so damned dirty I didn't even want to eat the fish out of it."

"I've been using it for coffee water, you know, after I boil it."

"Man," he said, "you're lucky you haven't gotten sick. And you still might, later on."

Then he asked about things that interested him. Had I seen any wildlife? Had I had any problems? How did I get around the big dams? How had the Mexican people treated me? I reported that the Mexicans had treated me very well, that their warm receptions had been one of the highlights of my trip.

"Hmm," he said, "I would have thought they'd have killed you several times by now."

—•◆•—

A few miles after I left the B. P. agent, I entered a straightaway that ended on the Texas side in front of a large Tudor-style mansion surrounded by finely manicured grounds. I assumed this signaled the approach to Brownsville. Midway down the long straightaway, I found a dead *huisache* on the riverbank, and there was just enough space to set up camp between the shore and the wall of river cane growing on the bank. I sawed six sections of firewood from the tree. Then, hearing a voice close by above the river cane, I thrashed through the thick cane to scout the area above my intended camp.

I emerged from the river cane to the tenth fairway of the River Bend Golf Course and Community. What I had mistaken for a mansion was actually the clubhouse. Senior couples dressed in polo shirts and nylon slacks chased their golf balls around in electric carts. Although I was dressed in a life jacket and dirty jeans, everyone treated me respectfully. I found a groundskeeper mowing the grass underneath two neat rows of orange trees and inquired about a store. He directed me to the pro shop, and when I expressed reservations about finding anything of use to me in there, the man said, "What are you looking for?"

When I reeled off my list of staples, he assured me I'd find beer, fruit juice, and ice there, so I decided to make the long walk down the fairway, past the clubhouse, and through the mobile home community.

The pro shop did offer what the groundskeeper had promised, but the prices were so steep that I left empty-handed. I retraced my path through the quiet streets, waving cheerfully to residents sipping cocktails in lounge chairs, and studying the license plates of their Winnebagos and SUV's. Most came from faraway places like British Columbia, Iowa, North Dakota, and Ontario. All were Anglos, and the only Hispanics I saw were three groundskeepers and four guys resurfacing a tennis court next to the clubhouse. It occurred to me that I could wander around this private country club neighborhood with impunity only because I was white.

—◆◆◆—

I pressed on because the groundskeeper estimated I was still "at least seven miles" from downtown Brownsville, and, translating that into river miles, I feared I could have as many as twenty miles to go. One mile later I reached yet another rock crossing. Despite a much easier portage route on the Mexican side, I landed above it on the Texas side, at the base of a mowed trail leading up to a pump house. From there, I saw I had a good chance of being able to navigate the drop in the canoe, so I lingered for a couple of minutes studying my route. As I did so, a police vehicle arrived on the Mexican side. Two officers stepped out of the shiny pickup truck and walked to the water's edge opposite where I had landed my canoe. One waved to me, and I responded by pointing down at the rapid, then flashing a tentative thumbs-up sign, my way of soliciting their opinion on my running the drop. The larger of the two then waved his arms and emphatically shook his head. I took this as a sign that I should carry around the hazard.

An hour later I found another gorgeous beach camp, and after my ritual scouting for signs of human footprints and finding none, I felt safe, even though a highway ran along the bluff on the Mexican side across the narrow river. I slapped coyote droppings into the river with my paddle and then dug a deep hole in the sand for my fire. It would be my last night camping alone, a bittersweet evening. Still more than sixty miles from the Gulf of Mexico, I was already beginning to miss the river.

After the noisiest night of my entire trip, I awoke feeling remarkably fresh. The raccoons had chattered all night in the forest above camp. Not to be outdone, dogs on the Mexican side had barked. Beaver tails had thumped the water near my tent. A water pump on the Mexican side had droned ceaselessly. I reasoned that with such a racket, no single sound could have startled me awake—hence my rested feeling.

I reached the next rock crossing after a surprisingly remote stretch of river, given that I was wedged between two cities that totaled some three-quarters of a million people, most of them on the Mexican side in Matamoros—the biggest river city this side of Juárez, edging out Reynosa by only a few thousand people. Because the rock crossing is only two miles from the downtown bridge that separates the two cities, I was amazed to find not a single person at the dam. I had hoped to find a portage trail on the American side, but its riverbank was thick with river cane. The Mexican side was so much easier and safer that I decided to carry on that side, and risk being spotted by the Border Patrol or by the Mexican army. From above the dam, I could see nothing on the Mexican side but tilled fields stretching in all directions, ending at lines of trees that shielded any view of residential Matamoros.

As I was loading the canoe beneath the rock crossing, a B. P. vehicle appeared across the river. I knew I'd have to paddle over and identify myself. When I had crossed halfway, a young Hispanic agent leaped from his truck and ran down the embankment toward me, ready to intercept me the moment I set foot on shore. As I neared, he shouted, "¿Hasta dónde vas?" (Where are you going?)

I answered in a mix of languages, "Hasta el mar, pero I speak English."

My English settled him immediately, and he seemed unconcerned that I had portaged on the Mexican side. His curiosity about my trip centered on something that nobody yet had asked me about.

"When was the last time you had a shower?"

"I bathe in the river every other day," I answered.

"That's not a shower. Man, you're probably dirtier when you get out than before you went in. You could get sick going in that water."

"So far, it's been working fine."

"So when was the last time you had a shower? I mean a real shower with clean water."

"Falcon Lake State Park two weeks ago."

He made a disgusted face. "Man, I couldn't live like that. I take a shower before work, after work, when I go to bed. I couldn't sleep if I wasn't clean."

He said that the first of Brownsville's bridges lay only a couple of bends away, and not far after that, I would enter downtown and arrive at the second bridge. Having heard so many erroneous distance reports over the preceding weeks, I wanted reassurance; he assured me I could walk there in thirty minutes or less.

"You're just about there. You probably can't see it from down there, but from my truck I can see the Matamoros water plant. After that, it's just one more bend in the river and you'll be at the first bridge."

I thanked him and turned my canoe downriver. He took a few steps up the embankment, paused for a moment to watch me paddle, and then called out an unusual good-bye: "Stay clean!"

—◆◆◆—

After repeated floods—some caused by upriver rains, others by hurricanes—in the early nineteenth century the city fathers of Matamoros were forced to move the city from the riverbanks to higher ground a couple of miles inland. Above the river, a wall defends Matamoros from floodwaters, and few structures are located below it. As a result, from the river I saw fewer people in Matamoros than I'd seen even in some tiny villages. Most notably, I saw no signs of the Mexican army. Aside from the flood wall around the city's perimeter, numerous signal towers rising from beyond the wall, and four international bridges connecting it to Brownsville, I saw little evidence of this city of half a million people.

That was just fine with me.

In contrast to Matamoros, Brownsville is the most visible of all the American towns and cities I'd passed on the Rio Grande. I could see much of the downtown area as I paddled the straightaway between the first two bridges, and I found this sight comforting. For one thing, it meant I would have little difficulty getting to shore to locate Jesse. Also, knowing I was visible from the American side gave me a sense of security I hadn't expected. If anything was to stop me from completing my trip to the Gulf, it would more than likely be human, and I could expect to find it within the city limits of Brownsville/Matamoros.

As I paddled toward the end of the straightaway right in downtown Brownsville, I saw that a B. P. agent parked high up on the bank next to the duty-free store had noticed my approach, and I decided he was my likeliest source of assistance. As I neared, the agent left his truck and bounded down the first tier of the embankment to watch me. When I drew within earshot, I called up, "Can I land the canoe here? I need to use a telephone."

"Sure," he answered, sounding friendly. "Go ahead and leave your canoe down there and meet me up at my truck."

My honor roll of amicable and helpful Border Patrol agents grew longer the further I moved through the Rio Grande Valley, but B. P. veteran Pete Lozoya vaulted to the top of the crowded list. When I reached his truck, he greeted me with a wide grin and a warm handshake, saying, "I've been working the river here nine years, including two years on boat patrol, and I've never seen anybody in a canoe. Where are you coming from?"

As I recounted my story, Pete punctuated each of my statements with an enthusiastic "Wow!"

"Man," he said, "I'd love to do something like that. I love the river. It's so peaceful down there." He spoke as if the river were hundreds of miles, rather than hundreds of feet, away. After I declined his offer of a cigarette, Pete added, "This job is so boring when they stick me up here in this truck."

A thickset man in his early thirties, Pete had an infectious smile that suggested he was an undying optimist. And something about his congenial nature suggested that when he busted people who were merely crossing illegally, he did it reluctantly, with a keen understanding of the poverty and squalor they were attempting to escape. I sensed a large-hearted, selfless man, someone who'd coach Little League baseball or volunteer at his church.

"Can you tell me where the nearest store is? I need to use the pay phone," I said.

"Here, use my cell. Make as many calls as you want to," Pete said. "If I can't use the phone to help somebody, what's the point of having it?"

I phoned Jesse, who answered immediately. Astonishingly, he had just entered downtown Brownsville and was a mere two blocks away.

As Pete answered my questions about what to expect further downriver, an Anglo man interrupted us. "Excuse me," he said, nodding hello to Pete and turning to direct his question to me. "Is that your canoe down there?"

"Yes, sir. Is someone stealing from it?"

"Oh no, I was just walking across the bridge from Matamoros and I saw you walking up from the river. I bought a canoe last year and I've been wanting to take it on the river. I guess I had always thought it was illegal, so I'm glad to see someone else down there first."

—◆◆◆—

Except for accompanying me on an overnight raft trip from Columbia Solidarity Bridge to Laredo the previous May, Jesse had been frustrated in his attempts to explore the Rio Grande, largely because he didn't own a boat. Now he hoped to combine a longer river trip with reporting on the river experience for his newspaper. Jesse is, literally, a good camper, eager to assist in chores and enthusiastic about exploring beyond the periphery of camp. He's as much at home bathing in the Rio Grande as he is showering with indoor plumbing. Furthermore, he handles adversity well. When he and had I paddled my largest, slowest raft down a thirty-three-mile section of the Rio Grande leading into Laredo in vicious head winds and hundred-degree temperatures for two days, his only complaint had been a cheerful, "This is a little slow, but I'm loving it."

Jesse arrived in his newspaper's SUV while I stood talking to Pete Lozoya, and I was immediately struck by how his appearance contrasted with mine. With a collared blue shirt and pleated khaki pants on his six-foot-four-inch frame, he looked as if he were about to enter the office rather than a canoe, while the gel in his hair made him resemble a college kid on his way to a nightclub. I introduced him to Pete, and they conferred on where to find a landing from which Jesse could easily load his gear into my canoe. Despite his great height, Jesse has a knack for putting people at ease; his soft Missouri drawl helps. Pete took to him right away. He offered to lead Jesse back upriver to an easier access, while I paddled the canoe a quarter mile upstream to the landing.

By the time I reached it, a small crowd had gathered. A newspaper photographer had joined Jesse, and two B. P. vehicles were parked beside Pete's truck. The photographer, named Delcia, had snapped numerous pictures of my entrance to the narrow cove below the group of vehicles. The Border Patrol agents stood above her, amused at all of this. When I landed the canoe, Jesse was already pitching bags of gear and food down the embankment toward my boat. "I think he has more gear for three days than you have for three months," Delcia said. "How are you ever going to fit all of that and both of you in that canoe?"

·•◆•·

Jesse and I charged out from shore and pointed the canoe downriver for the last fifty-five miles to the Gulf. As had occurred the first time he joined me, the canoe sides now dipped perilously close to the water line. Jesse seemed even more eager than I to put Brownsville behind us, and he dug his paddle into the water. We raced under the main bridge, passed the old Fort Brown—now the campus of University of Texas at Brownsville—and soon reached Veterans Bridge, marking the edge of Brownsville.

I remarked that I was disappointed to have passed Matamoros without having seen a single Mexican soldier. Jesse turned and gave me a dubious look. "Man, you've been drinking way too much river water."

Several miles later we passed the fourth of the international bridges, and below it we pulled over for lunch. Other than the traffic noise from the bridges, the river seemed a world away from the two cities. Flying fish called mullets skipped just above the current at times; at other times, they leaped high into the air, often four feet above the water line. Carp and alligator gar thrashed the water beneath the canoe, startled by our sudden appearance. Herons squawked on the shoreline. We saw no people along the shore, and river cane blocked our view of any development above the banks.

After lunch we arrived at the final rock crossing, a nasty drop cluttered with boulders. We were just about to pull in on the Mexican side when I noticed two B. P. vans parked downriver. We could see that on the Mexican side the carry around the dam was clear of brush and trees and that a well-worn path reached the river at the top of it. The Texas side offered far more difficult access, and only reluctantly did we steer the boat into shore there.

A steep trail led down from the B. P. access road above the river, and I carried a load of gear up there. A hundred yards down the access road I could see four agents, two on horseback and two standing beside their vans, conversing. I waved in their direction, but none noticed me. Jesse and I toted a couple more loads up before any of them saw us, and when they finally did, they arrived in a hurry. Suddenly, we found ourselves surrounded by four wary agents. On the river below, three Mexicans had arrived to fish, and I could see them gazing at this amusing change of scenery: two gringos drawing the suspicions of the Border Patrol.

"What do you have in those boxes?" one agent said as he approached me, one hand cupping his nightstick, the other resting just above his holstered gun.

As I began to stammer an explanation, a second agent interrupted. "How did you get here?"

Within seconds, I was leading two agents down the trail to the canoe, where they took turns filtering through our gear. One of them, a junior agent, not long out of the academy, told me to dump out the clothes in my dry bag. The other young agent rummaged through my food box, taking particular interest in my first-aid supplies, half of which I'd stored in a zip-lock plastic sack. Jesse stood off to the side, discreetly snapping photos as the agents worked. Satisfied that we weren't carrying contraband, they asked us to produce identification. Neither seemed impressed with Jesse's press pass, and my college faculty ID was similarly dismissed. However, they allowed us to continue portaging the gear up from the river while one agent went to run a license check on us.

As we worked moving the gear up to the B. P. access road, the two agents on horseback hovered over us, smoking Marlboro cigarettes and making small talk. Both Hispanic and in their mid-thirties, they appeared to be the mentors for the younger agents, and I thought that perhaps we were part of a training exercise. The older agents were affable and curious. The younger agents had been businesslike and officious; they asked me to repeat answers they found less than satisfactory, and three times I had to state my place of employment. However, once their criminal check turned up no outstanding warrants, their tone changed, and the six of us fell into easy conversation, joking about the craziness of the canoe trip. Jesse took advantage of the changed tenor to interview all four agents, and they seemed to revel in the attention.

I went to scout for a path we could use below the rock crossing. Jesse then found one, but it presented a problem. He and I were conferring as the B. P. agents huddled ten yards away. Now, the most senior agent of the four said, "We'll load you in the vans and take you to a tractor cut down the river. It's easy to get in there."

They helped us load our gear and the canoe, and I climbed in beside it. Our caravan of two vans and two agents on horseback set off downriver, inching along the rutted road above the roar of the last rock crossing. A mile below it at the tractor cut, we unloaded the van. As far as I could see on the U.S. side, freshly tilled fields extended across the flat delta. The agents spotted fresh tracks, and they left on foot to follow. Jesse trailed after them, leaving me to carry the gear to the river's edge. When he came back, he said, "Listen to this. Those guys found some wet underwear in the field up there where whoever crossed the river had changed clothes. I picked up the underwear and the brand name was No Boundaries. How's that for irony?"

—◆◆◆—

The B. P. agents knew of a camp another mile downriver, and said they'd meet us there. We launched the canoe into the narrow, winding river, now forty-seven miles from the Gulf.

"Let's have a beer," Jesse said as we rounded a bend and dropped out of view of the access road.

"Let's have several," I joked, as we rested our paddles and let the canoe drift in the lazy current.

"Those guys turned out to be really nice," Jesse said as he popped open a can and stretched his back. "It didn't look too good when they first saw us, but they were cool."

"Border Patrol agents have been the best part of this trip these last two weeks. I've been amazed at how nice they've been, and it's gotten so that I look forward to seeing them."

"Man," Jesse retorted. "That doesn't sound at all like the Bowden I know. Hanging out with the Border Patrol? The next thing I know you'll be telling me you don't like Mexicans anymore."

"That's not going to happen. I can guarantee you that's never going to happen."

In camp we grilled hamburgers on coals at the side of the campfire, and as the sun dropped below the horizon, Border Patrol lights came on to illuminate the fields above our camp. Although we couldn't see the actual lights, their beam was strong enough to send a wide swath of soft light into the night sky, more light than both Brownsville and Matamoros offered upriver. The agents on horseback paced the cliff above us, and their silhouettes looked eerily beautiful. We were giddy with excitement about our camp and our B. P. "chaperones." And Jesse was ecstatic to be out on the river, camping and sleeping under the stars. To my surprise, I found it fun to have his company. He sat by the fire taking notes as he asked me question after question about my adventure, while I paced around the flames, keyed up about how well our first day together had gone, eager to see what tomorrow would offer.

For the first time all trip, I felt confident I would reach the Gulf of Mexico. I sensed that the end of the trip might be its nadir, but for this one night, I wasn't going to allow any regret for the trip's ending to interfere with the bliss of camping on a gorgeous river bend on a fine spring night, fireflies sparkling in the riverside darkness, our bellies full with the first meat I had eaten in weeks. Neither raccoons nor coyotes interfered with deep and dreamless sleep that night.

Poison

Mar. 4–5

We awoke to a March morning chilly by Rio Grande Valley standards, and one of our B. P. chaperones visited our camp wrapped in a heavy coat with a fur collar. Jesse and I stood by the fire drinking coffee in our shorts. "Aren't you all freezing?" the young agent asked.

Refreshed by the cool morning, we broke camp purposefully, wanting to get on the river before the gulf winds began blowing the current against us. I'd experienced the great transition from Brownsville to the Gulf on land: the highway passes through miles of forest leading to the tidal estuaries of the sea, where the trees diminish in size and then disappear altogether. Within six miles of the Gulf, the surrounding land looks more like Cape Cod than South Texas. I anticipated seeing a similar change on the river.

Instead, we rounded bend after bend and saw little change from the river cane-lined shores I had seen for a hundred miles. Though I had expected us to pass through bayous before entering the delta tide flats, I found that both sides of the river were farmed, and we could hear the noise of tractors working the fields above the river. On one turn, we saw an orange grove that extended from the river to the Texas-side horizon. Only Sabal Palm Grove, a preserve of native woodland, offered any change in riparian scenery.

On the Mexican side, we heard a lot of highway noise, and a couple of hours from camp that morning, we rounded a bend to find three Mexican guys fishing with spools of fishing line wrapped around Coke bottles. Above them sat a large utility truck with a hydraulic bucket, and one of the fishermen wore a bright yellow hard hat. As soon as I saw them, I angled the canoe for shore. Earlier I had told Jesse that I no longer had much appetite for talking with Mexicans fishing because I was sated from my hundreds of conversations with them, all of which followed the same constricted pattern. Now, when I told Jesse I was pulling into shore to talk to them, he turned and said, "Man, I'm beginning to worry you might have swallowed a lethal dose of river water. I thought you didn't want to talk to any more fishermen."

"This is different," I replied. "Now that I have you here to watch the canoe, I'm going in to shore to find some beer. Notice that they all have beers in the grass at their feet."

The three men welcomed us and assured me there was a store a short walk away. I offered to treat them to some beer. The man in the hard hat directed the youngest of the three, a kid already tipsy from drinking, to drive me to the store in the immense company truck. Jorge Sánchez, from Matamoros, stumbled to his feet and warmly shook my hand. We climbed into the truck cab, and he said they'd aborted their workday at midmorning because air-conditioning units they were supposed to install had not arrived at the jobsite.

On our way down the rutted ranch road from the river to the highway, I asked Jorge about the soldiers.

"They just left. And I'm glad they did. Things were tense around here for a couple of months. I mean, they don't bother you so much as they slow you down. Checkpoints. Inspections. So now things move faster, and it's better."

"Why were they here?" I asked as we reached the paved highway. "Look down there," he said, directing me to gaze eastward. "Just down there, two gringos were murdered a couple of months ago. The authorities said it was an accident. But around here the people say those gringos were in the drug business. They had a lot of money and they were buying cocaine. I don't know if it was a bad deal or maybe someone was robbing them, but those gringos never went back to Tennessee." He paused to sip his beer just as a police car passed in front of us. "With all respect to you, my friend, it doesn't seem right that these drug dealers in Mexico kill each other every day and the army does nothing, but when two gringos get killed, our army arrives. We think, 'Which people are you protecting? Mexicans or gringos?'"

Jorge followed me to the beer cooler. I pulled out a couple of six-packs of Tecate. "What kind of beer do you guys drink? I'm buying."

"Well, we prefer American beer. It's more expensive here, but if you can't afford it, we'll drink the same as you're buying."

I bought them two six-packs of Miller Lite and a sack of ice, and Jorge was grateful. There's nothing quite like cold beer for improving international relations. He asked about my trip, and by the time we made it back to the riverbank five minutes later, Jorge was calling me "Superman" and insisting I return to visit Washington Beach, a pristine stretch of coastline south of the Rio Grande delta. I assured him I'd be back. Then Jesse and I climbed into the canoe just as the afternoon winds began to roll the river water back toward Brownsville.

◆◆◆

At the point where we'd met the three fishermen, the Rio Grande reaches the southernmost point on its long trip to the Gulf of Mexico, dropping to a latitude of 25.49 degrees, a full six degrees below my starting point in El Paso and only slightly more than two degrees latitude above the Tropic of Cancer. For comparison's sake, the southernmost point in Texas lies further to the south than approximately 200,000 square miles of Mexico—more than one-fourth of the whole nation, including the entire states of Sonora and Baja

California Norte. Only a tiny slice of the very bottom of the state of Chihuahua lies further south.

At this point, the river promptly turns north for its final push to its mouth at Boca Chica, a peninsula immediately below South Padre Island. The river seems in no hurry to reach the sea, meandering slowly around bend after bend. At two points, it turns back and heads due west for nearly a mile. With flows now greatly diminished by the agricultural, commercial, and residential demands of the Rio Grande Valley, the current turns sluggish and fickle. Surface water seems to delight in being pushed back upriver by the gulf winds, and large waves roll back upstream every afternoon. River flows, which measured 1,700 CFS only two hundred miles back, have been siphoned down to a mere 300 CFS. During the drought of the 1990s, the Rio Grande often didn't have enough water to reach the Gulf of Mexico; it ended in sand dunes.

As Jesse and I paddled this stretch, we were often startled by leaping mullets. One aggressive fish shot across the river by skipping above the surface until it collided head-on with the stern of our canoe, making a sickening thud. Another leaped right into Jesse's lap and just as quickly launched itself back into the air. A third spiraled right through the loop in my arms as I paddled, high-jumping the width of the canoe in one leap.

Another common sight on this leg of the trip were floating Mexican beer coolers, large rectangular tubs bearing the logo of a national beer. We couldn't determine whether they were used to convey people across the river or had just been tossed into the water after picnickers finished their revelry on shore. Around every bend, we found a cooler marooned in some spot between the head winds pushing it upriver and the lazy current coaxing it downriver.

About midafternoon we landed beside three men fishing with a large net on the Mexican side; they seemed uncertain about what to make of the appearance of two gringos invading their turf. Jesse explained that he was a reporter for an American newspaper, but his interest in them seemed to further confuse them, and they fumbled their way through answers to his many questions. Although they had been catching fish, fifteen minutes into Jesse's interview they suddenly excused themselves, loaded their gear into an old Crown Victoria, and drove away.

"I think you scared them away, Jess," I noted as he fastened his life jacket.

"It's a funny thing about Mexicans I interview. If I can't keep them around for forty-five minutes, I can't get them to open up. It takes about that long."

—◆◆◆—

This stretch of the river didn't offer many camping possibilities, and after a long day fighting head winds and rolling waves, we settled for a narrow strip of beach below tilled fields. For the first time all trip, I saw no tracks or scat of either raccoons or coyotes. Likewise, the beavers seemed to have disappeared. In their place, the flying mullets popped out of the water beside camp, nearly always leaping three times before they disappeared. While I cooked tortellini in pesto sauce, Jesse grilled me with questions. He scribbled the answers in a journalist's notepad the size of a folded road map, filling an entire page with just one of my sentences.

I've always been an intensely private person, one who is fond of saying that the only bad thing about boating alone is I can't figure out how to go without me. I don't like being the center of attention, even when I'm by myself. One of the reasons I love rivers so much is that while floating them, I become part of them. I usually don't find people interesting, and perhaps the one I find least interesting is myself. Being the subject of Jesse's interview, then, was one of the most uncomfortable hours of my entire trip. I couldn't understand why I had to be the focus of Jesse's article. I argued that I wasn't even the focus of my own trip; the river was. The beauty of the river was that I lost myself in it.

You go for weeks not having to articulate anything beyond simple questions about fishing or the distance to the next rock dam, and you realize that so much of our language developed as a time-killer for people with the luxury of having time to kill. On the river, I found very little use for language. In consequence, I found it difficult to express anything Jesse could capture in a measured quote. For instance, "How has this trip changed you?" he asked.

"I don't want to go back. That's how it's changed me."

"What do you mean?"

"I mean I don't want to go back. This is perfect. The camping, the river, the fishing, the elements, the sense of purpose. Mexico on my right. Texas on my left. I want the river to go on forever."

"But obviously it's not going on forever, and two days from now, you're going to have to go back. How do you think you'll see things then?"

"I think I'll spend the rest of my life looking for something this perfect." I said. "The good thing is I know exactly where to find it."

<hr>

We were about to turn in for the night when the roar of a boat motor cut through the darkness, pressing in deafening waves toward our camp. Seconds later, a large trawler running upriver without lights swept past, and its wake crashed into shore. Then the pilot cut the motor and eased the boat into a 180-degree turn. Suddenly a searchlight filled our camp with a blinding shaft of light. Instinctively, I waved. As the boat trawled slowly to shore, I whispered to Jesse, "Well, this ought to help fill out your story."

Four Border Patrol agents sat aboard the boat, and as it edged toward us, one leaped from his swivel chair on deck and approached the bow. His unbuttoned trench coat twirled like a cape as he jumped up. I could barely make out his face in the darkness, noting only a crew cut and the stern look of a drill sergeant.

"What the hell are you doing in there?" he shouted angrily.

Jesse snapped a picture with his flash camera, and the agent barked, "Hey, no pictures!"

In the light of Jesse's flash, I saw that the other three agents, all younger than the man on the bow, wore heavy jackets and ski masks like those I associate with bank robbers.

"Why no pictures?" Jesse asked.

"Because I said so!" He edged closer to the bow. This didn't seem the sort of man who settled disputes amicably.

The man interrogated us, and as I answered his questions, his attitude gradually softened, though nothing in his voice ever approached friendly. The younger guys in the back of the boat were considerably more congenial. Again I had the sense that I was part of some training run. The chief interrogator swaggered back and forth on the bow, lighting a cigarette, grudgingly answering my questions. One of the younger agents asked how we bathed, and when I told him I bathed "in the river," the lead agent said, "This river is full of poison. People die from simple contact. You're going to wish you hadn't gotten in it."

"As much as I needed a bath, I think bathing in contaminated water was better than not bathing at all. Hey, do you all know how many miles to the Gulf?"

"You have twenty-six miles. You get in that boat first thing in the morning and you'll be there tomorrow." It sounded more like an order than an approximation of distance.

When they left, navigating upriver with the use of night vision goggles, we heaped wood on the fire and opened beers. I fell into a fit of giggling while imitating the agent's gruff final order.

"So what do you think about his saying the river is full of poison?" Jesse asked. "That was a pretty heavy statement. I got the idea I might wake up deformed."

"If you wake up at all. I wouldn't put it past that asshole to come by here in the middle of the night and empty his automatic weapon into our skulls."

—◆◆◆—

An hour out of camp the next morning, we found a flatboat with an outboard motor anchored mid-river on a long straightaway. A bearded blond guy sat back near the outboard and a petite girl sat near the bow. They appeared to be working fishing lines as we approached, perhaps baiting them on the floor of the boat. As we neared, I saw the words "Texas Tech University" stenciled on the side of the boat.

"This might be interesting," Jesse said. "Pull up alongside them so I can ask them some questions."

The guy introduced himself as Caleb Huber, a graduate student from Texas Tech, who was studying a fish called the common snook for his Master's thesis. He introduced us to his undergraduate assistant, Tamara Young, a pretty Hispanic girl with an angelic smile.

"What's your thesis about?" Jesse asked, his notepad at the ready.

"It's on the common snook's habitat preference and gonad development."

"Gonad development?" Jesse asked, fighting to suppress a smile.

Caleb explained that snook, a small basslike fish, spawn in the Gulf and live in fresh water. All snook are born males, and as they mature they change genders, becoming females as adults. Their population has been declining in recent years, and Caleb's studies centered on trying to determine the cause of that decline. He hypothesized that it could have been environmental deterioration of the fish's habitat, or perhaps overfishing by the Mexicans.

"How bad is the water here?" Jesse asked.

"Well, Tamara and I just tested it a few minutes ago," Caleb said, "and it's pretty clean. Not quite clean enough to drink, but it's pretty good."

Caleb said he spent three days a week on the river. Had he encountered any problems in the two months so far? Jesse asked. "You know," Caleb said, "when I first started coming out on the river, I was pretty scared. People try to get you to believe being here is extremely dangerous. The first few times I expected to have trouble, but everyone's been really nice. I mean, I still carry a gun, but I haven't had a single problem here."

Jesse was also curious about the research tools Caleb carried aboard, and Caleb showed off a few of them. "I even have a device which measures current." He extracted a metal instrument that looked like a small hand-held scale and dipped it into the water. After a moment, he withdrew it and said, "The current is 0.1 meters per second."

"What's that mean in CFS?" I asked.

"It means there's no current. It's essentially a lake all the way from here to the Gulf."

⸺♦♦♦⸺

Jesse and I had to paddle hard much of the day due to head winds. Plus, for the first time, we were experiencing the slightest suggestion of a tidal effect. During the night the river had dropped about a foot, and all day it rose slowly as the tide came in. The winds that accompanied the incoming tide were considerably harder to battle than any inflow of water. We worked hard; as soon as we tried to take a rest in the boat, the river promptly pushed us backwards.

The meetings with Caleb and Tamara and the B. P. the previous night provided us with high-powered ammunition for humor. Fighting laughter, Jesse said, "Man, can you imagine going to parties and when they ask you what you do, you have to reply: 'Oh, I study gonad development in the common snook'?"

"Hey, now that you mention it, what's the difference between a common snook and other snooks? And do they all change to women?" I said.

Laughing helped to keep our minds off the difficult job of paddling. As we progressed, the narrow river had gradually widened, stretching to more than two hundred feet across by midafternoon; we had begun the day with the river a third as wide. The banks became less steep as the river expanded: at our camp, we had been twenty vertical feet below the surrounding countryside, but by midafternoon we were only about three feet below it. This meant that we had little protection from the relentless winds, and on long straightaways, the waves tried to roll us upriver.

We began seeing run-down fishing shelters on the Mexican side, and we stopped to investigate one, a ramshackle hut not much larger than a small bathroom. Weathered buoys, dilapidated traps, and beer cans littered its yard. It had no door, and inside only a crude wooden bench. Though it didn't look sturdy enough to withstand the high winds of tropical storms raging in from the Gulf, everything about it suggested that it had stood there near the shore for a long time. Perhaps the tenants reconstructed it with the same weathered lumber every time a storm leveled it.

—◆◆▶—

Late in the afternoon we passed Palmito Ranch, one of the most historic sites on the Rio Grande. From the river, you can't see it, and I recognized it only because on the Mexican side of the river there sits the last ranch before the Gulf of Mexico.

On May 13, 1865, Union forces defeated Confederate troops on the battlefield at Palmito Ranch. Unbeknownst to the troops engaged in the battle, the Civil War had already ended; exactly thirty days before, General Robert E. Lee had surrendered at Appomattox, Virginia.

As we paddled past, I thought of that battle as a harbinger of the future of the border and the river. A hundred and forty years later, the border remains disconcertingly out of step with the two nations it divides. You get the feeling that we continue to fight battles in wars that have already been lost.

El Mar

Mar. 6

In camp, we could smell the sea. The tide flats stretched out in all directions, as smooth as the tilled fields that had bordered the river for the last two hundred miles. I had outlasted even the river cane. Downriver, to the east, we could see the lighthouse on the point at Bagdad, and it looked enormous rising out of the sand. Jesse dipped his finger into the river water to taste for salt and, uncertain whether he'd detected a trace of the sea in the river, asked me to try.

"No thanks," I said. "If we can see the lighthouse, I know we're close."

Only the routine of setting up camp, collecting wood, and burning a campfire kept me from feeling disoriented. Never one to love the sea, I felt out of my element on a body of water that now bore a closer resemblance to a tidal estuary than a river. The Rio Grande had stretched to some four hundred feet wide, and its current was determined by tidal influence. Gulls replaced raccoons as the resident scavengers. Windswept sand flats replaced farms and orchards above the riverbanks. Finally, after 1,260 miles of walking paths littered by the undocumented workers who traversed them, I found the riverbanks were clean.

Jesse tried again to get me to open up for an interview, but I resisted his questions. I felt little but disappointment at reaching the end. Although nearly every muscle in my body had ached for weeks, I had never tired of the river and the toil I endured traveling it. Knowing every night that the next day would bring a full slate of work was a continuing source of comfort. The uncertainties of navigating a new stretch of river, of bypassing obstacles like rapids and dams, and of finding a store where I could buy supplies—these were the challenges that sustained me. The finality of making last camp was sobering. Talking about it didn't help; reminiscing about highlights of the trip would only serve to make me miss the river more.

Driven by routine, I was doing things exactly as I had done them for the past sixty-nine days. I boiled water for coffee, wrote in my journal, took down the tent, drank exactly six cups of water, cooked breakfast, and loaded the canoe. I meticulously double-tied all the gear in the canoe despite the fact that the wide, still river offered no danger of capsizing the boat. Jesse stood by watching me. "Do you really think we need to secure everything that well?"

"I don't expect you to understand this," I replied, "but, yes, I do."

During the night, the tide had gone out and left the river a full ten feet from the shore where we'd landed, so we had to push the loaded boat across the slick sand. As I steadied the back end, Jesse climbed aboard, and then as he braced, I boarded. Immediately, the wind began pushing us upriver, and our first few paddle strokes merely arrested the backwards movement. We soon powered our way forward, and around the first bend we met Caleb and Tamara on their way upriver to do more research. They informed us we had five or six miles of river left before the Gulf, although, looking at the Bagdad lighthouse, which appeared so close, I thought their estimate seemed too long.

With vigorous paddling, we passed bend after bend but appeared no closer to the lighthouse. An hour out of camp, we landed on the Mexican side near a cluster of fishing huts. Off to the north, across the Laguna Madre, I could see the high-rises of South Padre Island spearing into the sky. To the south, the tide flats stretched as far as I could see, disappearing into the horizon. Suddenly, the wind died.

For over two weeks, I had canoed into head winds and fought a relentless battle against them. It seemed as if the winds had wished to prolong my trip, to keep me from reaching my goal, and now I had a feeling that these same winds, which had seemed adversarial all trip, had in fact been my ally. It was as if they knew that I didn't want to reach the end, and they had complied by prolonging the trip. Only now, with the Gulf of Mexico just a couple of miles distant, they relented. I felt they were communicating with me, surrendering in a sense, saying, "Hey, we're tired too. You've stood the test. Now take a victory march in peace. We'll give you that."

◆◆◆

At the end of a long straightaway, which seemed to bring us near to the base of the lighthouse, Jesse stopped paddling and craned his neck toward the sea. "Do you hear that?" he said, almost whispering.

Ahead, the low roar of the sea sounded like a river rapid. The smell of ocean was strong, and straight ahead of us it looked as though the river ran smack into a wall of sand dunes.

"Let's get there before the wind kicks up again," I said. "It seems to be giving us a window of opportunity."

As the river bent south, we saw a long straightaway extending a mile or more parallel to the dunes. I had a sinking feeling that we had missed a turn and had somehow paddled into an estuary that would dead-end. We paddled forward, and within a few minutes, the lighthouse at Bagdad disappeared behind a sand dune.

"Jesse, is it possible we took a wrong turn?"

"I don't know, man," he said, laughing. "But if we did, that would be a first. I can imagine the headline now. River Adventurer Lost on Rio Grande, Unable to Follow Current."

A flatboat paddled by two Mexican men and a woman approached us, which seemed to confirm that we'd indeed strayed off course. I angled the canoe toward them, and they greeted us cheerfully. "Which way to the mouth of the river?" I called in Spanish.

"Just follow the river. It bends up ahead and then ends at the sea over there," one man said, pointing back in the direction we had come.

The river bent, this time moving due east in a wide swath, taking us tantalizingly close to the surf. Then it bent yet again and followed north along the base of the dunes, back in the direction of the lighthouse. In total, we had traveled three miles to gain less than half a mile. We passed beneath the base of the lighthouse, and the river began to bend east again. As we rounded this bend, we saw a row of pickup trucks parked on the sandy banks of the river, which suddenly narrowed, and as we completed the bend, the Gulf of Mexico opened before us. The surf pounded into the narrow river channel. As Jesse snapped pictures from the bow of the canoe, I couldn't keep the canoe moving forward against the onrushing tide, so I steered into shore, still fifty yards short of the Gulf.

On the Mexican side of the river, dozens of people fished and drank beer. One man sold seafood from a step van, from which he blasted tropical music through a lone speaker. An intrepid fisherman cast his line from chest-deep water in the channel. Others fished on the calmer water a hundred feet upriver. Kids thrashed in the small waves near shore. The American side was empty.

—◆◆◆—

Boca Chica ("Little Mouth") is a peninsula, with the mouth of the Rio Grande at its southern tip, Laguna Madre on its northern tip, and the Gulf on its eastern flank. State Highway 4 reaches Boca Chica north of the river's mouth. When the tide permits, vehicles can drive the three miles of hard-packed sand from the end of the highway to the river. The absence of people at the mouth of the river on the American side on a warm, sunny March Sunday can only mean that the tide is up, blocking vehicle access.

Jesse had left his truck in Brownsville, so he planned to hitch a ride the twenty-seven miles back to town. Our plan called for him to leave as soon as we reached the river's end; meanwhile, I would carry all the gear to a spot a quarter mile up the beach, high enough that even high tide wouldn't reach it. Instead of heading out, though, Jesse lingered for about fifteen minutes, watching the fishermen on the Mexican side.

"I'm surprised you're taking out here," he said, while gazing across at the party on the opposite beach. "It seems more your style to take out over there and go back through Mexico."

I watched him walk down the beach, stopping to talk to some people parked a half mile away, trying to persuade them to give him a ride to the beginning of the paved highway. But they didn't move from their lawn chairs, and I could barely make out his lanky frame as he walked past them. A few minutes later, those same people hurriedly packed their truck, and they too disappeared in the direction in which Jesse had gone. This confirmed that the rising tide was about to cut me off from the rest of the beach. I resigned myself to the fact that I'd likely be stranded for hours, and went about the work of portaging my gear across the hot sand. It seemed only fitting that after I had spent the winter on water, water would at the end isolate me from the road back to the world I had little desire to reenter.

Epilogue: *Pesadillas*

IN THE WEEKS AFTER MY RETURN TO LAREDO, I sensed that a few of my acquaintances were embarrassed that their dire predictions about my trip had proved inaccurate: not only had I not been the victim of an assault or a gunshot, but I didn't even gloat about having achieved my goal. Since I didn't report being terrified the whole time and relieved that the trip was over, some friends believed I was more *loco* for liking the trip than I had been for attempting it.

My transition to life at home was not easy precisely because *life* was so easy. I missed the sense of purpose I had had on the river, the challenge of navigating, the struggle of keeping myself supplied with food, the uncertainty about what lay around the next bend. The novelty of laundry facilities, nearby stores, and indoor plumbing lasted less than a week. After that, I was homesick for the river.

I was haunted by the fact that I hadn't traveled the entire Texas-Mexico border by raft or canoe, instead biking the section from El Paso to Presidio because of rumors that the river there was impassable. But in fact every stretch of the Rio Grande Tony and I had seen had offered clear passage. I now doubted the credibility of those who had warned me against attempting this run; after all, nearly everyone had admonished me about doing the trip, period. I believed that if I could run the urban sections of the Rio Grande during the most violent period in border history, I could overcome the obstacles—if they existed—created by salt cedar. But due to the scarcity of water below El Paso, I would have to wait until winter—when farmers stopped the irrigation that drained the river—to make this run.

◆◆◆

In August I canoed from Eagle Pass to Laredo because that had been a favorite stretch of the trip seven months before, and I wanted to experience it in the heat of summer. On my wintertime trip, I'd been terribly cold for the six days it took me to paddle between the two border cities, so it was delightful to face the challenging rapids knowing a capsize might bring relief from the heat rather than the threat of hypothermia. With all the trees full of leaves, I could see no trace of the trash I had seen below Eagle Pass, and the islands where I had camped in winter were now overgrown with high weeds. I saw many more people, but none crossing the river as they had in winter. Mexican families picnicked on the banks, men fished, and children played in the shallows near shore. Everyone was friendly and curious. My days were full of charming encounters with the Mexican people. And I walked to the store in Hidalgo, where I found the same two women watching a *telenovela*. I knew better this time than to disturb them before the commercial break.

I spent much of the fall—when I wasn't teaching classes—preparing for the canoe trip below El Paso in early December. Hayesy wanted to go along, even though in the ten months since I'd left him in Ciudad Acuña, he had ingested a steady diet of Fox News Channel horror stories about the border. When we launched our two boats on a cold December morning, my assurances that we'd be safe didn't appease him. A Border Patrol agent who visited our first camp told about a recent shoot-out between drug runners on the Mexican side and B. P. agents on the American side, further feeding Hayesy's paranoia.

For two days, we had superb boating as the river sliced through the outer reaches of El Paso Valley's agricultural belt, but on Day Three, the Rio Grande plunged us into a netherworld of salt cedar. At times, the growth of overhanging branches was so thick we had to saw a path—from our seats in the boats—just to make any forward progress. Countless barbed-wire fences blocked the channel, all requiring us to portage. Where trees had fallen into the river, we had to carry around them. Every time the river split around an island, only one of the two channels would extend all the way to the end of the island, and we didn't know which channel it would be; the other channel would splinter into dozens of micro-channels that disappeared into the dense salt cedar growth. Our progress was dismal: one day we traveled less than two miles, and the next not even a mile. Hayesy became stomach-sick, and we couldn't decide whether it was due to drinking water from dirty water jugs or to inhaling dust of the dozens of salt cedars we had sawed just to clear our way. For once, people had been right about the river, *damn it!*

On the sixth day, we met a man named Carlos—a ranch hand new to the area—chopping wood near where we had to slip the boats under a barbed-wire fence. He said he worked on a small ranch a ten-minute walk from there, owned by a man who worked near El Paso during the week and came to the ranch on weekends. Carlos expected him to arrive later that night.

At camp the next night, we heard voices nearby on the Mexican side, and I called to them. Soon seven men emerged from a trail across the river from our camp, led by Carlos's boss, Manuel Hernández.

"We've been looking for you all day," Manuel said in Spanish. "I'll take you wherever you want, but you can't continue in your boats. The river is *una pesadilla* (a nightmare) below here."

I had no option but to accept Manuel's ride back toward El Paso, put Hayesy on a plane to Boston, and salvage my vacation by floating the Lower Canyons alone.

◆◆◆

The following year, in August, I canoed the Eagle Pass–to–Laredo stretch yet again. The idea that I could drive upriver for two hours, start canoeing, and land five or six days later a couple of blocks from my apartment in Laredo appealed to me enough that I expected to do the trip every August for years to come.

Late in the afternoon of my second day on the river, I approached a rapid about three hours past the ledges of Guerrero. I smelled something horrible, and I worried that a dead cow or javelina might obstruct the channel I intended to run. Along the Mexican shore, I could see what river runners call a "cheat lane," a narrow channel that bypassed the worst of the rapid, so I cut the boat toward it. Just as my canoe dropped into the cheat lane, I passed a human body lodged on the rocks right next to my canoe. The odor overwhelmed me, but the stench didn't compare to the hideousness of what I saw: the corpse had no head, and scavengers had opened his torso to feed on his internal organs.

I had discovered my first dead body in the river.

The following morning I met two Mexicans working on a water pump about fifteen miles below the spot where the corpse was lodged. I asked them what we should do about it. One guy retreated and stood fifty yards away, waiting for me to leave. The other guy dropped his head as if embarrassed, and said in Spanish, "There is nothing we can do. These things are very complicated, so it's better to leave it alone."

When I arrived home two days later, I called Jesse Bogan to ask him what to do. Since the body was close to the Mexican shore, I thought Mexican officials would retrieve it, and because of his job as a border reporter Jesse had many Mexican contacts. He made some phone calls, and within the hour an official from Piedras Negras phoned to ask me questions. I answered as thoroughly as I could, and said it would be very difficult for them to reach the body unless they went by boat. How would they know exactly where to find it? he asked. I replied in Spanish, "No problem. You're going to smell it from a long way off."

Two days later, an official from the Mexico consulate in Laredo phoned, and his tone made me feel like a suspect in the case. He asked the same questions repeatedly, as if to catch me in a lie. When my patience grew thin, I told him I had given him all the information I knew. He said, "What do you do for a living?"

"I teach at the college."

"So you were doing scientific research?"

"No, I was taking a vacation trip."

"I see," he said skeptically.

I never learned whether they bothered to retrieve the body.

———◆◆◆———

In December, Hayesy and I rafted the Lower Canyons. Four days before reaching Langtry, we found a dead man lying face down in the river only thirty feet from the Texas-side bank. He appeared to have been shot in the head, and I saw what seemed to be fresh blood and brain matter on the back of his skull. Since the corpse had drifted into shallow water near the point where a rough ranch road comes close to the river, I wrote a note describing the appearance and location of the body, and left the note between two rocks in the middle of a large X that I carved in the dirt in the road. Hayesy and I continued downriver.

In Langtry we were met by the Border Patrol, who had found both my note and then the corpse the day before. The agent told us we had to go to the sheriff's office in Sanderson to fill out a statement. There the deputies treated us well, serving us coffee and asking if discovering a corpse had ruined our trip. I wrote a three-page statement detailing our actions from the moment we found the body until we arrived at the sheriff's office. After they thanked us for taking the time to write the statement, the chief deputy said, "Don't worry. You're not suspects."

During my first thirty-seven trips on the Rio Grande, I never found a corpse. Now, two trips in a row, I'd had such grisly encounters.

The previous December, when Manuel Hernández had helped Hayesy and me, he'd walked us through his tiny village on the dirt road linking Juárez with the outback—the same road Tony and I had biked—and lamented the fact that few people remained. "Things are changing," he said, "but not always for the good."

"Has everyone left to go over there?" I asked, pointing in the direction of the U.S.

"Either over there," he said, "or down there." He pointed to the ground.

Late that same afternoon we reached a small village near El Porvenir, Chihuahua, the town across the international bridge from Fort Hancock. There we met Manuel's wife's brother-in-law, a handsome Fort Hancock native named Juan Garibay, who would later drive us across the river to his hometown. Before we were introduced, Manuel took Juan aside to explain how he had come to be carrying two gringos and their boats in the back of his pickup. I could see Juan shaking his head as he listened, but they were out of earshot. Finally, Juan walked over to us, smiling, and said in English, "Man, the river isn't like it used to be. You can't go down it anymore."

He added, "Crazy gringos, you all need to find something better to do with your lives."

THE MOUNTAINEERS, founded in 1906, is a nonprofit outdoor activity and conservation club, whose mission is "to explore, study, preserve, and enjoy the natural beauty of the outdoors...." Based in Seattle, Washington, the club is now the third-largest such organization in the United States, with seven branches throughout Washington State.

The Mountaineers sponsors both classes and year-round outdoor activities in the Pacific Northwest, which include hiking, mountain climbing, ski-touring, snowshoeing, bicycling, camping, kayaking, nature study, sailing, and adventure travel. The club's conservation division supports environmental causes through educational activities, sponsoring legislation, and presenting informational programs.

All club activities are led by skilled, experienced instructors, who are dedicated to promoting safe and responsible enjoyment and preservation of the outdoors.

If you would like to participate in these organized outdoor activities or the club's programs, consider a membership in The Mountaineers. For information and an application, write or call The Mountaineers, Club Headquarters, 300 Third Avenue West, Seattle, WA 98119; 206-284-6310. You can also visit the club's website at www.mountaineers.org or contact The Mountaineers via email at clubmail@mountaineers.org.

The Mountaineers Books, an active, nonprofit publishing program of the club, produces guidebooks, instructional texts, historical works, natural history guides, and works on environmental conservation. All books produced by The Mountaineers Books fulfill the club's mission.

Send or call for our catalog of more than 500 outdoor titles:

The Mountaineers Books
1001 SW Klickitat Way, Suite 201
Seattle, WA 98134
800-553-4453
mbooks@mountaineersbooks.org
www.mountaineersbooks.org

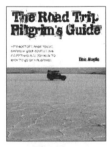